Pitt Series in

Russian and East European Studies

Parables from the Past

The Prose Fiction of Chingiz Aitmatov

Joseph P. Mozur, Jr.

University of Pittsburgh Press
Pittsburgh and London

Pitt Series in Russian and East European Studies no. 22
Published by the University of Pittsburgh Press, Pittsburgh, Pa., 15260
Copyright © 1995, University of Pittsburgh Press
All rights reserved
Manufactured in the United States of America
Printed on acid-free paper

Designed by Jane Tenenbaum

Library of Congress Cataloging-in-Publication Data

Mozur, Joseph P.
    Parables from the past : the prose fiction of Chingiz Aitmanov /
Joseph P. Mozur, Jr.
        p.   cm. — (Pitt series in Russian and East European studies ; no. 22)
    Includes bibliographical references and index.
    ISBN 0-8229-3791-3. — ISBN 0-8229-5531-8 (pbk.)
    1. Aitmatov, Chingiz.   I. Title.   II. Series: Series in Russian and East
European studies ; no. 22.
PL44.9.A36Z78   1994
891.73'44—dc20   93-45921
                                                              CIP

A CIP catalogue record for this book is available from the British Library.
Eurospan, London

For Petra

Preface

As soon as the wolf had crept up to the herd,
Chypalak cried out from within its gut,
"Hey! Shepherds, wake up!
I, the grey wolf, have come to steal a lamb."
—Kirghiz folktale

Chingiz Aitmatov is one of a number of prominent writers who, under conditions of censorship, published their works exclusively in Soviet literary journals in the years following the Khrushchev cultural thaw. His works were immensely popular among a broad Soviet readership and were particularly well received in the non-Russian republics of the former USSR. There, readers admired Aitmatov, a Kirghiz, for his all-union success in a country whose dominant language and culture was Russian. They looked upon Aitmatov as a defender of the Soviet Union's non-Russian cultures, capable of getting his message through despite the numerous layers of censorship.

Yet Aitmatov was equally popular in the Russian republic. Russian readers valued Aitmatov's ability to depict the issues of the day in intensely human terms against a background of Central Asian oral history. While readers in Moscow and Leningrad tended to be more critical of the aesthetic side of Aitmatov's fiction, their criticism was often based on false assumptions. Although Aitmatov wrote in Russian, he remained a Kirghiz. His style was not the polished idiom of classical Russian literature, but combined the politicized language of Soviet contemporaneity with the lyricism of Kirghiz oral folklore. His works were written to engage the emotions and elicit the reader's protest against oppression and cruelty in Soviet society. As such Aitmatov's fiction was and remains compelling reading. New editions of his works continue to appear and enjoy particular success in Western Europe.

Aitmatov's fiction does not fit neatly into a literary movement or school. The dominant literary grouping in official Soviet letters in the 1960s and 1970s was a movement known as Village Prose. Among the movement's prominent names were Valentin Rasputin, Vasilii Belov, and Viktor Astaf'ev. Although Aitmatov shared their antiurban bias, respect for the prerevolutionary heritage, and concern for the natural environment, he was never considered part of the movement because of the non-Russian settings of his works and his own non-Russian ethnicity. Neither can Aitmatov be placed within the short-lived movement of the 1960s that came to be called Youth Prose. Although Aitmatov was of the same generation as Vasilii Aksenov, Anatolii Gladilin, Iurii Kazakov, and Vladimir Voinovich and first gained literary recognition at the same time they did, he shared with them only their strong anti-Stalinist convictions. He rejected outright their ironic, irreverent attitudes toward the optimistic teleology of Soviet life at the time.

Nor does Aitmatov's fiction have much in common with Urban Prose and the works of its primary representative, the talented writer Iurii Trifonov. In his masterpieces, Trifonov portrayed the moral dilemmas of the urban intelligentsia. Aitmatov, because of his provincial background, avoided depicting the city, and urban characters play only marginal roles in his prose. Finally, while several of Aitmatov's works deal with World War II, he cannot be included among the writers of War Prose, the other major literary grouping of Soviet writers in the post-Thaw period. Unlike Vasil' Bykau, Iurii Bondarev, and Viacheslav Kondrat'ev, Aitmatov was too young to serve in World War II, and thus the war is depicted in his work only as it impacted the daily lives of villagers in the Soviet hinterland.

Perhaps the best of post-Thaw official Soviet letters can be captured under the generic rubric of "moral prose" or "the literature of moral opposition," terms popularized by Grigorii Svirskii in his 1979 *tamizdat* study of Soviet literature.[1] Such categories accurately describe how talented Soviet writers viewed their work before the fall of Soviet totalitarianism. If censorship allowed neither criticism of the political structure nor questioning of the ideological underpinnings of Soviet power, then the writers of Village Prose, Urban Prose, and, for the most part, War Prose could depict the negative consequences of one-party rule and its monopoly on ideology only in terms of basic human morality. Yet in the portrayal of the negative sides of Soviet life, Aitmatov distinguished himself from his colleagues by his successful and innovative use of Central Asian myth and folklore. In a country where the vast majority of the citizenry could never hope to travel abroad and where the authorities suspiciously controlled access to information on life outside the Soviet state, Aitmatov's work satisfied a thirst for the exotic while bringing attention to bear on the important issues of his day.

Although Aitmatov had epigones, notably in the non-Russian republics, and although by the late 1970s Soviet critics began to call his works and those of his followers "mythological prose," pointing to its affinity with the fiction of Gabriel García Márquez, no clearly defined literary school ever emerged. By referring to García Márquez, whose loyalty to socialist ideas made him a welcome authority for the Soviet cultural establishment, critics sought to co-opt Aitmatov's works for socialist realism.

While there were other major players on the post-Thaw Soviet literary scene, as well as a number of writers publishing important works in *samizdat* ("self-published" literature that was circulated underground) and *tamizdat* (literature written in the Soviet Union but published in the West), Aitmatov certainly ranks as one of the most prominent authors writing for publication in the Soviet Union. His work in the 1970s and 1980s represents better than that of any other Soviet writer the limits of permitted dissent in official belles lettres. Moreover, the intense discussion in the Soviet press provoked by the appearance of many of Aitmatov's works allows his works to serve as useful points of reference in approaching post-Thaw Soviet fiction. Finally, the composition, characters, and Central Asian atmosphere, as well as its immense popularity among Soviet readers, make Aitmatov's fiction unique in Soviet letters and thus deserving of scholarly attention.

In their analysis of post-Thaw Soviet literature, Western scholars, with few exceptions, have concentrated on the works of Russian Soviet writers. This book represents a first attempt to examine in a comprehensive way the work of a prominent non-Russian Soviet writer. In this discussion, special emphasis is placed on the Kirghiz

dimension of Aitmatov's fiction, an aspect that has been sorely neglected in the critical reception of his work in Soviet literary journals.

Parables from the Past introduces English readers for the first
time to the works of a Soviet writer from Central Asia and comple-
ments two other recent publications on contemporary Soviet prose,
Josie Woll's monograph on Trifonov, *Invented Truth: Soviet Reality
and the Literary Imagination of Iurii Trifonov,* and Kathleen Parthé's
study, *Russian Village Prose: The Radiant Past.*

Acknowledgments

M y interest in Chingiz Aitmatov began in graduate school at the University of North Carolina, Chapel Hill, where in 1983 I completed a Ph.D. dissertation on the author. Upon graduation, I became interested in the work of other non-Russian Soviet writers and published articles and reviews on Vasil' Bykau, Ion Drutse, Olzhas Suleimenov, as well as other writers from the non-Russian republics of the former Soviet Union. A fellowship received in 1991 from the Center on East-West Trade, Investment, and Communications at Duke University provided me with the time and resources necessary to complete this book on Aitmatov.

The Center also enabled me to conduct several interviews with Chingiz Aitmatov and generously funded a trip to Kirghizstan in June 1991. Special thanks go to the Center's director, Professor Jerry Hough, as well as to the fine libraries at Duke University and the University of North Carolina in Chapel Hill. The staffs of both libraries were always eager to assist me in any way.

I also thank the Department of Foreign Languages and the Research Committee at the University of South Alabama for support of travel to Luxembourg to interview Aitmatov and for funding several trips to the Summer Research Laboratory on Russian and Eastern Europe at the University of Illinois in Champaign-Urbana. I am indebted to the Research Laboratory in Champaign-Urbana for several summer fellowships and to the interlibrary loan section of the University of South Alabama for its speed and efficiency in obtaining needed research materials.

I am grateful to Abdyldazhan Akmataliev, Director of the Kirghiz Institute on Language and Literature, and his colleagues who received me warmly in Bishkek and answered my many questions about the Kirghiz dimension in Aitmatov's works. Special gratitude also goes to a prominent Kirghiz-American, Azamat Altai, formerly of

Radio Liberty, who offered valuable suggestions during the later stages of my research.

Last but not least, I would like to thank colleagues whom I consulted when planning the book or who read the manuscript at different stages of my work: Paul Debreczeny, professor at the University of North Carolina, Josie Woll, professor at Howard University, Peter Rollberg, professor at George Washington University, Thomas Lahusen, professor at Duke University, and Ada Mayo, professor at the University of Minnesota.

Note on Transliteration and Translation

Russian words and names appearing in bibliographical references and in the body of the text are rendered according to the Library of Congress system of transliteration (without diacritical marks). Infrequent exceptions are made in the body of the text to account for established English usage, that is, *Tolstoy* for *Tolstoi*, *Dostoevsky* for *Dostoevskii*, *Yeltsin* for *El'tsin*. Unless otherwise indicated, all translations from Russian texts are my own. Kirghiz words and names are transliterated from the Cyrillic using the same system.

Titles are given in English, whether or not they have been translated. Details of publication, including title as originally published, can be found in the notes and bibliography.

Parables from the Past

Introduction

" "The mission of literature is to express the essence of the human spirit, of man's spiritual quest," Chingiz Aitmatov remarked to a Western interviewer during the culturally stifling years of the Brezhnev regime.[1] The attempts of Brezhnev and his minions to subjugate all facets of Soviet culture and society to the interests of the Communist party produced what historians and political observers would later call the era of stagnation. In responding to questions pertaining to the mission of literature, the Soviet writer was expected to speak about building socialism or creating positive heroes for emulation by the masses.

It was not by chance that Aitmatov's simple statement, disarmingly straightforward and apolitical, appeared in a Western publication. Yet the author's words can be viewed as the creative principle that has guided his work since the 1970s. On other occasions during those years, Aitmatov spoke of the need for literature to concern itself with the eternal problems facing mankind, issues that existed centuries before the creation of Soviet society and the so-called new Soviet man. After the advent of glasnost, the author continued to elaborate on the concept of "man's spiritual quest," postulating the existence of "eternal values" common to all mankind[2] and speaking of a "divinely inspired" common spiritual foundation, which must be preserved and developed by modern man.[3]

Such an artistic stance, which views the present day through the prism of the experience of past generations, had, of course, little to do with the demands of socialist realism for *partiinost'* (party-mindedness) and *ideinost'* (correct ideological stance) in literary works, concepts that for decades were used by Soviet ideologues to harness literature to the Communist party's tasks of the day. Aitmatov's major works—*Farewell, Gul'sary!, The White Ship, The Piebald Dog Running Along the Seashore, The Day Lasts More than a Hundred Years,* and *The Place of the Skull*—played a substantial role in freeing Soviet letters from just such ideological shackles.[4]

Indeed, the major themes in his fiction—the juxtaposition of pre-revolutionary values and revolutionary moral relativism, the struggle with despotism, the need to protect the environment and national cultures from the arrogant insatiety of the powerful—reveal the party's failures and the negative sides of life in the Soviet state. While Aitmatov had no monopoly on those themes, prominently represented in both Urban and Village Prose, he managed to present them in much more urgent terms than his contemporaries publishing in the Soviet Union.[5] There is a clear apocalyptic mood pervading the presentation of those themes in Aitmatov's works that probably only Valentin Rasputin's *Farewell to Matyora* (1976) and *The Fire* (1985) approximate.

Although the Soviet state struggled to deflect, indeed to prohibit, strong social criticism in Soviet letters, Aitmatov continued to call attention to its ills. But he never stepped over the line separating reform-minded writers from dissidents. Such circumspection and willingness to work within the given system enabled him to become a major cultural figure in the USSR during the 1970s and 1980s. Aitmatov was fully cognizant, however, of the danger of being turned into a "servant of the party"[6] and was generally successful in maintaining a high degree of artistic and ideological independence. He was viewed by many as a loyal liberal seeking evolutionary change from within. Others considered Aitmatov to be a non-Russian writer conveniently manipulated by the regime to create the false impression of tolerance in Soviet letters and success in the country's cultural policies toward the national republics.

The controversy continues into the 1990s and is hardly limited to Aitmatov alone. Numerous talented works published in the USSR during the 1970s and 1980s, a time when many Soviet writers were forced to leave the country or write for *samizdat* and *tamizdat*, have been viewed as something less than real literature. Young Russian postmodernists have begun to deride the efforts of the 1960s generation of Soviet writers, ridiculing their idealism and their hope that the oppressive regime could be reformed.[7] Yet works like Aitmatov's *The White Ship* and *The Day Lasts More than a Hundred Years*, Vasil' Bykau's *The Dead Feel No Pain*, Rasputin's *Farewell to Matyora*, and Iurii Trifonov's *House on the Embankment*, despite the conditions of censorship in which they were created, challenged Soviet readers to question the state of their society, with its secretiveness, ubiquitous suspicion, lack of compassion, and readiness to condemn those who think for themselves. Ultimately, such works of fiction served as a catalyst for the social and political changes of the Gorbachev years.[8]

Compared to Bykau, Rasputin, and Trifonov, Aitmatov enjoyed a favored status in the Soviet cultural establishment, which was a source of envy and resentment for some Soviet writers and intellectuals. For decades, beginning in the 1960s, he served on a number of editorial boards, including that of *Literaturnaia gazeta* and *Novyi mir*. His official durability is best evidenced by the length of his service, from 1967 until 1990, on the editorial board of *Novyi mir*, where he weathered several editorial upheavals. For his belles lettres, Aitmatov was awarded the Lenin Prize in 1963 and two State Prizes of the USSR in 1966 and 1983.

Yet despite all the official honors bestowed upon him, Aitmatov consistently used his most-favored status in Soviet letters to question, rather than to affirm, the existing political and social order. Throughout the 1970s and 1980s his fiction condemned the neo-Stalinist behavior and totalitarian thinking of Soviet citizens and officials and promoted tolerance toward religion and believers. Those efforts culminated in 1986 with the publication of *The Place of the Skull*, a novel depicting a Christian hero fighting to save Soviet youth from narcotics addiction. Significantly, Aitmatov links the addiction to hallucinatory drugs to the ideological cul-de-sac of Marxism-Leninism.

Long before the abolishment of Article 6 of the Soviet Constitution, which guaranteed the leading role of the Communist party in Soviet society, Aitmatov's fiction called into question the party's right to its ideological monopoly. At a time when it seemed impossible to imagine any kind of reform in Soviet nationalities policy, indeed when it was unthinkable to discuss the issue openly and frankly, Aitmatov's fiction cautiously broached the sensitive subject of Moscow's language and cultural policies in the non-Russian republics. While Aitmatov was held up to the West as an example of the success of "internationalism" in Soviet linguistic and cultural policy, he was always keenly aware of the discrepancy between theory and practice, frequently forcefully addressing the need to protect the rights of the languages and cultures of the country's ethnic minorities. Indeed, Aitmatov has characterized the danger of losing the "lesser" languages of the world as a form of "global degradation of the human spirit."[9]

Ironically, it is precisely Aitmatov's strong stance on strengthening the Kirghiz language and the emphasis on the Turkic national heritage in his fiction that for years made it more difficult for him to publish his works in his native republic than in Moscow. The most conservative opponents of the expression of the Turkic national heritage in literature were to be found in Frunze (now Bishkek). There, the authorities, in exaggerated efforts to please Moscow, sought to stifle all expression of what might be interpreted as bourgeois nationalism. As recently as 1984, one powerful Russified compatriot— Tendik Askarov, then head of the Kirghiz Writers' Union—purposely slighted Aitmatov by leaving his works unmentioned in a major article on the development of contemporary Kirghiz letters.[10] Today, Aitmatov concedes that one of the major reasons for his decision, in 1966, to write in Russian rather than in Kirghiz was his fear that his controversial works would never see the light of day in Kirghizstan.[11]

During the years of Mikhail Gorbachev's perestroika, Aitmatov's status as an all-union public figure continued to grow. In 1989, Gorbachev nominated Aitmatov to chair the Supreme Soviet's Commission on Issues Pertaining to the Development of Culture and Language, which had the power to make major corrections in the linguistic and cultural policy of the Soviet Union. The Aitmatov Commission recognized the legitimate rights of the languages of the Soviet Union's national minorities and created the legal framework for their development in the future. In the same year, he served on the Yakovlev Commission, which finally recognized the authenticity of the secret protocols to the Molotov-Ribbentrop pact of 1939. In 1990, to stress the importance of the intelligentsia in his reform efforts, Gorbachev appointed Aitmatov, along with Valentin Rasputin, to the Presidential Council.

From October 1988 to October 1990, Aitmatov worked as editor of the prestigious literary journal *Inostrannaia literatura* and was instrumental in returning or introducing to Soviet readers the works of such important authors as James Joyce, Arthur Miller, Vladimir Nabokov, Isaac Singer, Jean-Paul Sartre, Henry Miller, Salman Rushdie, and others. Soviet censorship, and the smoke screen of socialist realism charged with covering it, had the goal, as one Western critic observed, of breaking "that slender thread that ties contemporary Soviet literature to the West."[12] During his short tenure at *Inostrannaia literatura*, Aitmatov saw to it that those ties were strengthened.

After four years of actively participating in the political processes transforming Soviet society, Aitmatov requested from Gorbachev and received, in November 1990, the position of Soviet ambassador to Luxembourg. At the time of this writing (1993), after the collapse of the Soviet Union, he resides there still, as Russian ambassador. Aside from his duties as diplomat, he has remained very active as a writer, traveling frequently in Europe to read from his works to enthusiastic audiences and to cultivate his international contacts. His most recent work, a collection of philosophical dialogues and literary discussions with Japanese Buddhist leader Daisaku Ikeda, was, significantly, first published in German.

Aitmatov's fiction represents a unique synthesis of his Central Asian heritage with the Russian-European literary tradition. His belief that Soviet society was too quick in turning its back on centuries of accumulated cultural experience, as well as his rejection of its

dehumanizing utilitarianism, account for the author's persistent return to the mythic past for ethical lessons. This orientation toward
the past, which flows naturally from his Kirghiz cultural heritage, is
responsible for what Aitmatov calls *mnogoplanovost'* (multilayered
narrative) in his prose fiction. During the years of stagnation, he
believed this approach to Soviet reality to be a powerful means of
"extracting literature from its one-dimensionality, in which it [had]
abided so stubbornly and for so long."[13] His best fiction integrates
many differing literary and paraliterary genres into the narrative. Aitmatov transforms the material of myth, legend, and folklore into literary subplots, which, when introduced into the primary narrative
line, function as parables, providing lyrical and moral commentaries
on the events portrayed in the more central, realistic plot line.

The significance of the parabolic in Aitmatov's fiction cannot be
overemphasized.[14] Together with the numerous folklore elements
Aitmatov weaves as intermezzos into the main plot lines of his narratives, it explains the universal relevance and appeal that many of
his works acquire, their ability to transcend the specific time and
space of their settings. Etymologically, the word *parable* has two
roots: *para* (alongside of) and *ballein* (to cast, place, or throw). The
word implies that one thing is understood or fully appreciated only
in juxtaposition to or in comparison with another.[15] Aitmatov's folklore parables not only interpret but enhance the meaning of the author's portrayal of events in the main narrative plane. The parabolic
subplots—frequently presented as memory flashbacks of specific
characters—not only provide additional information and flesh out
characters, but also structurally model plot situations. They thus reflect and concentrate in more poignant form the larger, more complex issues in a work.

Like biblical parables, the folklore subplots are polyvalent and
can submit to multiple interpretations. Such polyvalence permits a
free, creative response from the reader: "The parable is a form of
discourse that appeals not only to the fascination of the human imagination with metaphor, or to the joyous perception of a surprise or
paradox, but to the most basic of human qualities: freedom."[16] In
Aitmatov's prose, the reader is challenged to find the answer, the key
to understanding the interrelationship of the parable and the central

plot. While the author's contemporary heroes may or may not completely comprehend the parable's message, the reader must grasp the greater context to appreciate the work fully. This very quality gives Aitmatov's works a high degree of ambiguity, which, in turn, has helped ease the way of his fiction through Soviet censorship. Frequently, his folklore parables function as screens disguising the author's critical attitude toward phenomena of Soviet life.

The folklore intermezzos play an equally important role in creating the narrative mood in Aitmatov's prose fiction. Most of the author's works end tragically. The lyrical style of the subplots, as well as their own tragic conclusions, serve to heighten the reader's sense of loss. Defying socialist realism's demand that a work of art have an underlying positive orientation, Aitmatov leads his readers through a series of tragic events that culminate in a powerful feeling of catharsis. His hope is openly didactic: the readers will resolve to better themselves and society. In this manner, the writer believes, Soviet literature can aid Soviet citizens in finding their true humanity and thus their way out of the moral degradation brought about by decades of totalitarianism.

In this study I examine Aitmatov's literary career—his personal "transition from Gorky to Dostoevsky," which one critic sees as the pivotal change undertaken by Soviet writers in the 1980s.[17] Aitmatov's literary evolution is truly remarkable. He began his career very much a prisoner of the literary models of the late Stalin era, freed himself from the one-dimensional portrayal of Soviet reality during the Thaw years, and, in the Brezhnev period of stagnation, drew increasingly on the oral tradition of his people to develop his unique parabolic genre. In my analysis of Aitmatov's fiction, I focus special attention on the folklore sources of his parables and demonstrate how knowledge of them can expand the reader's appreciation of the text. The literary and political context in which Aitmatov's major works appeared is also discussed at some length because of its relevance in explaining the response of Soviet readers to the publication of each of his major works. *The White Ship*, *The Day Lasts More than a Hundred Years*, and *The Place of the Skull* became literary events at the time of their publication. While some Soviet readers greeted

Aitmatov's works with enthusiasm, others found much to criticize. Yet virtually everyone read them.

In discussing Aitmatov's fiction, I limit myself to an analysis of those works that best reflect his parabolic genre: *Farewell, Gul'sary!*, *The White Ship*, *Early Cranes*, *The Piebald Dog Running Along the Seashore*, *The Day Lasts More than a Hundred Years*, and *The Place of the Skull*. These four novellas and two novels, Aitmatov's most popular works, also provide the greatest insight into his worldview.

The advent of glasnost brought radical change to the established rhythm and structure of the literary process in the Soviet Union.[18] After struggling so long against the many barriers constraining and inhibiting Soviet literature, Aitmatov compares his feelings in the new literary situation to those of a man "standing in confusion before a vast plain, not knowing what to do." "The new freedom," he notes, "seems boundless, and we must exert great effort to be worthy of that freedom."[19] Such freedom may compel the writer to reexamine his understanding of the role of literature in his country, as well as the genre that made him one of the most popular writers publishing in the Soviet Union in the 1970s and 1980s. The era of Soviet totalitarianism and social stagnation has come to an end; closer examination of the culture of that period is just beginning.

1

Aitmatov and Kirghizstan

Chingiz Torekulovich Aitmatov was born on December 12, 1928, in Sheker, a small *ail* (village) in the Kirov district of northern Kirghizstan, not far from the present border of Kazakhstan. Until 1936 the area was part of Kazakhstan. Aitmatov's paternal ancestors belonged to the clan of Sheker and for generations lived in that area of the Talas valley. The *ail*, where Aitmatov spent much of his boyhood, is located at the foot of legendary Mount Manas, the highest peak in the Talas mountain range. Manas shares its name with the Kirghiz oral epic (over 500,000 lines in verse!), which relates the exploits of the legendary Manas, a sort of Kirghiz Il'ia Muromets, who defends the Kirghiz lands against a host of mighty invaders.

More than just a collection of adventures concerning a central hero, *Manas* is the receptacle of the Kirghiz national heritage, a virtual ethnographic and cultural treasure chest. The epos has served as an inexhaustible source of inspiration for Aitmatov and other Kirghiz writers. Indeed, Central Asian critics have attributed the rapid rise of Kirghiz letters directly to the republic's time-honored epic tradition.[1] Its first compiler, Chokan Valikhanov (1835–1866), a Kazakh ethnographer and friend of Dostoevsky, referred to the epic poem as the *Iliad* of the steppes and pointed out that the epos contained information on "customs, geography, religion, medicine, as well as on international relations."[2] Through the centuries, the wealth of Kirghiz culture and folklore was preserved by singers of the epos, the revered *manaschi*, who kept it alive from generation to generation by reciting from memory improvised renditions of it. As a youth Aitmatov heard performances by Saiakbai Karalaev (1894–1971), one of the "last great *manaschi*," and has expressed his deep regret that the ancient art has been lost forever.[3] A leading Kirghiz expert on Aitmatov's work notes the significance of the author's firsthand encounter with the living epos:

> Today, much time has passed, and things have become clearer. We can assert with confidence that in the persons of Saiakbai Karalaev and Chingiz Aitmatov there occurred an historical meeting of two epoi— the ancient epos which was dying and the modern epos which was being born. Such an immediate, tangible encounter with the great ancient epos, of course, could not help but leave its indelible mark on Chingiz Aitmatov's work and life.[4]

In a number of ways, Aitmatov's perception of his vocation stems from his understanding of the role of the *manaschi* in prerevolutionary Kirghiz society. Through the centuries. the *manaschi* inspired and encouraged the Kirghiz nation in its darkest hours. They preserved the national heritage in times of defeat and foreign occupation, often performing for their compatriots at secret gatherings in the mountains. In performances lasting several days, they reminded the people of their nation's greatness and evoked the invincible Manas, a Kirghiz warlord who in the eighth century fought to liberate his downtrodden nation from Chinese occupation.

Aitmatov has pursued a similar social mission in his creative work, seeking to remind a denationalized Kirghiz intelligentsia of the dignity of their national heritage. His very first journalistic articles were dedicated to linguistic and cultural issues;[5] citing numerous examples, he makes a strong appeal to translators to show greater respect for the Kirghiz language. Although his art was never limited solely to a Kirghiz agenda, his stance on Kirghiz culture made him immensely popular in the republic. The Kirghiz people took particular pride in the success of Aitmatov's works beyond the boundaries of his national republic and saw in him a man who, in both his commentaries and belles lettres, was able to go over the heads of the Russified Kirghiz leadership and criticize the effects of Moscow's policy of aggressive sovietization toward Central Asia. Aitmatov's influence in post-Soviet Kirghizstan remains great, and people in Bishkek speak candidly about his role in brokering the victory of Askar Akaev, Kirghizstan's first democratically elected president.

Manas, together with a number of smaller Kirghiz oral epics, most notably *Kodzhodzhash*, resonates throughout Aitmatov's fiction. His prose possesses a distinct oral quality, with numerous refrains and subplot digressions punctuating the narration. As in the performance of a *manaschi*, such elements retard the portrayal of events and "serve to heighten the expression of the conceptual basis of the composition."[6] An air of improvization pervades his fiction, with abrupt shifts in styles, themes, and even genres. Aitmatov has frequently been criticized by Russian critics precisely for such sudden shifts, perceived as lapses in literary style. In particular, critics abhor the intrusion of journalistic style into Aitmatov's narratives. Indeed, when one compares such sections with the more polished passages elsewhere in the same work, the contrast is striking.[7] An impression is created that Aitmatov, like a *manaschi*, chooses to relax during certain parts of the "performance," only to renew its intensity later.

Despite such perceived stylistic deficiencies, which are more striking for occidental readers, Aitmatov's major fiction became highly popular reading in European Russia. His novellas and novels portrayed real human drama, at a time when Soviet citizens longed for literary works that told the truth about their time and society. The depiction of negative characters in Aitmatov also appears to be a *Manas* legacy. Aitmatov's villains consistently emerge as unrelentingly powerful and evil, threatening all around them. Characters like Orozkul, from *The White Ship*, Tansykbaev, from *The Day Lasts More than a Hundred Years*, and Bazarbai and Ober Kandalov, from *The Place of the Skull*, are in many ways various hypostases of one and the same epic evildoer, modern versions of Kongurbai or Dzholoi, Manas's awe-inspiring enemies.

Although parts of *Manas* were recorded and published before the Russian Revolution, serious compilation and study of the epos began only in the 1920s. Aitmatov himself worked for years as the editor of the Kirghiz Academy of Science's most authoritative edition of *Manas* to date and has stressed the necessity of saving it for future generations of Central Asians. The publication history of the epos has been far from smooth, however, with ideological guardians, both Kirghiz and Russian, throughout most of Soviet history opposing the appearance of many of its sections, which they considered narrowly nationalistic or unduly positive in portraying the prerevolutionary past. In 1937 *Manas* was condemned for its "bourgeois-clerical" philosophy, and its Kirghiz compilers were arrested. In the late 1940s and early 1950s, the label was changed to "feudal-clerical," and again arrests were quick to follow.[8]

As a student in Frunze in 1952, Aitmatov witnessed firsthand the bitter struggle between the proponents and detractors of the epos. The two camps were divided along ethnic lines. Most of the detractors were non-Kirghiz, unable to read the epos in the original, whereas Kirghiz scholars rallied to defend their cultural heritage. Yet the controversy was eventually decided in Moscow, to the detriment of *Manas* and other Turkic national epics. In a publication by the Academy of Science of the USSR, *Manas* was vilified for its "pan-Islamism, bourgeois-nationalism, military adventurism and disdain for the toiling masses."[9] Although that decision was eventually reversed after the death of Stalin, the effect of the anti-*Manas* campaign was felt for decades in Kirghizstan. As recently as 1987, Aitmatov condemned those who continued to take an ideological approach to the epic, saying that it was "stupid to try to make a thousand-year-old epic fit the political needs of the day."[10]

The geographical location of Aitmatov's native *ail* also seems to have imbued the writer with an epic view of man and life, an ability to see the human experience in a greater historical context—to grasp the essence of humanity apart from its entanglements in the affairs of the day. The legendary mountain's hold on the writer's artistic imagination is particularly evident in a passage from an essay Aitmatov wrote on his childhood:

> I become excited whenever I approach Sheker and see in the distance
> the blue-white snows of Manas, shining brightly in the inaccessible

heights of the sky. And if you lose yourself for a minute, if you stare only at that peak, at the sky, then time seems to lose its essence. The sense of the past disappears. No, you think to yourself, nothing has happened, nothing has changed, everything in the world is just as it was ten, twenty, and maybe a hundred and a thousand years ago. Manas stands as it has stood. And the clouds floating above it are one and the same clouds.[11]

The epic view of humankind is prominent in all of Aitmatov's mature fiction, eternal human values and the timeless wisdom of the natural world serving as prisms through which the humanity or morality of his characters are perceived.

But Aitmatov's view of the world has been determined by more than geography. Northern Kirghizstan, having been exposed at different times in its turbulent history to Lamaism, Hinduism, Islam, and Orthodox Christianity, has been characterized as a "Weltanschauung faultline dividing different civilizations."[12] Whereas the Islamization of Uzbekistan to the south and the west occurred rapidly after the Arab invasion of the area, the piedmont of northern Kirghizstan was spared the incorporation into Dar al-Islam by the sword. Islam thus came to the area relatively late through the proselytizing of Sufi wanderers. They adapted Islam to the underlying pantheistic (shamanistic) beliefs of the Kirghiz. The nomadic way of life of the Kirghiz made them particularly immune to the influence of theocentric religious systems. They held fast to their pantheistic and anthropocentric beliefs, with emphasis on wisdom, morals, and spiritual secularism.[13] Only in the late nineteenth century did Islam begin to occupy a greater place in the Kirghiz consciousness. Nevertheless, many of the old shamanistic and totemistic beliefs continue to live on today in rural areas of the republic, in the form of fairy tales, myth, and superstition. Their influence pervades Aitmatov's fiction. Some of the key elements of the shamanistic worldview among the Kirghiz are the sense of unity and participation with Creation, the belief that man lives under the watchful eye of the spirits of his ancestors, and faith in pantheistic intercessors.[14]

This close contact and sense of identity with the natural world greatly influenced the way the Kirghiz viewed human existence and history. Unlike the Judeo-Christian concept of time, which posits a beginning and end to Creation and hence a linear view of time imparting a sense of purpose to humankind's movement through time and history, the primal nature religion of the Kirghiz saw the universe as perpetual and time as cyclical, similar to what philosophers today call Indo-Hellenic time.[15] The observable repetition of nature's cycles of birth, death, and decay suggested to societies with primal religions a cyclical view of history, or "eternal recurrence," analogous to that of the Greek stoics, who believed—on the evidence of the cyclical movements of the heavenly bodies—that "the whole history of the Earth is exactly, and even identically, repeated in each cycle."[16]

Although a cyclical view of time is characteristic of many rural cultures and, as Kathleen Parthé has illustrated, is clearly evident in the fiction of Russia's Village Prose writers,[17] other factors contribute to its historical prevalence in Kirghizstan. In the Eastern religions of Buddhism and Confucianism—a glance at the map will remind us of Kirghizstan's proximity to both India and China—a similar view of human existence in time can be noted. The emphasis is on the "conviction that man [is] an integral part of nature or the universe, and that he should not strive to set himself over and against it as having a unique form of being or destiny." The observable cycle of birth, death, and decay in the natural world was viewed as a reminder to man "to live in conformity to nature, cheerfully accepting ultimate annihilation as occasioned by the physics of the universe."[18]

The pre-Islamic worldview of the northern Kirghiz was peculiarly past-oriented. For the proper harmonious functioning of human relations in society, the Kirghiz relied on the experience of those who were older or who had gone before them. Hence the worship of ancestors, the *arbak*, and reliance on their wisdom allowed the Kirghiz to make sense of the world and reinforced their confidence that they were not upsetting the sacred balance so evident in the natural world. The Kirghiz did not see history as transporting humanity to a higher developmental stage or bringing it closer to the fulfillment of a divine plan. History was, like nature itself, cyclical, allowing today's situation to be evaluated morally with respect to past generations. This approach to history is very much alive in Aitmatov's fiction. It is perhaps the quality that most distinguishes him as an Asian writer.[19] In his works, the present often tragically repeats the past, and the author invites his readers to contemplate their place in the world in the context of the historical experience of centuries of human civilization.

While traditional Islam eventually spread throughout northern Kirghizstan and Kazakhstan, it generally encountered deep-seated anticlericalism in the population. Sufi Islam, however, allowed a "smooth transition from shamanistic rites and concepts to what was thought to be Islam" and, in fact, included much of the old ethnic traditions. Sufism adapted itself to the natural ethnic structures of the Kirghiz. Indeed, Sufi ties paralleled tribal fidelity to the seven ancestors, and often the *shaykh* was an *aksakal* (white beard, or tribal elder).[20] Yet to date, Islam has exerted far less influence on Aitmatov's fiction than have the tenacious survivals of shamanism or even Christianity. Its absence is conspicuous. The fact that Aitmatov chose to portray a faithful Christian as the central character in his most recent novel, *The Place of the Skull*, is quite telling. When Islam is portrayed in Aitmatov's work, however, as in his classic *The Day Lasts More than a Hundred Years*, it appears more in a Sufi or *jadid* (secularized) form. Aitmatov's indifference to traditional Islam—the dominant religion in today's Central Asia—is not just the result of his own secular upbringing but an attitude that stems from his rejection of any and all forms of religious fundamentalism or ideologies with "pretensions of possessing the final truth."[21]

Chingiz Aitmatov is a bilingual author. He has written and published successfully in both his native language and Russian. In this he is similar to such well-known non-Russian Soviet writers as Vasil' Bykau (Belorussian) and Ion Drutse (Moldavian). Aitmatov prides himself on translating into Kirghiz works that he wrote and first published in Russian. It should also be noted that he prefers to speak Kirghiz at home.[22] Western specialists have characterized the author's literary Kirghiz as "the modern reference linguistic standard," and his works in that language are "perfectly pure from gratuitous Russian lexical and idiomatic *zasorenie* (littering)."[23] In a short autobiographical sketch, Aitmatov humorously credits his bilingualism to a whim of fate. The writer's paternal grandfather, Aitmat, suffered financial ruin from a fire that destroyed the family's water mill. Deciding to improve his lot, the impoverished grandfather left

Sheker with his twelve-year-old son Torekul (1903–1938) to find employment building a railroad tunnel near Maimak for the Arys'-Pishpek (Frunze) line of the Russian railroad.

As a consequence, Torekul, Aitmatov's father, had the opportunity to study in a Russian-Tartar school (*russko-tuzemnaia shkola*) in Aulie-Ata.[24] There, he became literate in both Kirghiz and Russian. Like many of the educated native elite in Central Asia, Torekul Aitmatov welcomed the Russian Revolution for its promise of putting an end to the political abuse and cultural insensitivity of the tsarist administration in Turkestan.[25] The degree of native frustration with Moscow on the eve of the revolution was demonstrated in the massive and bloody uprising against the tsarist administration and Russian settlers. Thousands of people on both sides perished in the turmoil, while others fled across the border into China.[26]

In 1921, Torekul traveled to Moscow to study at the Kommunisticheskii universitet trudiashchikhsia vostoka (Communist University of Toilers of the East), which trained specialists for party work in Central Asia. After his return to Kirghizstan in 1924, he occupied a number of important party positions in Kirghizstan—he headed the Kirghiz Oblast Committee's Department for Propaganda and Agitation, worked as secretary of the Dzhalal-Abad District Committee, and became people's commissar of the Industrial and Trade Department of the Kirghiz Autonomous Republic. His work in the party organization eventually gained him the position of second secretary of the Kirghiz *obkom* (Oblast Committee).[27] Torekul's keen interest in Russian culture was shared by his wife, Nagima Khamzaevna Aitmatova (1904–1970), who came from a prosperous Tartar merchant family and was, likewise, highly educated for her time. Together, the parents acquainted their children with Russian culture, language, and literature.

Familiarity with Russian literature at an early age was to have a lasting effect on Chingiz Aitmatov. Pushkin, Dostoevsky, Turgenev, and Tolstoy all fired his youthful imagination. The classics of Russia's golden age taught him to believe in the power and lofty mission of great literature. He came to share Tolstoy's belief that literature has a role to play in morally bettering humankind. This sense of ethical mission pervades all of Aitmatov's fiction and converges naturally with a similar Kirghiz understanding of the purpose of art and literature.

While Aitmatov became acquainted with Russian culture through his parents, the Kirghiz way of life and the Turkic national heritage were passed down to him by his paternal grandmother and aunt. Torekul Aitmatov, whose party career had brought him back from Moscow to Kirghizstan in 1924, settled in Frunze (Bishkek), the future Kirghiz capital. He never lost contact with Sheker, however, and would send Chingiz to the *ail* to spend the summer with his mother, Aiymkan Satan-kyzy. Aitmatov's grandmother would take the future writer along with her during summer migrations to high pastures in the mountains. This childhood experience instilled in Aitmatov a love for the rich culture of his native land. During the migrations, Aitmatov learned the age-old, pre-Islamic traditions and rituals associated with the nomadic way of life, as well as the fairy tales, myths, songs, and legends of his people—a heritage destined to reappear in the author's fiction. His lifelong fascination with folklore genres he attributes directly to those early summers spent with his grandmother. In later years his aunt, Karagyz Aitmatova, would assume Aiymkan's function as mediator of Kirghiz culture. Aitmatov was fortunate to have experienced that culture firsthand, because much of it was doomed to disappear following the forced sedentarization and collectivization of the Kirghiz in the 1930s.

Aitmatov's formal schooling began in Frunze, where he entered first grade in a Russian school. The following year, 1935, the family moved to Moscow, in conjunction with Torekul's studies at the Institute of Red Professors, a party school of higher learning established to train party-minded university instructors as well as cadres for positions in the central administrative bodies of the party and Soviet government. There, Aitmatov was enrolled in a Russian school and completed the second grade. In 1937, tragedy struck the family when Torekul Aitmatov was accused of "bourgeois nationalism" and arrested. The same fate would be shared by most of the students and former students of the institute. On the eve of his arrest, however, Torekul managed to arrange for his family's quick departure by train from Moscow to Sheker. The last time Aitmatov saw his father was through the window of the departing train.[28]

This event was to have a deep impact on Aitmatov's prose. Indeed, the author has never completely freed himself from the agony of being deprived of his father at an early age.[29] Throughout his works, the reader encounters heartrending depictions of young boys who lose their fathers. In *The White Ship*, for example, the boy hero perishes as he makes a desperate attempt to swim to his father, who he believes works as a sailor aboard a ship on Lake Issyk-kul. In *The Day Lasts More than a Hundred Years*, two boys watch tearfully as their arrested father is taken away from them by train. The loss and injustice experienced by Aitmatov's family are also articulated in the biting sarcasm accompanying scenes depicting Stalinist and neo-Stalinist bureaucrats.

Aitmatov speaks of the tragic irony of the railroad tunnel that Aitmat and his son Torekul built before the revolution. He notes that the railroad brought not only happiness, new culture, and civilization to his region, but also totalitarianism and misery:

> The railroad brought us everything, so to say. On that railroad my father left to study in Moscow. On the same line he returned in a prison wagon for his investigation. The same railroad was used to take him away to the north somewhere, perhaps to Chukhotka, or maybe he disappeared somewhere else. Who knows? . . . It was as if Father and Grandfather built that tunnel for our fate.[30]

Whenever Aitmatov has occasion to travel by rail through the tunnel, regardless of the hour, he stands in silence at the window because, in his words, "my soul won't let me do otherwise."[31] It is in a sense a religious place where the spirits of his father and grandfather reside.

For fifty-three years, Aitmatov had no idea of how his father had perished or where he was buried. Then the incredible occurred. In the summer of 1991, the remains of Aitmatov's father were found in a mass grave on the territory of an NKVD (People's Commissariat for Internal Affairs) recreational facility called Chon-Tash (Big Rock), located on the outskirts of the Kirghiz capital. The sensational discovery stunned Aitmatov, compelling him to believe in the mystical presence of "higher justice" in the world, a force that knows no "statute of limitations" and lies "outside the sphere of our daily lives."[32] The site contained the remains of 138 Kirghiz intellectuals shot by firing squads on November 6, 1938, the eve of the anniversary of the October Revolution. Their execution by the NKVD represents, in Aitmatov's words, nothing less than the "intellectual genocide" of the Kirghiz nation.[33] Those murdered were young and talented. Their average age was between thirty and thirty-five. Conclusive evidence pointed to the fact that Torekul Aitmatov was among the dead:

> Among the things found was a death sentence with a bullet hole in it— apparently it was put in my father's pocket—which proved that those were his remains. Everything had disappeared, rotted away: the bodies of the unfortunate people, their footware, and clothing. But pieces of paper, a document from that time with the name of Torekul Aitmatov on it, survived. [That document is] a typewritten text of three pages that is so well preserved that it can be read. . . . All of this, of course, stunned me. And especially the horrible document which had lain buried for half a century in the ground and which I saw with my own eyes.[34]

Using that document and KGB archives in Bishkek, investigators were able to reconstruct the list of those executed on that day in November. All 138 individuals have since been identified.[35]

Torekul's family arrived safely in Sheker at the beginning of September 1937. Aitmatov recalls that kolkhoz activists and the *selsovet* (village council) soon made life miserable for the family of "an enemy of the people." Close relatives, however, came to the family's aid. Torekul's brother, Ryskulbek, courageously helped the family acquire food and fuel for the winter. In mid-October 1937, a month and a half after the family had arrived in Sheker, Ryskulbek himself was arrested in the night by people in uniform. At the time, Aitmatov shared a bed with his uncle, and he recalls vividly his feelings upon waking up and finding himself alone. The experience of losing yet another father figure was traumatic. The family never saw Ryskulbek again.[36]

When the NKVD finally responded to the request of Aitmatov's mother for information on her husband, they cynically informed her that Torekul Aitmatov had been sentenced to ten years' incarceration without the right of correspondence. That willful misinformation was delivered to the family by special NKVD courier after Torekul's execution.[37] Such was the atmosphere of hostility in which Aitmatov completed the second and third grades at a Kirghiz school in Sheker. Years later, he would write that during those difficult childhood years he would dream of sacrificing himself in a heroic deed "to prove in such a way the innocence of my father before the Soviet state."[38]

The family's fortunes improved somewhat in 1939, when Aitmatov's mother found employment as an accountant in Kirovskoe, the regional administrative center. For the next three years, Aitmatov again attended a Russian school. Yet after the outbreak of World War II, food shortages made life so unbearable in Kirovskoe that Nagima Aitmatova took her family back to Sheker, where she found work at a kolkhoz for a "subsistence norm" in food products.[39] Thus by the age of fourteen, Aitmatov, unlike most of his peers, had experienced an alternating exposure to Russian and Kirghiz cultural environments and had become fully bilingual.

The war years in Sheker were harsh for the fourteen-year-old Aitmatov. At a time when all the men were away in the army, Aitmatov's literacy in both Russian and Kirghiz made him the most educated youth in the *ail*. As a result, Aitmatov was drafted to be secretary of the village soviet.[40] His duties brought him into close contact with all the families in the area, and when called upon to collect taxes from the impoverished people in that difficult time, he deserted to join a tractor brigade rather than fulfill what he considered so inhuman a duty. He was almost brought before a tribunal for his recalcitrance. The war as experienced by Aitmatov in a destitute village deep in the hinterland was later to find expression in much of his early work and became pivotal in *Early Cranes*.

After the war, from 1946 to 1948, Aitmatov studied veterinary science at a *tekhnikum* (vocational school) in Dzhambul (Aulie-Ata), Kazakhstan. The choice of veterinary medicine was a prestigious one for a young Kirghiz man. Like their northern neighbors, the Kazakhs, the Kirghiz had for centuries believed that human spirits lived on in livestock, and the possession of healthy animals was viewed as a great blessing. This veneration of animals would later surface repeatedly in Aitmatov's fiction. Indeed, it is one of the most prominent features of Aitmatov's prose. Beginning with *Farewell, Gul'sary!*, animals are presented as man's lesser brothers and are at times endowed with greater wisdom than the people among whom they live. Often, the animals play the role of the hero's alter ego or function as a moral yardstick by which the humanity of Aitmatov's characters is measured.

In 1949, Aitmatov enrolled at the Kirghiz Institute of Agriculture in Frunze. He proved to be an excellent student and was even awarded a Stalin stipend in his second year of studies. By the end of 1951, however, Aitmatov's background as "son of an enemy of the people" caught up with him, and he was suddenly deprived of the stipend. He also sensed an equally rapid change in the attitudes of his colleagues and teachers toward him. Upon graduation in 1953, he felt himself to be an *izgoi* (an outcast), and he did not insist on entering graduate school, although several departments had sought his enrollment.[41] The rejection he experienced at the Institute of Agriculture turned out to be a blessing in disguise. Aitmatov began to channel more of his energies into literature. Within five years of his graduation, his name would be known throughout Kirghizstan.

Before Aitmatov became a writer, four important factors contributed to the formation of his view of life and the world. The first was the Kirghiz cultural experience, with its cyclical concept of history, its understanding of man as part of nature, and its legacy of religious diversity. Perhaps the richness and depth of Aitmatov's Kirghiz cultural experience helped to make him resistant—after a brief period of literary apprenticeship—to one-dimensional portrayals of reality or calls for ideological conformity. It explains the writer's comprehensive approach to Soviet reality, resulting from an innate receptivity to ideas and philosophies from different cultures. It accounts for the writer's efforts—especially striking in *The Place of the Skull*—to find a common denominator for worldviews as disparate as totemism and Christianity.

The second influence was Russian culture, which Aitmatov acquired through his parents and the schools. His intimate knowledge of the Russian language gave him direct access to the classics of Russian literature and, in the end, made it possible for him to reach a wider circle of readers. A third influence was that of the writer's provincial upbringing, which instilled in him a strong rural bias. His fiction—like that of Tolstoy and that of many other Russian writers—

reveals the belief that city life corrupts. Indeed, Aitmatov generally avoids depicting the city in his works. The city is the place where moral values are lost, and consequently it is there that his villains reside or dream of living. In this he has much in common with Rasputin, Belov, and other Village Prose authors. Aitmatov also shares with them a concern for the natural environment.

Finally, there is the trauma of losing his father. The arrest and execution of Torekul Aitmatov during Stalin's purges resulted in the writer's literary idealization of the relationship between fathers and sons and helps explain the determination with which he has put his fiction in the service of de-Stalinization. After the discovery of the Kirghiz "Katyn'" in 1991,[42] Aitmatov will, no doubt, continue to probe the abyss of the Stalin years in his future writings as well.

2

First Steps

Aitmatov began his literary career as a translator. While still a student at the Kirghiz Agricultural Institute, he felt strongly drawn toward literature and decided to make a contribution to Kirghiz letters by translating two popular works on World War II: Valentin Kataev's *Son of the Regiment* (1945) and Mikhail Bubennov's *White Birch* (1947). When he presented his translations to a publishing house, he learned that both works had already been translated and would soon appear in print.[1] Far from being discouraged, however, he began to write short articles and essays for Kirghiz newspapers, including two on the art of translation,[2] and in 1952 published his first literary works—three short stories: "Newsboy Dziuio," "Ashim," and "We March Onward." All three stories appeared in Russian language publications.

After graduation from the Agricultural Institute, Aitmatov worked as a veterinarian specialist and continued to publish short stories: "Water Lords" in 1953, "On Dry Fields," and "White Rain" in 1954, and "Difficult Crossing" in 1955.[3] With the exception of "On Dry Fields," this second set of early stories was written in Kirghiz and first published in Kirghiz journals. Their publication opened the doors of the Writers' Union for Aitmatov and subsequently gained him an invitation to study at the Gorky Literary Institute in Moscow, in 1956 and 1957.

The early short stories are all narrated in the third person, a voice that proved difficult to handle for the beginning writer. The plots tend to be simplistic, and a lack of psychological motivation for the characters' actions is typical. Aitmatov himself would later criticize them as "imitative and having little to do with real life."[4]

Certainly an embarrassment to Aitmatov today, "Newsboy Dziuio," for example, portrays the hard life of a newspaper boy in U.S.-occupied Japan, whose growing political awareness prompts him to participate in a signature drive for a world peace petition. The narrative descriptions tend to be verbose, and the narrator's voice has a declamatory ring: "There went an American. Oh, how Dziuio hated him! He could painfully step on Dziuio's foot with his heavy shoe. More than once had Dziuio felt their coarse blows to the back of his head."[5] The story is complete with an appeal to Stalin, in whom the boy puts his faith for a better future. Aitmatov never included "Newsboy Dziuio" in any subsequent collection of his works. Its anti-American sentiment and its inclusion of Stalin in the role of deus ex machina were quite in keeping with the literature and propaganda of the Zhdanov years. "Newsboy Dziuio" is an indication of the power literary stereotypes had on a young provincial writer.

Aitmatov would subsequently recall his attitude toward Stalin at the time as being very complicated. Although Stalin was ultimately responsible for the deaths of his father and uncles, he was unable to accept that truth fully. His father's sister, Karagyz Aitmatova, who was illiterate, would curse Stalin in his presence and would try to open his eyes to the abominable nature of the regime, but to no avail. Looking back on his youth, Aitmatov recalls that the schools and media of the time had succeeded in fully indoctrinating him. By 1953, however, perhaps in connection with his becoming an outcast at the institute, he had become more and more convinced that his aunt was right. When Stalin died on March 5, 1953, Aitmatov went alone to the funeral ceremonies in Frunze. He remembers, "On the one hand I understood that the people were sincerely moved, but on the other hand I knew and felt that at last that monstrous force was departing."[6]

Aitmatov's mixed feelings and awakening were, no doubt, shared by millions of Soviet citizens of his generation.

The short stories "White Rain" and "Water Lords" can be placed within the mainstream of Kirghiz literature at the time, reflecting as they do the conflict of the new and old in Central Asia. It was ideologically appropriate to affirm the new and progressive in socialist Kirghizstan. Thus, in "White Rain," a girl alarms her tradition-minded mother by going to work in a Komsomol brigade plowing virgin land. There, the heroine secretly marries, grievously disappointing her mother. In the end, however, the mother suddenly accepts her daughter's new way of life when she realizes how important the work of the brigade is in the virgin lands. In "Water Lords," a similar generational conflict occurs between a father and son. The title refers to the men (*sypaichi*) who build weirs in mountain streams to divert water into irrigation ditches. The profession was critical for Kirghiz agriculture, requiring a lot of experience and just as much guesswork. Often many hours of work were destroyed by the caprice of a rising river. In Aitmatov's story, the son of a *sypaichi* insults his father by suggesting that building floodgates would be more efficient than the work of the *sypaichi*. Father and son become estranged. As the story concludes, however, the son returns as an engineer to build the floodgates, and upon seeing the project the father forgives him.

In both "White Rain" and "Water Lords," the representatives of the old accept the new, yet the psychological motivation for such a transformation is unconvincing. The plot scheme is typical of much of Kirghiz and Soviet literature at the time, and Aitmatov's versions suggest that literary models had a much greater influence—however short-lived—on the young writer than the folklore of his "backward" *ail*.

Much of this early work fits neatly into the rubric of socialist realism, whether one uses Vladimir Voinovich's humorous but simplistic definition of the term ("Socialist realism is praise of the leadership in terms they can understand") or approaches socialist realism with the aid of Bakhtin's chronotope, as Katerina Clark does. Clark stresses the significance of the deep structure of socialist realist works, noting that they generally display "two orders of time and place," which "gives shape to both characters and events."[7] As in

"White Rain" and "Water Lords," the ordinary time of the present is contrasted with the future time of communism. The central figure in a socialist realist work thus becomes, in Clark's words, a "harbinger of the Great Future."

The spatial duality of socialist realist works is expressed in the inevitable contrast between the urban center of political authority and a microcosm of Soviet society at a distance from the capital. In "Water Lords," for example, the son returns from engineering school in the city to correct a problem in the province. Clark admits that "the precise pattern of the two time-places has changed more than once, but the convention of having two orders of time-place has remained."[8] Socialist realism was thus a dynamic aesthetic system. Yet central to it was what Geoffrey Hosking calls "an impoverished image of man which [was], in large measure, accepted by the oppressed themselves."[9] In the future, Aitmatov would seek to destroy that image of man, substituting it in his fiction with spiritually autonomous heroes. In so doing, he has proved himself adept at manipulating both the surface and structural features of socialist realism.

The short story "Difficult Crossing"—which has also appeared under the title "On Baidamtal River"—is the best of Aitmatov's early stories, and no doubt played a large role in his admission to the Gorky Literary Institute in Moscow. "Difficult Crossing" contains a number of ingredients that would characterize the mature Aitmatov—the conflict is highly dramatic, the hero is faced with a difficult moral decision, and nature plays an important role in reflecting the psychological state of the hero. The main character of the story, Nurbek, deserts his sovkhoz after wrecking a tractor on a steep hillside. His high opinion of his abilities has caused him to disregard the warnings of his more experienced fellow workers and to attempt to plow on the dangerous slope. After the accident, Nurbek flees into the mountains, where he is later found, half-dead, by a hydraulic engineer near the river Baidamtal. The engineer's daughter, Asiia, nurses the runaway back to health. Asiia's cheerful outlook on life and pride in her work appeal to Nurbek, and, by contrast, his own reckless actions begin to appear more and more shameful to him. He therefore decides to leave the family secretly and to continue his flight.

To do so, he must cross the flood-swollen Baidamtal by means of a hand-powered cable car. As he draws near to the other side of the river, however, the winch jams and the car stops. Nurbek manages to reach the other side of the river by walking the remaining four meters on the cables. Safe on the other bank, he begins to run when he is suddenly struck by the thought that Asiia and her father would not be able to return the car to their side of the river. Knowing Asiia's resolve and self-confidence, Nurbek realizes that she would risk her life on the cables in an attempt to retrieve the car. Therefore, at great risk to his own life, Nurbek crawls along the cables to the other bank to obtain the necessary tools to repair the car. The experience tempers his character, and upon completion of the repairs he resolves to return to the sovkhoz to face responsibility for his actions.

Despite the melodramatic character of the short story, Aitmatov succeeds in creating believable dialogue and in resisting the temptation of a happy ending. Although Nurbek decides to return, the conclusion is open-ended: the reader is left to surmise the outcome of both his return and his relationship with Asiia. Reading the story today, one is inclined to dismiss it as insignificant. Yet in the context of the Kirghiz literary scene in the 1950s, "Difficult Crossing" appears quite innovative. Moreover, it brought Aitmatov his first taste of fame when it was made into a successful radio play.[10]

In 1956, Aitmatov became a member of the Communist party and was subsequently accepted into the Writers' Union of the USSR. In the same year, he began advanced literary studies at the Gorky Institute in Moscow. He was admitted both on the merit of his early stories and on the basis of what might be called Moscow's "affirmative action" policy toward non-Russian writers from the national republics.[11] Aitmatov's studies in Moscow proved to be a turning point in his literary career. He arrived in the Soviet capital at a time when the literary thaw was gaining momentum. The year 1956 witnessed Nikita Khrushchev's first steps toward the de-Stalinization of Soviet society. Vladimir Dudintsev published his sensational *Not by Bread Alone*, and the first Soviet edition of Dostoevsky's antisocialist novel *Besy* (The Possessed) appeared. It was an exciting time to be in Moscow, and Soviet writers were filled with optimism about the prospects of greater literary freedom.

Aitmatov no doubt learned much he would never have been exposed to in distant Kirghizstan. In Moscow, he was able to participate in a rich and diverse cultural life, which in and of itself greatly expanded his understanding of literature. Finally, the course work at the institute taught him much about literary theory, poetics, and the writer's craft. All of this would come together and contribute greatly to his further liberation from literary schemata. Twenty years after completing the institute, Aitmatov recalled what he had come to realize in Moscow: "I had to free myself from the shackles of sentimentalism and naturalism, which my former 'provincial' notions about 'real' literature had put upon me. I had to stop living what I would call the 'unreal' lives of my literary heroes, who were only pretending to be people. Overcoming my youthful and naive illusions was thus connected with the need to become myself, to understand who I was as a person, as an author."[12]

One of the striking changes to occur in Aitmatov's work after his arrival in Moscow was his shift from short story to novella, which later proved to be his favorite and perhaps most successful genre. The year he graduated, 1958, saw the publication of his first two novellas—*Face to Face* and *Dzhamilia*. After his graduation, Aitmatov returned to Kirghizstan to work as an editor of *Literaturnyi Kirgizstan*, in 1959 and 1960, and later, from 1961 to 1965, as special correspondent for *Pravda* for the Central Asian republics. His four years' experience as a journalist deepened his appreciation for the life in his own republic, and during that period he produced a number of successful novellas dealing with various aspects of contemporary Kirghizstan: *My Poplar in the Red Scarf*, *The Camel's Eye*, *The First Teacher*, and *Mother's Field*. With the exception of *Face to Face*, all of the novellas of this period are narrated in the first person. Uniting them also is the author's concern with the difficult role of women in Soviet Central Asia.

Face to Face tells the story of a Kirghiz deserter during World War II, who secretly returns to his native *ail*. His wife, Seide, is at first beside herself with joy at the thought of having her husband, Ismail, alive. But when hiding his presence becomes more and more difficult for both of them, Seide witnesses her husband's gradual loss of humanity. Ismail eventually sinks so low as to steal and slaughter a cow, a poor widow's only resource to sustain her children.[13] Shocked and torn by grief for the widow's great misfortune, Seide realizes that she herself is indirectly responsible for the crime. She therefore betrays her husband to the NKVD. Ismail throws down his weapon and surrenders when Seide approaches him with their child in her arms. Aitmatov was later to admit that the conclusion of the novella was psychologically implausible[14]—a woman, especially in view of her social position in Central Asia, would be unlikely to betray her husband. Though Aitmatov sought to motivate Seide's actions by making her husband's crime appear heinous, the solution remains unconvincing.

Sixteen years later, the same conflict would be taken up by Rasputin in *Zhivi i pomni* (Live and remember), 1974. In Rasputin's popular novel, however, the deserter's wife, Nastena, perishes with her unborn child rather than betray her husband, who has similarly lost his humanity. Yet such a realistic portrayal of the dilemma of choosing between private and public allegiances would almost certainly have been impermissible in Soviet letters at the time *Face to Face* was published. When Aitmatov wrote his novella, the subject matter alone was provocative enough. In Kirghizstan, for example, he faced severe criticism for allegedly slandering the reputation of Kirghiz fighting men. Also, his portrayal of near-starvation in the village was viewed as casting doubt on the effectiveness of the victorious Soviet wartime economy.[15]

In March 1990, Aitmatov republished *Face to Face* in *Literaturnyi Kirgizstan* and included a new chapter, which, he maintains, was intended to be part of the 1958 original but had to be scrapped due to "considerations of censorship."[16] The new chapter concerns itself primarily with the portrayal of Ismail's mother and her relationship with her son. Ismail emerges as a more plastic, believable character, but the story still falters on the issue of Seide's motivation. The most important new dimension of *Face to Face*, however, is the linking of the war theme to the dispossession of the kulaks in Kirghizstan. In the new version, Ismail dreams of fleeing with his family high into the Chatkal mountains to his mother's brothers, who had there found refuge from the unjust dispossession and deportation carried out during the party's collectivization campaign. Such linkage would, of course, have been impossible in 1958. As late as 1982, Bykau's classic *Znak bedy* (Sign of misfortune) was rigorously censored for portraying Belorussian collaboration with the Nazis as a consequence of party-inspired class warfare in the Belorussian village during the 1930s.

Despite a degree of woodenness in the author's depiction of his characters (reminiscent of his early short stories), there is much in *Face to Face* that anticipates the mature Aitmatov—the dramatic nature of the clash between good and evil in Seide's conscience, the integration of folklore genres (songs) into the narrative, and the choice of a controversial subject.

Dzhamilia, also published in 1958, brought the thirty-year-old writer international fame. The plot of the novella is simple but again controversial—a young Kirghiz peasant woman falls in love with a disabled veteran and betrays the husband her extended family has chosen for her. The affair develops while the husband is away at the front. The heroine, Dzhamilia, eventually leaves her native *ail* with her newfound love, Daniiar, just as her husband is convalescing from his wounds in a hospital. The novella's innovative twist to the stereotyped depiction of Soviet women—unflinching in their faithfulness to their men at the front—was quite provocative at the time. And in contrast to *Face to Face*, Aitmatov succeeded in making the motivation of his characters convincing. Dzhamilia emerges as a personality, a unique human being whose actions are consistent with her character and her psychology. In keeping with the spirit of the Thaw, Aitmatov's heroine gains the sympathy of the reader by choosing dignity and personal happiness over the obligations and behavior her social milieu demands of her. The triumph of the personality is the theme of *Dzhamilia*.

Dzhamilia is narrated in the first person, through the eyes of the heroine's brother-in-law, Seit, who was fifteen years old at the time of the events yet as narrator is much older, having completed school and become an artist. Indeed, Seit tells Dzhamilia's story to explain why he has devoted his life to art. As Dzhamilia's brother-in-law, it had been his family duty to protect her from any attempts on her fidelity in the absence of her husband. Consequently, he accompanied Dzhamilia everywhere and thus witnessed her falling passionately in love with Daniiar. Through Seit, Aitmatov presents an objective picture of the patriarchal way of life in the *ail*, with all the intricate responsibilities and taboos established by tradition and implied in the social reality of the extended family. But Aitmatov refrains from depicting Dzhamilia's milieu as unduly oppressive. He chooses not to resort to this stereotyped approach toward the tenacious *perezhitki* (remnants, cultural survivals) of prerevolutionary Kirghizstan. Indeed, Dzhamilia is happy and respected in her family at the time she meets Daniiar. Their love is free of the social entanglements created by patriarchal society. Seit recognizes this and keeps their relationship a secret. The youth sees in their love the beauty of freedom.

Fortune smiled on Chingiz Aitmatov. *Dzhamilia* came to the attention of Louis Aragon, a prominent French author and communist, who translated it into French and wrote an enthusiastic introduction, proclaiming Aitmatov's novella to be the "most beautiful love story in the world."[17] That endorsement literally put Kirghizstan on the map for European readers and resulted in an invitation to Aitmatov to tour France and Western Europe, a trip he made in 1964. The author had suddenly become a non-Russian writer of all-union stature. From that time on, the Soviet cultural establishment would hold Aitmatov up to the West as proof of the success of the Soviet Union's cultural policy toward non-Russian Soviet peoples.

The novellas written by Aitmatov in the early 1960s reveal the impact of his growing experience—as special correspondent of *Pravda* in Central Asia, he traveled extensively and broadened his knowledge of his homeland. He continued to work hard at his fiction, and his work of that time bears the evidence of his experimentation with different literary forms and points of view. In *My Poplar in the Red Scarf*, for example, the unhappy love story of a young truck driver is told by three first-person narrators. *The Camel's Eye* breaks with Socialist Realism's clichéd stereotypes of noble proletarian and weak-willed intellectual. The hero of the story, Kemel', is a sensitive youth who is brutalized by the villain, Abakir, who hates the youth because of his erudition and idealism. Their work together in the virgin lands turns into a duel of wills. While beaten physically, Kemel' prevails spiritually over his proletarian opponent. The portrayal of the negative Abakir is exceptionally successful; he would later become the prototype of a number of negative characters in Aitmatov's fiction.

In the novella *The First Teacher*, Aitmatov reinterprets the literary concept of the positive hero. The novella tells the story of Diuishen, a semieducated Komsomol member who goes to a Kirghiz *ail* in the early 1920s to teach the children to read and write. Diuishen makes up for his lack of education by enthusiasm for the ideals of the revolution. The story of his life is narrated by a woman academician who was in Diuishen's first class as a little girl. Because he saved her from becoming a *tokol* (a second wife) of a crude sheepherder and later enabled her to study in the city, she is deeply indebted to him and defends him when, nearly forty years later, the intelligentsia in the *ail* laugh with disbelief at the thought that Diuishen, now the village mailman, could ever have taught anyone anything. There is a quixotic quality in Aitmatov's portrayal of Diuishen, a man who first takes a beating for his ideals and then, years later, after Soviet power and institutions are firmly established in the *ail*, becomes a figure of ridicule among the educated young people.

The character of Diuishen in *The First Teacher* was Aitmatov's answer to the prose of his young Russian colleagues of the early 1960s, whose distaste for the positive heroes of socialist realism moved them toward a total break with the concept of party heroes obsessed with the collective goal of building communism. In the fiction of Vasilii Aksenov, for example, the positive hero was replaced by irreverent antiheroes à la J. D. Salinger. Both the protagonists and their authors display bold disdain for the slogans of the time. While he shared the young writers' dislike of "classical Socialist Realism"[18] and the odious positive heroes populating such prose works, Aitmatov's background and ideas on the moral purpose of literature put him at odds with them. In the press, he spoke out against their approach and by so doing placed himself on the side of party conservatives who eventually suppressed youth prose. In an open letter appearing in *Komsomolskaia pravda*, Aitmatov criticizes Yevgenii Yevtushenko, Vasilii Aksenov, and Andrei Vosnesenskii, and asks rhetorically: "What will we tell the next generation? What pictures of the life of our time will we bequeath to those coming after us? Have you thought about the fact that we have yet to create any vivid, profound, or complex portrayals of Soviet people in the 1960s?"[19]

Here Aitmatov is arguing against the antiheroes of youth prose, not attempting to resurrect the clichéd concept of the positive hero. Aitmatov felt that Soviet literature needed characters who could appeal to a wider circle of readers and not just reflect the disillusionment of urban youth. There were still positive heroes to be found, in Aitmatov's view, but they did not reside in the city. They lived in the provinces among the simple people who had borne the bulk of the hardships of collectivization and war.[20] The positive character Aitmatov presents in *The First Teacher*, therefore, is devoid of the heroic trappings of his stereotypical predecessors. Despite the aura surrounding Diuishen in the narrator's eyes, the reader sees him also for what he is—a "little man" in the venerable tradition of Russian letters. The positive hero has "fallen" in Aitmatov's prose and, as a result, has become more human and believable. Aitmatov's subsequent positive heroes would share Diuishen's modest character.

Mother's Field represents perhaps the most significant step in the writer's literary maturation. The novella's form—consisting of a dialogue between a distraught widow and the Earth—is an abrupt departure from the tenets of classical socialist realism. A third voice, the author's, functions as a dramatist's voice and gives only the initial "stage directions." The composition and theme are reminiscent of Wolfgang Borchert's play, *Draussen vor der Tür* (The man outside). Borchert was first published in the USSR in *Inostrannaia literatura* (July 1958), with an afterword by Heinrich Böll. Both Aitmatov's novella and Borchert's play deal with the difficulty of starting life anew after experiencing the horrors of war. Borchert's hero returns to Germany from a Soviet POW camp at the end of World War II and takes his grief to the river Elbe. The Elbe refuses to allow the hero, Beckmann, to commit suicide, and Beckmann must come to terms with life in the rubble of postwar Germany.

In Aitmatov's novella, the heroine, Tolgonai, seeks solitude in a harvested field, where she tells Mother Earth how much she suffers from the loss of her husband and three sons to the war. She finds consolation in the fact that her grief has been shared by many before her and that the Earth suffers with all mothers who have experienced the loss of their children. She also comes for advice—how is she to tell the truth to the illegitimate son of her only daughter-in-law, whose despair at the loss of her husband led to an unwanted pregnancy and death in childbirth? Like Andrei Sokolov, the hero of Mikhail Sholokhov's novella, *Sud'ba cheloveka* (The fate of a man), 1957, Tolgonai does not despair of life as, blow by blow, her happiness is destroyed. The form of the imaginary dialogue evokes an aura of primitive yet deep religiosity. Quite innovative at the time for Soviet letters, this departure from the tangible and the real reflects a deeply ingrained Kirghiz view of the world—Tolgonai's dialogue with the Earth corresponds to the Kirghiz cult of Umai-ene, the goddess of human and earthly fertility.[21] Hence the dialogue between a Kirghiz peasant woman and a timeless deity endows the heroine's story with universal significance and makes her sorrow stand for that of all women who have lost their men in war. The author's efforts to seek the universal in the specific is also borne out by the way his illiterate heroine speaks in the lofty manner of a seer.

The three voices in the novella—the Earth's, the author's, and Tolgonai's—speak in condemnation of war. There is no effort to portray the Soviet Union's role in World War II as just and thus elevate Tolgonai's suffering to a higher level than that of German mothers, for example. While acknowledging the heroism of Soviet soldiers, Tolgonai adds, "but nothing, no glory can bring my son back to life. Ask any mother; no mother dreams of such glory. Mothers bear their children for life, for simple earthly happiness."[22] Such a view of the war, in the opinion of a number of Soviet critics at the time, invariably led the author into compromising the proper Soviet ideological position. Pavel Glinkin's monograph on Aitmatov, published in 1968, best captures the spirit of the times:

> Tolgonai did not see firsthand the horrors that fascism brought. Consequently, her ideas about what had occurred are in many ways incomplete; as a result her consciousness does not distinguish between a just war and an unjust one. . . . But that which the simple Kirghiz woman did not do, the author, Aitmatov, somehow should have accomplished. His voice as author should have "introduced corrections" into Tolgonai's ideas and viewed them from a higher ideological position. Unfortunately, that did not take place, and therefore the general idea behind

Mother's Field was coated over by a metaphysical, socially and histori-
cally undifferentiated, evaluation of the war. The monologue form of
the work, a story narrated by a mother, thus created the contradiction
in the objective appraisal of historical events.[23]

Socialist realism, of course, demanded that the author's position
toward the events portrayed in a literary work be clearly defined. Yet
Aitmatov revealed in *Mother's Field* an inclination to make his own
stance in his fiction ambiguous. Thus on the realistic plane, Tolgonai
sees her sons as heroes of a righteous cause; yet on the more powerful
nonrealistic plane of her dialogue with Mother Earth, the emphasis
is placed not on the specific but the universal, that is, on the tragedy
of all wars. Such a technique is the cornerstone of Aitmatov's mature
fiction. Frequently, the mythic or folkloric plane reduces the political
and social complexities of contemporaneity, depicted in the realistic
plot line, to simple universal categories of right and wrong.

In April 1963, Aitmatov was awarded the Lenin Prize for the
publication of *Tales of the Mountains and Steppes*, which included
My Poplar in the Red Scarf, *The First Teacher*, *The Camel's Eye*, and
Dzhamilia. The award can be considered recognition of both Aitmatov's artistic achievement and his generally acceptable ideological
stance. In this context, it is important to keep in mind that Aleksandr
Solzhenitsyn's *A Day in the Life of Ivan Denisovich* was published
in 1962 yet nominated for the Lenin Prize in 1964. At the time of
publication, the award was blocked by conservative functionaries,
despite broad support for Solzhenitsyn's novella. The choice of Aitmatov in 1963 enabled those opposing Solzhenitsyn to defer for a
year the inevitable controversy connected with Solzhenitsyn's nom-
ination. For the next three years, Aitmatov published no new works.
The fall of Khrushchev and the trial of Joseph Brodskii in 1964 signaled the end of the regime's liberal attitude toward Soviet writers.
When Aitmatov broke his silence in 1966 with the publication of
Farewell, Gul'sary!, it became clear that the writer had entered a
new stage in his development.

Prior to *Farewell, Gul'sary!*, Aitmatov's novellas were mostly
written in the first person, a form that he now came to view as too
limiting. Beginning with *Farewell, Gul'sary!*, Aitmatov has preferred
the third person, with heavy reliance on internal monologue to por-

tray his characters more fully. Accompanying this change is an increasing use of the folklore and oral legacy of Central Asia to elucidate parabolically the events depicted in the main plot line. As a consequence, his works became longer, leading to the publication in 1980 of Aitmatov's first full-length novel, *The Day Lasts More than a Hundred Years*. *Farewell, Gul'sary!* also marks a shift in the language of Aitmatov's fiction. While his early work was translated from the Kirghiz by the author with or without the aid of professional translators, beginning with *Farewell, Gul'sary!* Aitmatov has written his works directly in Russian. The language change—partially motivated by greater conservatism in the Kirghiz literary establishment[24]—also signaled Aitmatov's growing concern with problems whose implications transcend the confines of his native republic. Borrowing his images from the cinema, Aitmatov notes the significance the Russian language has for him in his art: "To write and, consequently, to think in Russian means the same to me as filming for the wide screen. The experience of another language, with its greater literary and cultural seniority, is constantly present, and helps me involuntarily, almost unnoticeably to expand my frame of vision."[25]

3

Farewell, Gul'sary!
Coming to Terms with the Stalinist Past

Farewell, Gul'sary! represents a major advance in Chingiz Ait-matov's literary career. Not only is the novella aesthetically superior to all of his fiction published before 1966, it also signals a greater willingness on the part of the author to confront the controversial issues of contemporary Soviet life. The subject matter of *Fare-well, Gul'sary!* is thus more complex and provocative than that in Aitmatov's award-winning *Tales of the Mountains and Steppes.* The central conflict in the novella addresses the problem of political morality in the Communist party, which, at the time of the novella's publication in *Novyi mir*, in March 1966, was approaching its fiftieth anniversary in power.

Farewell, Gul'sary! appeared within weeks of the scandalous trial, in February 1966, of dissident writers Andrei Siniavskii and Iulii Daniel. Aitmatov's novella, as well as the brilliant war novel *Mertvym ne bol'no* (The dead feel no pain) by the Belorussian writer Vasil' Bykau, which appeared in *Novyi mir* that January, were eclipsed by coverage of the trial in the Western media. Both works reveal the extent to which the Stalinist legacy was alive in Soviet society of the 1960s and shed light on the limits of the "permissible" in Soviet letters at a time of growing political reaction. For months after the sentencing of Siniavskii and Daniel to seven and five years, respectively, of hard labor, the Soviet authorities were besieged with protests from prominent public figures, both in the West and in the Soviet Union. Particularly disturbing, no doubt, were the protests of Communist leaders from Western Europe, for example, French poet Louis Aragon, who had done much to popularize Soviet literature in France and Western Europe. The awarding of the Nobel Prize to Mikhail Sholokhov the preceding October was also quickly forgotten in the public uproar.[1]

Within weeks of the appearance of *Farewell, Gul'sary!*, Aleksandr Solzhenitsyn submitted part 1 of *Cancer Ward* for publication in the same journal.[2] Though Solzhenitsyn's novel is more powerful politically, delving philosophically into the inherent immorality of Communist ideology, both works probe the excesses of the Stalinist past and its legacy in the Soviet Union of the 1960s. The affinity between the works of the two writers was stressed two years later by Aleksandr Tvardovskii, editor of *Novyi mir*, who, in a desperate effort to save Solzhenitsyn's novel from the censors, wrote a letter of appeal to the first secretary of the Writers' Union of the USSR, Konstantin Fedin. In his letter, widely circulated in unofficial channels through *samizdat*, Tvardovskii emphasizes both writers' love of truth and depth of realistic portrayal and notes that the work of such writers as Aitmatov, Solzhenitsyn, and Sergei Zalygin has little to do with "short-lived" literature, which "smoothes over and impoverishes reality according to a standard, given scheme."[3]

Tvardovskii's maneuver failed miserably. Konstantin Fedin was hardly in the mood for liberalism in the wake of the Siniavskii-Daniel trial and the uproar created by Solzhenitsyn's open letter to the Fourth Congress of the Writers' Union in May 1967. For party conservatives like Fedin, it was not the similarities but the differences between Aitmatov's and Solzhenitsyn's works that were critical. In *Cancer Ward*, the Communist party is not seen as offering much hope for a better future. Aitmatov's novella allows some hope to remain, and despite his grievances, the main character, Tanabai Bakasov, still sees the party as the legitimate means to realize his cherished ideals. He continues to hope that the party and Soviet authorities will finally begin to respect such basic human values as sincerity and justice. Aitmatov, no doubt, like many Soviet citizens at the time, shared such guarded optimism, despite the evidence to the contrary following Nikita Khrushchev's fall from power. The Soviet invasion of Czechoslovakia in 1968 eroded much of that optimism, and the tragic mood in Aitmatov's fiction intensified after that date, as well.

Aitmatov's assessment of Stalinism in *Farewell, Gul'sary!* demonstrates a grass-roots bias. His novella expresses the belief that, despite the bloodletting and untold cruelty of the Stalin era, the revolutionary ideals of freedom and justice for the masses of Central Asia survived the disaster and continue to be safeguarded from neo-Stalinist ideologues and bureaucrats by hardworking, rank-and-file party members. Thus while condemning the excesses of Stalinism in his novella, the author makes it clear that faith in the original ideals of the 1917 revolution lives on.

Yet while his hero retains his faith in the ideals of the revolution, Aitmatov by no means portrays the post-Stalin Communist party as capable of rekindling those ideals in contemporary Soviet society. In *Farewell, Gul'sary!*, the sins of the past have not been overcome, and the party hierarchy of 1966 is depicted as still embracing opportunists with Stalinist mentalities, hostile to any real democratic reforms. Twenty-five years after the novella's appearance, such party functionaries demonstrated how they would seek to bring down democratic reforms in the Soviet Union, by their attempted coup d'état of August 1991. The point Aitmatov makes in his novella retained its relevancy throughout the 1970s and 1980s.

The composition of *Farewell, Gul'sary!* is complicated, presaging the author's *The Day Lasts More than a Hundred Years*. Two temporal planes, the present and past, alternate throughout the novella. The present, which in the novella occupies only about eight hours in Tanabai's life, serves as the frame for his reminiscences of the past, which account for over twenty years of his life and as such constitute almost all of the plot. In this manner, the past and the present are constantly contrasted, the past being evaluated retrospectively, from the vantage point of the present. There is only one date given in the novella (March 5, 1950, exactly three years before the death of Stalin), yet time periods and events in the narration can readily be ascertained using that date as a reference point.

The story is narrated in the third person, a departure from *Tales of the Mountains and Steppes* and *Mother's Field*. The narrative point of view frequently shifts from Tanabai's to that of his horse, Gul'sary, a name that in Kirghiz means "yellow flower." The name evokes both the beauty and the vulnerability of the animal. The reader is accordingly afforded a double vision of the main character—through Tanabai's own analyzing consciousness and through the naïve consciousness of Gul'sary. Gul'sary's perception and the *ostranenie* (the literary technique of "making strange") it makes possible are also extended to other characters and events in the narration. Moreover, since Gul'sary's life spans the time of Tanabai's reminiscences, it functions in many ways as a running commentary on Tanabai's life, clarifying and heightening the important events.

Two works of Kirghiz folklore, "The Lament of the She-Camel" and "The Song of the Old Hunter," are given important parabolic roles in the plot, determining the mood and style in large sections of the narration, tying together Tanabai's plot line with Gul'sary's, and reflecting in their structures the problems presented in the novella. No doubt, many Russian readers at the time saw the two songs merely as instances of oriental ornamentalism in Aitmatov's fiction and did not give further thought to their function in the novella's composition. Yet the two pieces in *Farewell, Gul'sary!* shed light on the author's assessment of Tanabai's actions and characterize more fully the moral issues the hero confronts.

Tanabai's plot line dominates all others in the novella. The narration opens and closes on a lonely country road. In this deserted setting, which serves as the frame for Tanabai's life, the reader first meets the main character as an old man riding a cart pulled by his onetime mighty steed, Gul'sary. Little is left of Gul'sary's past strength and stamina, and on that very night the aged horse is destined to die on the road. As Gul'sary's movement becomes slower and slower, Tanabai's reminiscences of his life gather speed.

The hero recalls his impoverished youth, during which he and his half-brother, Kulubai, worked as shepherds for a rich *manap* (landowner). When the revolution spread to Central Asia, Tanabai became one of its most fervent supporters—the certain promise of a better life led him to enter the party and later to embrace collectivization enthusiastically, even to the point of denouncing his own brother, who had since become moderately prosperous, as a kulak. Tanabai's longtime friend in the Komsomol, Choro Saiakov, took a moderate stance toward collectivization and tried to win hardworking men like Kulubai for the kolkhoz. Yet at Tanabai's insistence, Kulubai was expelled from the kolkhoz and exiled to Siberia, an act that made Tanabai a hated man in the *ail*. At that time, Tanabai felt that such a grievous sin against family and clan was justified, for he believed in the ideology of class struggle, and the kolkhoz was indeed becoming more successful. In the 1960s, however, Tanabai realizes the inhumanity inherent in his transgression.

After the war, during which Tanabai saw action on both fronts, he returns home to the kolkhoz, which had suffered severely from neglect in the war years. His friend Choro, now chairman of the kolkhoz, had done his best to keep it functioning during the war and was now struggling with the disastrous state of the postwar economy. Tanabai agrees to take on the most difficult and unpleasant jobs in the kolkhoz. First, he works as a blacksmith, then tends horses in the mountains (there he finds Gul'sary as a colt and rears him to become a spirited steed), and finally consents to work as a shepherd. To a large extent, it is his friendship with Choro that induces him to subject himself and his family to the harsh conditions such work entails.

Yet Choro's failing health soon causes him to step down from the position of kolkhoz chairman to that of party organizer. The long years of hard work and political maneuvering for the benefit of the kolkhoz have left him with a chronic heart condition. His replacement, Aldanov (the root of the name in Kirghiz implies deceit), soon reveals himself as a vain and sadistic bureaucrat. A clash with Tanabai becomes inevitable when he expropriates Gul'sary from Tanabai for use as his personal riding horse. Choro, whose years as chairman have taught him to avoid direct confrontation with one's superiors, urges his friend to submit to authority. Choro even encourages Tanabai to accept Aldanov's demand that he make an unrealistic pledge to the party to increase the stock in his herd of sheep. Despite Tanabai's heroic efforts to meet his pledge, the cold spring and the breakdown in feed distribution result in disaster, not only for his herd but for all the livestock in the region. When the party sends the regional prosecutor, Segizbaev, to Tanabai's herd to look for a scapegoat, Tanabai's wrath knows no bounds. Segizbaev, who has grown accustomed to men fearing him, insults Tanabai and threatens him with prison. To the horror of Choro, who accompanies the prosecutor, Tanabai attacks Segizbaev with a pitchfork. For this act, Tanabai is expelled from the party.

Years go by, and Tanabai appears to have been forgotten. He lives alone with his wife, working as a warden on an unimportant stretch of kolkhoz property. His friend Choro dies, but before his death he realizes his responsibility for Tanabai's misfortunes. Seven years after Tanabai's expulsion, Khrushchev's de-Stalinization campaign is launched at the Twentieth Party Congress, in 1956. The local party authorities ask Tanabai to seek reinstatement in the party. Although he sees improvements in the life around him, Tanabai does not take the step, for he feels his time has passed.

At this juncture in the hero's life, fate returns Gul'sary to him. His once-spirited horse is no longer of use to the kolkhoz, so it is given to Tanabai. Tanabai's care helps Gul'sary regain his health, but the mistreatment and age of the horse have taken a heavy toll. It is in this state that Tanabai harnesses the horse to pay a visit to his son and daughter-in-law in the city. There, he discovers that his son has become a spineless party bureaucrat. His daughter-in-law ridicules him for the years he worked as a shepherd and holds him responsible for his son's missed promotion. Insulted, Tanabai walks out on them. On the road home, Gul'sary's strength gives out, and his slow dying causes Tanabai to reminisce and reassess his life. Gul'sary's death makes Tanabai aware of his own approaching end, and, overcome by loneliness, he resolves to write Choro's son, requesting his aid to enable him to return to the party. On this sad yet "optimistic" note, the novella closes.

This seemingly positive ending, however, is deceptive. On the surface, it displays the trappings of the upbeat conclusions of classic socialist realism—a new day is breaking when Tanabai lifts his eyes skyward to see a wild goose flying across the sky in pursuit of his flock. Mentally, Aitmatov's hero vows to petition to be reinstated in the party. But a number of important elements in the plot of *Farewell, Gul'sary!* contradict the apparent optimism and reveal the author's fear that the process of de-Stalinization was in grave danger. Aitmatov completed his novella in 1966 and had no illusions about the short-term prospects for greater freedom and tolerance in the Soviet Union. Like many Soviet citizens, he realized that the brief period of liberalization had come to a grinding halt with the ascension of Leonid Brezhnev to power and the arrest of Joseph Brodskii in 1964, followed by that of Andrei Siniavskii and Iulii Daniel in 1965.

All of these events were certainly on Aitmatov's mind at the time he was writing the novella in 1965. The threat of re-Stalinization was perceived as very real at the time.[4] Aitmatov's hero is well aware that the party is far from living up to the ideals of basic human morality. This realistic depiction of the political situation is emphasized in the novella by the fact that seven years after Tanabai's expulsion and Choro's death, as well as after the Twentieth Party Congress, Ibraim, a petty opportunist who willfully contributed to Tanabai's fall and who fully cooperated with the Stalinist bureaucrats, has become chairman of the kolkhoz Tanabai now belongs to. This is the post once held by Choro, a weak but good man. Thus the change can be seen as a step backward. Also, the hostile attitude of Tanabai's son and daughter-in-law toward their father reveals that Tanabai's "crime" is still in the records and can have a negative impact on the career of his son many years after the fact. Moreover, it is ironic that Kerimbekov, the new regional party secretary, makes his offer of party membership to Tanabai while accompanied by Ibraim. Thus the author makes it clear that, along with the reformers, many Stalinist opportunists have found positions in the party hierarchy. Perhaps this explains Tanabai's delay in accepting the offer.

Tanabai's desire to return to the party is, therefore, not intended to be primitively didactic. Aitmatov avoids the conventional linear progression of post-Stalinist socialist realist works: the party made mistakes, the party has corrected them, the party now can do no wrong. Instead, Tanabai's decision is motivated by a yearning to recapture his faith in the ideals of his youth. It is in part an effort to overcome the existential loneliness of old age. Since the novella has an open ending, the reader never finds out whether Tanabai in fact writes the letter to Choro's son. The logic of the narration makes such a positive outcome unlikely. Indeed, the narrator reminds the readers just several pages from the conclusion that Tanabai had made similar decisions in the past about rejoining the party, but at the last minute had changed his mind. Tanabai thus remains a tragic figure. His creation constitutes an important step in Aitmatov's advocacy for the tragic in literature, a concept whose legitimacy in Soviet letters was yet to be officially sanctioned.

Soviet reviews appearing in the central press were favorable. Critics pointed to the novella as a good example of the further maturation of the literatures of the Soviet Union's non-Russian nationalities.[5] *Farewell, Gul'sary!* was praised for its "balanced portrayal" of Soviet reality. While not denying the intensity of its social criticism, the critics generally underscored the positive note on which Aitmatov's novella ends and concurred that the novella imbued Soviet readers with "confidence and faith in Soviet ideals."[6] Further developing the imagery in the final scene of the novella, in which Tanabai is depicted on a deserted road gazing upward at the flight of a lone goose struggling to catch up with his flock, one critic remarked, "Tanabai will catch up with his comrades because the situation in the country has changed radically. Dull, apathetic bureaucrats like Kashkataev and Segizbaev have been exposed, and the party has placed insurmountable barriers in the paths of deceivers and careerists. . . . Tanabai will rejoin his comrades because honesty and truth have prevailed."[7]

In Frunze, the novella angered the Kirghiz literary establishment. At the July 1966 Congress of the Kirghiz Writers' Union, Aitmatov and his work became the target of bitter criticism. The relentless depiction of contemporary corruption in Kirghizstan was too much to bear for party officials. Tugel'bai Sydykbekov (b. 1912), regarded as the father of the Kirghiz novel, attacked Aitmatov mercilessly for what he considered the author's cavalier treatment of reality. Sydykbekov attributed Aitmatov's popularity to irresponsible critics outside Kirghizstan who were enamored of the oriental exoticism in the author's prose.[8] In such criticism, one could sense the degree to which Aitmatov had irritated the literary generals in the Kirghiz Writers' Union by circumventing their authority and publishing *Farewell, Gul'sary!* directly in Moscow. It was clear to them that Aitmatov had finally escaped their tutelage, a process that had begun with the publication of *Dzhamilia* in 1958.

Perhaps the best assessment of Aitmatov's novella was published outside the Soviet Union by Marxist critic Georg Lukács, who refers to the novella as a tragicomedy:

> In this novel we see the way in which the brutal bureaucratic manipulation of the Stalin system turned against those who, for all their sectarian prejudices, worked enthusiastically to bring about the socialist revolution, undaunted by the sacrifices demanded of them. We see how until their own tragic downfall, they were able to preserve their inner human commitment to the revolution in the midst of the destruction of their own existence. Their personal fates are thus not merely comic but rise to the level of tragedy and tragi-comedy.[9]

Indeed, the tragedy of Tanabai Bakasov, a rank-and-file party member on a small kolkhoz in Kirghizstan, stems from the fact that he has been deceived, without fully understanding how it has happened. In his youth he welcomes the revolution's promise of freedom and equality, only to discover at the end of his life that he has helped create another class of exploiters.

Yet it is the subplots in *Farewell, Gul'sary!* that truly subvert the apparent optimistic conclusion of the central narrative strand. If Tanabai's plot line, tragic as it is, has at least formally a hint of an optimistic ending, Gul'sary's plot line serves to accentuate the depth of the hero's tragedy. Indeed, the horse's story has a parabolic function relative to Tanabai, formally marked by the narrator's shift to a lyrical style in passages concerned with Gul'sary. The same stylistic shift would later be observed in all Aitmatov's works with subplots based on myth and legend.

The device of comparing or contrasting the life of a horse to that of a man is hardly new for Russian literature. From classical Russian literature, examples include Leo Tolstoy's "Kholstomer" (The strider) and Frou-frou from *Anna Karenina*, as well as Aleksandr Kuprin's psychological portrayal of a race horse in "Izumrud" (Emerald).[10] Aitmatov's novella also shares a number of features with Ivan Turgenev's *Mumu*, especially in its use of an animal as a measuring stick for the characters' humanity. Yet of the works mentioned above, Aitmatov's depiction of the lives of Gul'sary and Tanabai has the most in common with Tolstoy's short story. In "The Strider," the author of *War and Peace* contrasts the natural life of a horse to that of a man. Through the point of view of his horse-hero, Kholstomer, who is endowed with human intelligence, Tolstoy reveals that the main character, Serpukhovskii, has senselessly squandered his life. The story closes with the death of both horse and man. In *Farewell, Gul'sary!* the horse dies, and the hero becomes acutely aware of his own approaching end.

Yet in Aitmatov's novella the contrasts in Gul'sary's and Tanabai's lives are less important than the parallels. While Gul'sary does not possess the human intelligence and insight of Kholstomer, the immediacy of the animal's emotional response to the world around him makes him a viable literary character. Through Gul'sary, Aitmatov demonstrates that one's treatment of animals is a reflection of one's attitude to all of the world of nature and, indeed, to fellow human beings. In this sense, Tanabai and Gul'sary are treated alike, wittingly and unwittingly, by all the characters in the novella.

The juxtaposition of man and horse also finds expression in the Kirghiz view of the world. The nomadic Kirghiz considered the horse the most important of animals.[11] Unlike early Russian literature and folklore, Kirghiz folklore has carefully recorded the names of both its heroes and their horses. The names of Manas and his lieutenants, for example, are always mentioned together with those of their horses.[12] Even the Kirghiz word for horse, *dzhanybar* (having a soul), points to man's close relationship to the horse.[13] Georgii Gachev notes the important role of the horse in age-old Kirghiz epics:

> It is the mediator between the natural world order and the artificial one, created by man. And since man is also a being of the middle kingdom, that is a creation of nature and "art," there is nothing closer and more intimate to him than the horse. That is why the horse can function for the Kirghiz as the most universal "body of account" both in the world of moral maxims and abstract concepts.[14]

In *Farewell, Gul'sary!*, Gul'sary plays the role of Tanabai's spiritual double and also serves as an absolute moral yardstick by which the actions of all the characters are measured.

Gul'sary, significantly, is described as *inokhodets* (literally, different gait), which, in view of his fiery and uncompromising character, can be equally applied to Tanabai.[15] From the very beginning of the novella, the oneness of Tanabai and Gul'sary is stressed by a number of details. In the first chapter, Tanabai feeds the failing Gul'sary the flat cakes his wife has baked for him. Throughout the novella, the various combinations of the refrain, "an old horse and an old man," emphasize their oneness. Quite frequently, Tanabai uses the first person plural when speaking to Gul'sary, making no distinction between himself and his horse. For the other characters in the novella, of course, this unity of personality and fates is not so obvious. Yet for Tanabai and, consequently, the reader, the treatment of Gul'sary by all the other characters in the novella is always seen in two dimensions: in relation to the horse himself and in relation to Tanabai.

Gul'sary is born in a mountain herd under an open sky, a symbol for freedom throughout Aitmatov's works.[16] The birth of Gul'sary roughly coincides with Tanabai's return to his native kolkhoz after the end of the Second World War. The sense of freedom Gul'sary experiences as a colt is shared by Tanabai after his demobilization. Tanabai sees life as beginning anew: "And now finally that real life would begin; the life which we had struggled for so long, and for whose sake we had fought and died during the war."[17] After Tanabai takes over the herd, he breaks in Gul'sary. Becoming a saddle horse does not mean a loss of freedom for Gul'sary. He is allowed to run free in the herd, and when saddled he enjoys carrying a rider (393). Gul'sary's gait and spirit soon make him famous throughout the region, and Tanabai becomes inseparable from his steed, even riding him on his nocturnal visits to his mistress, Biubiuzhan. Gul'sary shows the fire in his spirit at the equestrian games on the first May. But soon the political climate changes, and hopes for a better life are dashed by the party's crackdown on its victorious citizens. This change is signaled in *Farewell, Gul'sary!* by the arrival of Aldanov as new kolkhoz chairman. Soon Aldanov sends Ibraim, who heads the kolkhoz's stud farm, to request Gul'sary for his personal riding horse. Tanabai reluctantly fulfills the chairman's demand and immediately senses in him a potential enemy. Gul'sary rebels over the loss of freedom, and the narrator likens his stall to a prison.

At first Gul'sary manages to flee from his captor, once by throwing the chairman from his plush saddle, and twice by making his way to the herd in hobbles, which the narrator refers to as *kandaly* (shackles), stressing thereby Gul'sary's prisoner status and evoking the image of human suffering. When Tanabai curses Aldanov in the presence of the stable boys who have come to return Gul'sary, the chairman decides to castrate the horse, an act symbolically aimed at Tanabai. Aldanov sees both animals and people as objects over which he must extend his power. Ibraim, his helper, understands well the connection between Gul'sary's castration and Tanabai's political subjugation.

After gelding, Gul'sary becomes a horse devoid of personality; like a machine, he dutifully submits to all riders without distinction or preference. Thus in a scene that foreshadows the *mankurt* (men without memory) in *The Day Lasts More than a Hundred Years*, Gul'sary later carries the regional prosecutor, Segizbaev, who rides him into the mountains to accuse Tanabai unjustly of criminal negligence when the herd of sheep he tends for the kolkhoz begins to die in severe weather. Tanabai responds by attacking Segizbaev and inadvertently injuring Gul'sary. Tanabai's expulsion from the party and subsequent occupational demotion are paralleled by the gradual diminution of the horse's strength—first Gul'sary is harnessed to carts, then he is used to teach little boys how to ride, and finally, ill and abused, he is returned to Tanabai. Gul'sary's slow and painful death elicits only ridicule from the young and strong. A young truck driver passing Tanabai and Gul'sary on the deserted road tells him to kick the dying horse into the gully, muttering that the age of technology has come and that "such old men and horses" (397) belong to the past. The truck driver—whose profession makes him a typical representative of the proletariat—is depicted as a creature with no compassion. He adds insult to injury by urinating on the road in front of the dying horse. The driver's suggestion to push Gul'sary into the ravine to be finished off by the crows is, by implication, equally applicable to the aged Tanabai. This incident, occurring within hours of Tanabai's altercation with his son and daughter-in-law, gains additional significance and throws an even darker shadow on the optimistic conclusion. Soviet critics tended to overlook the significance of this scene. Indeed, the retrospective composition of the novella places the two events far apart from each other—the first occurring in chapter 3, the second in chapter 24. Thus the reader must reconstruct the proper sequence of events to discover the author's evaluation of the present and the context in which the novella's conclusion is placed.

When one considers the draconian spirit of the Stalin era, the punishment Tanabai receives for his physical attack on a high party official (a state prosecutor at that) is seemingly mild—expulsion from the party. Yet when seen together with the punishment Gul'sary is given for his rebellion—castration—his punishment takes on a deeper meaning and reflects the immorality and shrouded cruelty toward their subjects of those in power. In its function as parable, Gul'sary's story is a condemnation of those responsible for the spiritual castration of the Soviet people as a whole during the period of the cult of personality. The description of Gul'sary's castration makes it clear that Aldanov sees the act as an affirmation of his power over the recalcitrant and independent Tanabai. In the scene, the narrator emphasizes that connection, remarking that Aldanov "smiled in sincere hate and triumph, as if it weren't a horse lying before him, but a man" (436). Later, Aldanov gloats in the same way over Tanabai at the expulsion hearing, advocating the harshest punishment for his victim. Similarly, his helper at Gul'sary's castration, Ibraim, waits patiently to play the role of informer for the prosecution at the hearing.

But even before the scene depicting Gul'sary's gelding, his function as a universal "body of account" exposes the moral essence of Aldanov and Ibraim. Ibraim, who pretends to care for Tanabai's welfare, arranges to get Gul'sary for Aldanov in order to ingratiate himself with the new chairman. Gul'sary and Tanabai are mere pawns in his strategy. Similarly, Aldanov's arrogant and bullying attitude toward his subordinates is expressed in his treatment of Gul'sary. As a rider, he is often drunk, sitting awkwardly in the saddle. He irresponsibly organizes a race on a muddy field, whipping Gul'sary's head and jerking his bit. In this manner, all the characters in the novella are classified as good or evil according to their treatment of Gul'sary.

The problems depicted in the novella are developed further in the plots of two laments from Kirghiz folklore, which Aitmatov introduces into his narrative of contemporary Soviet life. The more important of the two is "The Song of the Old Hunter." At first glance, the piece seems to be the author's way of adding lyricism to Tanabai's feeling of loss at the death of his friend, but closer examination reveals its parabolic nature. In the context of the work as a whole, the song models the hero's life and emphasizes his personal responsibility for the deeds of the party.

"The Song of the Old Hunter" is sung to Tanabai by his wife, Dzhaidar, upon his return from Choro's funeral. Dzhaidar chooses the song to match Tanabai's mood of guilt and sorrow, caused by his quarrel with Choro before his death. The song itself is in the form of a *plach* (lament), a genre that enjoys an important place in Kirghiz folklore. Such laments are characterized by the hopeless despair of the lamenter and the emphasis on key words and ideas through monotonous repetition.

The song tells how an old hunter teaches his son, Karagul, to hunt. The son soon surpasses the father and begins to kill wildlife indiscriminately, sparing neither females nor their young. Soon he kills off the herd of the Gray She-goat, leaving only her and her mate alive. When she begs Karagul to spare her mate so she will be able to perpetuate her kind, the young hunter without hesitation shoots and kills him, too. Thus deprived of the possibility to procreate, the Gray She-goat begs Karagul to kill her also but warns that if he should miss, it would be his last shot. He shoots but only wounds her. In the pursuit that follows, the goat leads Karagul up a high cliff from which there is no way down. She leaves him there and curses him: "May your father cry over you as I cry for my murdered children and for the loss of my kind; may your father howl alone among the cold mountains, as I howl now.... I curse you, Karagul, I curse you" (502).

When Karagul's father, after searching for days, finds his son, the youth cries out from the mountain cliff, "I have been standing here for many days; I see neither the sun, nor sky, nor earth. Neither do I see your face, father. Have pity on me, father. Kill me, ease my suffering, I beg you. Kill me and bury me" (503). Just before sunset, the father aims and kills his son. He then throws down his rifle and sings his lament over the body of his dead son: "I've killed you, my son Karagul.... With my own hands I've killed you, Karagul" (503).

This particular lament is deeply rooted in the totemistic beliefs of the Kirghiz. According to these beliefs, the mountain goat was considered to be holy. The Kirghiz ascribed to its meat the power of purification and to its fur the capability of warding off evil spirits.[18] The hunting of such animals was, therefore, permitted but was associated with certain taboos. For example, hunters were warned not to kill more than a thousand of such goats. If a hunter violated the taboo, he would, upon killing the thousand-and-first goat, go blind or deaf or would kill his own son, mistaking him for a goat.[19] The folklore work that best expresses these particular totemistic beliefs is the ancient Kirghiz epic poem *Kodzhodzhash*, which Aitmatov re-interprets in his legend of the hunter Karakul. In *Kodzhodzhash*, the magical she-goat, Kaiberen, avenges herself on the merciless hunter, Kodzhodzhash, by leading him all over the Kirghiz mountains. Just as he is about to catch her, the she-goat prays to Tengri, the sky god, and Kodzhodzhash suddenly finds himself stranded on a cliff hovering between heaven and earth. There he remains, forever tortured by the fear of imminent death.[20]

The legend in the lament testifies to the close communion of man and nature among the Kirghiz and serves as a warning to those who might be so arrogant as to destroy such harmony. It tells of the vengeance of nature toward men who blindly destroy the natural environment. The theme surfaces again in *The White Ship* and *The Place of the Skull*. In *Farewell, Gul'sary!* it is linked to Tanabai's senseless violation of the natural law of his community during the mad rush to collectivize the Kirghiz *ail*. Like Karagul, Tanabai is arrogantly convinced of the righteousness of his cause. When his hardworking brother Kulubai turns up on the list of those to be dispossessed during the collectivization campaign, Tanabai pushes aside Choro's doubts and suggestions that the community needs such industrious people and blindly demands the repression of his brother: "If his name is on the list, then he is a kulak! There should be no mercy! For Soviet power I would not spare my own father" (468). Just as the hunter Karagul sets out to kill all the animals of a species (the gray mountain goat), when Tanabai comes to dispossess his brother he tells him that all people of his class have to be liquidated as enemies (468). The analogy is developed further in the depiction of Kulubai as wounded prey, thrashing about in a wheat field like an "animal in a trap" (469) before he is led off into exile. Kulubai is taken away, and in the merciless hunt for more and more enemies throughout the 1930s, many of the collectivizers themselves end up like Karagul, victims of their own inhumanity.

When Tanabai realizes that his and the party's reckless rush to have their way was a mistake, it is too late. He understands that those who urged caution and tolerance, like Choro, were right. At the end of the novella, Tanabai is alone, like Karagul, with no way to rectify the deeds of the past. In this sense, Aitmatov's inserted parable negates the glimmer of hope that Tanabai might return to find a place in a more humane party. By associating his hero with the hunter Karagul, Aitmatov brings the story of Tanabai to a tragic conclusion and finds a fitting image for the party's policy of class warfare in the Soviet countryside. Like Karagul, the party chases after its fleeting goals only to end up, metaphorically, on a cliff, leaving a trail of bodies in its wake below. Such is the price for violating the laws of civilized behavior. Aitmatov would again allude to *Kodzhodzhash* in his novel *The Place of the Skull*, where the theme is given an apocalyptic dimension. Yet in 1966 the disaster of collectivization could be broached only with caution. In his speech at the Twenty-eighth Party Congress in 1990, however, Aitmatov spoke in unambiguous terms:

> The division of society into classes is in the final analysis one of the forms of the same eternal immoral postulate "divide and conquer." I think we have had ample opportunity to grasp this from our own bitter experience of ideological inquisition, persecution, repressions, and liquidation of whole social groups and classes.[21]

In a broader sense, *Farewell, Gul'sary!* is itself one long lament—evoked by the rhythms and frequent refrains that pervade the narrative as a whole—on the tragedies in Tanabai's life: the loss of his friend Choro, his expulsion from the party, his alienation from his careerist son, the death of his beloved Gul'sary, and the acute awareness of his own approaching death. A sense of futility in all that Tanabai does runs through the narration. This mood is evoked by the refrain from another Kirghiz song, "The Lament of the She-Camel,"[22] which appears three times in *Farewell, Gul'sary!* and functions as a leitmotiv. In the song, a she-camel looks in vain for her lost foal. Milk from her overfilled udder pours onto the ground. This lament is also steeped in Kirghiz mythology, which holds the camel in special esteem. A Kirghiz ethnographer writes that at one time the Kirghiz believed that the camel possessed human characteristics, an attitude that found expression in a number of rituals. The birth of a camel, like the birth of a child, was marked by a feast (*zhentek*) lasting three days. The head of the mother camel was wrapped in a white cloth similar to the headdress of Kirghiz women. If a camel foal died, people consoled the mother camel, believing that she mourned and lamented her lost child as a woman would.[23]

The lament is played by Tanabai's wife after Gul'sary is taken away to Aldanov; it is called to mind when Tanabai discovers that Gul'sary has been gelded; and it is evoked again at the very end of the novella, after the death of the horse. The image of a mother camel calling out for her lost child, her milk flowing to the ground, invariably resonates as poignantly in the human world depicted in the novella. Thus it is not by chance that the final words of the novella are from this lament, once again underscoring the supreme tragedy of both the victims of collectivization and those who kept faith, like Tanabai.[24]

The Kirghiz folklore in *Farewell, Gul'sary!* emphasizes "the eternal and recurring nature of what matters in life (as opposed to political slogans, for example)"[25] and thus widens the novella's spectrum of associations. Together with the story of Gul'sary's life, the laments enable Aitmatov to realize the moral objectives of his novella parabolically, with a degree of ambiguity. The emerging parabolic dimension in Aitmatov's fiction provided the writer with a vehicle to marshal more fundamental criticism of Soviet history and of the political and social conditions existing in the USSR at the time of the novella's appearance. Like Aesopian language, the parabolic in his fiction requires that the reader see the interlocking details and allusions for the work to gain its full meaning.[26] Many readers failed to see the parabolic dimension or, as was the case with Soviet critics, perferred to limit their reading only to the surface, which would enable them to place the work in the socialist realist tradition. In *The White Ship*, Aitmatov's use of the parabolic would be further intensified, the folklore elements becoming an organizing principle in the narration.

4

The White Ship
Outcry in a Soulless World

In his early work, Aitmatov depicts the passing of the traditional patriarchal way of life in Soviet Kirghizstan. As was pointed out earlier, the conflict between the past and the present is resolved by the author with the victory of what was considered at the time new and progressive over the backward and traditional. Thus in *Dzhamilia*, the heroine abandons her husband and his extended family for love and a new life outside the tradition-steeped *ail*. Similarly, in *The First Teacher*, Altynai escapes the fate of becoming the second wife of an ignorant shepherd by leaving the *ail* for the city, where she gains an education and becomes a renowned academician.

Yet with the publication of *Farewell, Gul'sary!* and its use of age-old Kirghiz laments, a different attitude toward the prerevolutionary past of Kirghizstan emerges, expressed poignantly in Tanabai's belated appreciation of the yurt, a symbol of Kirghiz culture and the nomadic way of life of the past. As a young man, Tanabai actively fought for the liquidation of the yurt as a shameful relic of the past. Later, on the eve of the fiftieth anniversary of the revolution, when he is freezing in the mountains with his herd, he realizes his mistake: "How could he have failed to see the yurt as a remarkable invention of his people, in which every little detail had been tested by the century-old experience of generations" (432). Similarly, *The White Ship* stands as eloquent testimony to Aitmatov's own belated appreciation of the Kirghiz historical and cultural experience. Both the structure and content of the novella singularly reflect the age-old folklore of his people. Thus *The White Ship* voices a powerful plea to Soviet society to preserve the spiritual wealth of past generations.

Aitmatov's novella appeared in January 1970 in *Novyi mir*, at the beginning of the centenary year of Lenin's birth. For the celebration festivities, a giant illuminated portrait of Lenin graced the Moscow sky, supported by cables from a blimp hovering high above. The April 22, 1970, issue of *Literaturnaia gazeta* was devoted exclusively to Lenin and represented a new apogee of Soviet *bogostroitel'stvo* (god-building). Hundreds of volumes of scholarly studies, memoirs, and literary works on Lenin and his family were published throughout the year. To avoid anything that could have caused discord in the lovefest planned to honor the founder of the Soviet state, the party tightened its grip on culture in advance. In November 1969 the campaign against Solzhenitsyn culminated in his expulsion from the Writers' Union. In the summer of 1969 the editor of *Novyi mir*, Aleksandr Tvardovskii, was likewise severely criticized in the Soviet press by a number of influential party conservatives[1] and, in February 1970, forced to resign his position at the journal.[2]

For Mikhail Suslov, chief ideologue of the Brezhnev regime, and other neo-Stalinists seeking to bring de-Stalinization to an end, the resignation of Tvardovskii was the crowning victory in a decade-long struggle. Symbolic of that victory was the erection of a bust on Stalin's grave in June of the same year. For Soviet literature, the year 1970 was a tragic turning point. The award of the Nobel Prize for Literature to Aleksandr Solzhenitsyn at the end of the year unleashed an anti-Western barrage in the Soviet press and intensified the official campaign against the writer. Throughout the following decade more and more writers opposed to re-Stalinization would be forced into *samizdat* and *tamizdat*, while others seeking to publish in the Soviet Union would retreat to historical novels,[3] portrayals of rural and domestic life, or Aesopian language. Aitmatov would continue his struggle with Stalinist totalitarianism through the further use of prerevolutionary myths and legends as building blocks for his moral parables.

In an interview published after the appearance of *The White Ship*, Aitmatov noted that whereas in his previous novella folklore had served as a "device," in his latest work it had become a "concept," making up the main stratum of the narration.[4] Indeed, beginning with *The White Ship*, myths and legends in parabolic form become the organizing principle of the composition of Aitmatov' works and central in the expression of the author's cherished ideas.

Perhaps one of the factors facilitating the shift from device to concept was the publication of Mikhail Bulgakov's *Master i Margarita*.[5] Aside from its sensational content and history, the novel's appearance was significant for its legitimization of artistic innovation and religious themes. In his novella, *The White Ship*, Chingiz Aitmatov was the first Soviet writer to take full advantage of the new opportunites presented by the official publication of *Master and Margarita*. Just as Mikhail Bulgakov freely transformed the story of Christ's Passion from the gospels for literary purposes, Aitmatov would take a similar approach to the pre-Islamic myths of the Kirghiz. As if in a display of his appreciation of Bulgakov's work, Aitmatov would later reinterpret the Christ-Pilate encounter in *Master and Margarita* in his own portrayal of the Passion in *The Place of the Skull*.

On the surface, the plot of *The White Ship* appears unsophisticated. The hero is a nameless seven-year-old boy, whose fairy tales, as the narrator remarks laconically in the opening sentences, form the basis of the story. The action takes place on an isolated mountain outpost in a forest preserve overlooking Lake Issyk-kul. Three families live at the outpost: the warden, Orozkul, and his childless wife, Bekei; Bekei's father, Momun, and his second wife, a malicious old woman called Babka; and the family of Seidakhmat, a lazy young man who chooses to work in the forest preserve rather than find meaningful employment on the kolkhoz. The boy lives with his grandfather, Momun, having been deserted by his father and his mother, Momun's other daughter, who has since remarried and moved to a distant city.

Orozkul, a power-thirsty and sadistic man, uses his position of authority to tyrannize all the inhabitants of the outpost. He beats Bekei brutally and seeks to make life miserable for her and Momun, because Bekei has failed to bear him children. The boy, who suffers from the oppression around him, seeks refuge from the dark world of the grown-ups in an imaginary world of his own. His first fairy tale is his dream of turning into a fish and swimming out into Lake Issyk-kul to see his father, who, he believes, works as a sailor on the white ship he observes daily through binoculars. His second and favorite fairy tale is told to him by his grandfather. Momun tells the boy the myth of the Deer-mother, the protectress of the Bugu clan, to which the boy and his relatives belong. According to Momun's story, the Deer-mother saved the Kirghiz nation from extinction by leading the last two Kirghiz, a boy and a girl, from Siberia to the shores of Issyk-kul. As a sign of gratitude, the descendants of the boy and girl hold all deer in special esteem for centuries afterward. This relationship, however, eventually comes to an abrupt end when rich Kirghiz begin to violate the bond of gratitude by killing the deer for their antlers. Deeply grieved by the treachery, the Deer-mother leads the remaining deer from the Kirghiz forests and vows never to return.

The boy, like his grandfather, believes in the fairy tale and is understandably thrilled when he learns one day that three deer—a buck, a doe, and a fawn—have been sighted in their woods. The boy's longing for peace from Orozkul's tyranny is so strong that he comes to believe that the doe is the Deer-mother herself, who has forgiven the Bugu clan and wishes to bring harmony to the troubled settlement.

Yet happiness does not return. On the very day of the appearance of the deer, Orozkul beats his wife again and dismisses Momun from his job. Exploiting Momun's material dependency, Orozkul indirectly pressures the old man to shoot the deer. The boy is shocked when he discovers what his grandfather, the only person he looks up to at the outpost, has perpetrated. Seeing no more hope for his world after the Deer-mother has been slain, the boy escapes into his own fairy tale by imagining he has turned into a fish. He drowns in an icy stream as he attempts to swim to Issyk-kul to see his father on the white ship.

With the boy's death, both fairy tales come to an end. Aitmatov's novella was originally titled *Posle skazki* (After the fairy tale), with "The White Ship" as a subtitle in parentheses. The original title, which was more appropriate in view of the destruction of the central fairy tale, was changed by Tvardovskii in the novella's *Novyi mir* edition. Tvardovskii considered the subtitle more poetical.[6] The author has since changed the title back to the original, but most critics continue to refer to the work as *The White Ship*, which is also the name of its popular film version.

As the short plot synopsis reveals, *The White Ship* is an unmitigated tragedy. Whereas *Farewell, Gul'sary!* leaves the reader the illusion of an upbeat conclusion, the *Novyi mir* edition of *The White Ship* left nothing in its conclusion for Soviet critics to point to as optimistic—an innocent boy dies as a result of the unrelenting tyranny around him. The author completes his novella by stressing the boy's uncompromising attitude toward the surrounding oppression: "There is only one thing I can say now—you rejected what your child's soul could not accept. And I find consolation in this. You lived as a bolt of lightning, flashing brilliantly and then going out. But lightning is created by the sky. And the sky is eternal. And in this too I find consolation."[7]

The dismal world the boy rejects calls to mind the *samodurstvo* (petty tyranny) that appears in A. N. Ostrovskii's plays, and especially in *Groza* (The storm). Indeed, the parallels between Aitmatov's novella and the nineteenth-century play are so striking that it is surprising that they have been overlooked in Aitmatov criticism. Both Aitmatov's nameless boy and Ostrovskii's Katerina end their lives by drowning, leaving behind a world in which tyranny appears to have total sway. The boy hero's death and repudiation of that world create a powerful catharsis, motivating the reader to hate the evil in society that is responsible for the tragedy. Nikolai Dobroliubov's characterization of Katerina as the "ray of light in the kingdom of darkness" can equally be applied to the boy at the conclusion of *The White Ship*.[8] Aitmatov's words of consolation after the boy's death—"you lived as a bolt of lightning, flashing brilliantly and then going out"— particularly elicit this association.

The White Ship, however, was published over a hundred years after the appearance of Ostrovskii's play, in a country whose sole officially recognized literary method was socialist realism. True, after the death of Stalin the method came to be less rigidly applied to literature, yet at the time *The White Ship* appeared, in January 1970, Soviet literary criticism on the whole still continued to dismiss the tragic as incompatible with the optimistic teleology of socialist life. Thus it is understandable that Aitmatov's novella would produce considerable controversy for its portrayal of the negative in Soviet life as triumphant over the good. The dispute that ensued on the pages of *Literaturnaia gazeta* in July 1970 eventually compelled Aitmatov to defend his novella before his critics and readers.

The strongest criticism came from Anuar Alimzhanov, a Kazakh writer, who accuses Aitmatov of undue pessimism.[9] Alimzhanov protests, for example, that Momun's killing of the deer was implausible, because all his life he had served the good and because he must have known that in shooting the doe he was, in effect, killing himself and all that he had lived for. Moreover, Alimzhanov argues that the author took an essentially optimistic myth and transformed it into a pessimistic parable on the nature of mankind.

Another critic censures Aitmatov for neglecting social reality in his novella. The death of the boy, he argues, is contrived like an experiment, with the author "playing with his little hero" and leaving many things unclear or unexplained.[10] He mentions, for example, the lack of friends the boy should have had at school and the "infinite power of Orozkul over Momun," causing the latter to betray suddenly everything he had lived for and respected. The critic asks rhetorically, "Where is the portrayal of real life at the outpost, and where are the people on whom the boy's death would have had a horrifying impact?" Aitmatov quotes another reader who protested against the gloomy ending and who even naïvely suggested that the author should have concluded his work with the arrest of Orozkul; Momun could then be given a pension, and the boy sent to the city to a boarding school.[11]

In his defense of *The White Ship*, Aitmatov protested vigorously against what he viewed as an immature understanding of literature. He pleaded for the rights of tragedy in Soviet literature, and, referring to the tragedies of Shakespeare, in particular *Romeo and Juliet*, the writer pointed out that the apparent *bezyskhodnost'* (cul-de-sac) of the conclusion in the death of the heroes strikes a mighty blow at the evil of their times: "The history of Romeo and Juliet forces us to appreciate and understand the essence of the right to be free people. They gave their lives for that right. In doing so they are magnificent and powerful examples for the living."[12] The death of the boy in *The White Ship*, however, does not lead to a moral cul-de-sac. "There is a way out," Aitmatov notes, but "it lies outside the novella," with the reader. It lies in art's influence on the reader, its ability to engage the emotions and prompt the reader to build a "barricade" in defense of the truth that has been defeated in a given depiction of reality. Although physically the heroes may be unable to establish the truth, the reader is inspired to "fight" for it.[13] The nameless hero's uncompromising rejection of cynicism and cruelty is the important life-affirming element in the novella. Orozkul's victory is ephemeral; the spiritual and moral superiority of the boy remains unbroken.

This is the position on which Chingiz Aitmatov rests his defense. The discussion of the tragic being carried out in the official press on the pages of *Literaturnaia gazeta* provided legitimacy to the author's position on the permissibility of the tragic in Soviet letters. While it may seem incredible today, some twenty years after *The White Ship* was first published, that anyone could have questioned the rightful place of the tragic in literature, Soviet literary conservatives of the time viewed it as running counter to the "life-affirming" principles of socialist realism. Aitmatov's defense of such a basic principle helped open an important path for Soviet writers, by which they could continue their efforts to move beyond the bounds of classic socialist realism. Yet that path was far from trouble-free, and when Aitmatov subsequently submitted the novella for publication in book form,[14] he yielded to pressure to make several small corrections aimed at slightly mitigating the effect of the tragic conclusion.

Aside from its tragic conclusion, *The White Ship* made a lasting impression on its readers through Aitmatov's masterful use of Kirghiz folklore. The plot of the novella incorporates four different works of folklore—two legends, a fairy tale, and a myth—all told to the boy by his grandfather, Momun. The genre distinctions are of no consequence to the boy, and he calls all of his grandfather's stories *skazki* (fairy tales). The myth of the Deer-mother, having its origin in the totemistic beliefs of the Kirghiz, is given the central compositional role in the work. Yet all the pieces were modified by the author to give them a parabolic function vis-à-vis the tragic story of the outpost.

The two legends are told briefly, as if in passing. The first functions primarily to emphasize the isolated nature of the novella's setting. To explain to the boy why the winds of the valley are so strong, Momun tells how the fierce mountain wind, San-Tash, once drove away the invaders of the mountain valleys, leaving the inhabitants secure in their homeland. This legend—going back to the times when the Kirghiz retreated into the high mountains to save themselves from powerful invaders—introduces the reader to Momun's animistic worldview, according to which the forces of nature protect or punish human beings at will.

The second legend told by Momun instills in the boy a reverence for the songs and folklore of his people. According to the legend, a Kirghiz prisoner chooses death over life as a slave, on the condition that he be allowed to hear a native song before his execution. Clearly, this legend functions to characterize Momun's own veneration of his Central Asian cultural heritage in view of the increasing encroachment of modern European (Russian) civilization. This theme would appear later in Aitmatov's powerful image of the *mankurt* in *The Day Lasts More than a Hundred Years*. For the boy, it is a call to courage and loyalty to the culture of his people.

The fairy tale of Chypalak, a Kirghiz Tom Thumb (*mal'chik s pal'chik*), who is swallowed by a wolf but remains victorious, is told by Momun merely to entertain the boy; yet in the end, the tale comments parabolically on the author's conclusion to the novella as a whole. In the fairy tale, Chypalak cries out from within the wolf's stomach, "Hey, shepherds, wake up!" (34), thus preventing the beast from approaching the sheep herds unnoticed. In the end, the wolf is threatened by starvation and must give up his predatory life. Similarly, as Aitmatov would have it, his boy hero is devoured by *Orozkulshchina* (the despotism of Orozkul) yet continues to cry out his warnings to the readers.[15]

The myth of the horned Deer-mother is the most important element of folklore in *The White Ship*. Also told to the boy hero as a *skazka*, its significance is underlined by its central position in the novella (the fourth of seven chapters), and by its length, being many times longer than the other three episodic folkloric pieces combined.

In his review of *The White Ship*, the Kazakh critic Alimzhanov accused Aitmatov of altering the meaning of the totemistic myth on which his myth of the Deer-mother is based, in order to suit his pessimistic purposes.[16] Aitmatov indeed tailors essentially neutral mythic material into a moral warning to the egotistical and short-sighted. The author claims for himself, however, the right to create parables from the past, that is, to approach the cultural wealth of his people from a moralist's standpoint, selecting only those ancient myths and legends that are capable of saying something essential to contemporary humanity; if they do not meet that prerequisite, he suggests not resurrecting them at all.[17]

Yet besides the moral warning it embodies, the myth of the Deer-mother also reveals the inner world of the novella's characters, based on their attitude toward it. In this function, the myth in *The White Ship* plays a role similar to Gul'sary's in Aitmatov's earlier novella, serving as a universal moral standard according to which positive characters are differentiated from negative ones. The rich spiritual world of Momun and the boy is thus contrasted with the cynicism and disbelief of Orozkul and the other characters. Their belief in the Deer-mother, in the opinion of Vladimir Soloukhin, constitutes the crucial element of spirituality that runs through the world of the novella "as a water-shed" and which ennobles man, "making him better, purer, kinder, and more dignified."[18] The author's alignment with the spiritual world of Momun and the boy is evident everywhere in his narrative voice. Later, in an interview, Aitmatov remarked that people living without legends and myths are condemned to spiritual poverty and are incapable of understanding the modern world.[19]

Aitmatov's sources for the fairy tale of the Deer-mother reach deep into the totemistic past of the Kirghiz. A contemporary Kirghiz ethnographer points out that various aspects of totemistic ritual are still alive today, despite years of Soviet power and ideology in Kirghizstan, and notes the particular tenacity of the myth of the Deer-mother.[20] This testifies to the continual existence, albeit in weakened form, of a shamanistic worldview, which conceives of the human world as one with nature. People with such a view of the world are not prone to harm, kill, or eat the animal they consider themselves to be descended from. To do so carries many perils for the offenders. Among the consequences are infertility, sickness, and death.[21] In *The White Ship*, the shamanistic worldview reveals itself in all levels of the narration. Orozkul's rape of nature finds expression in his infertile marriage, and the death of the boy must be seen in the light of Momun's killing of the totem.

Of a number of totemistic myths in Kirghiz mythology, the story of the Bugu totem, the deer, is perhaps the best known. It was first recorded by the Kazakh ethnographer, Chokhan Valikhanov, in 1867.[22] Since that time, other variants of the myth have been recorded,[23] but Valikhanov's version seems to be the most common and apparently serves as the basis of the myth in Aitmatov's novella.

According to Valikhanov, two hunters, Kara-Murza and Asan, once discovered in the midst of a herd of deer a boy and girl with antlers. They killed the boy and captured the girl, who cried inconsolably over the body of her dead brother. As a result of her curse, neither Asan nor Kara-Murza would ever have children. The hunters took the girl to the tribal chieftain, who married her to his grandson. The girl's wisdom gained her the name Muiuz-baibiche (horned mother). Legend has it that a servant girl once drank the water with which Muiuz-baibiche had washed her head and miraculously became pregnant from it. The son she bore, Dzhelden (from the wind), became the father of the Bugu tribe. Thus the tribe came to venerate the Deer-mother (and all deer) as protectress of Issyk-kul and its surrounding valleys.[24]

Yet in considering Aitmatov's parabolic transformation of the myth, we should mention an older totemistic myth, that of the red dog tribe.[25] According to this myth, the daughter of a khan and her forty maids-in-waiting return home from a walk to discover their *ail* destroyed by the enemy. The only living creature left is a red dog, who later mysteriously becomes the father of the offspring of the princess and her forty maids. Valikhanov writes that the "children of the *kirk-kiz* (forty maids) came to be called the *kirghiz*, according to the number of their mothers."[26]

Both myths discussed here, as well as many similar totemistic myths, express a worldview of humanity as an integral part of nature, not above or even distinct from it. In and of themselves, the myths reveal no clear moral message or purpose. Totemistic myths tend to be morally neutral; it is Aitmatov who gives the myth of the Bugu its moral impact in the first place, transforming it into a account of humanity's fall from grace and consequent loss of the golden age.[27] Thus in telling the myth to the boy, Momun not only wishes the boy to share with him the lore of his ancestors but, more important, wants him to understand the source of evil in the world. Indeed, the boy's recollection of the myth in chapter 4 occurs at a time when Orozkul is on a drunken rampage, brutally beating his wife, Bekei, and humiliating Momun.

In Momun's fairy-tale version of the myth, which the boy recalls at such a trying time, the whole Kirghiz nation is assembled on the banks of the Enesai river (present-day Yenisei) to bury their chieftain. Suddenly, a hostile tribe appears and slaughters all the people and animals of the clan, save a boy and a girl. The two children are in the woods at the time of the massacre, having disobeyed their parents by secretly leaving the funeral repast. Returning later to the camp, they discover the slaughtered bodies. Their initial horror is soon replaced by terrifying loneliness. Fearing the prospects of being alone in the world more than any threat to their lives, they set out in pursuit of their people's murderers.

When they reach the enemy camp, the khan hands them over to a pockmarked, lame old woman, ordering her to push them off a high cliff into the river below. Just as she is about to push the children to their deaths, a doe appears and begs the woman not to commit the deed but, instead, to give the children to her to raise, in the absence of her two fawns, who were killed by hunters. The woman complies, yet warns the Deer-mother that "if the human children thanked her with black ingratitude, then she had no one to blame but herself" (44). The Deer-mother protects the children, carrying them from Siberia to Issyk-kul. There, she blesses the boy and girl, wishing them many descendants, and vows to protect them in the years to come. When their first child is born, the Deer-mother brings them a cradle on her antlers. To symbolize their bond of gratitude with the Deer-mother, the parents name their son Bugubai, after the Deer-mother (*bugu*, deer). Bugubai later marries a woman from an-

other tribe, thus founding the Bugu tribe.[28] Their descendants continue to venerate the Deer-mother and all deer, calling upon her at
times of war and distress.

For many years, the people live in harmony with their deer brothers until the sons of a rich Bugu decide to honor their father's memory by placing antlers on his grave. After the first deer are killed—
representing the violation of the covenant between the Bugu and the
deer—wholesale slaughter of the animals becomes commonplace.
The antlers become a status symbol for the rich. The Deer-mother
abandons Issyk-kul and leads the remaining deer to the other side of
the mountain range, vowing never to return.

In creating this version of the myth, Aitmatov combines elements
from the myths of the red dog and the Bugu tribe. But he eliminates
the element of magical conception found in both totemistic myths.
Instead, the children are reared by the doe alone, a situation reminiscent of that of Romulus and Remus, the mythic founders of Rome.
The author uses the beginning of the red dog myth, replacing the
princess and maids-in-waiting, who discover the destruction of their
ail, with the two children returning to the ravaged camp. The children's pursuit of their tribe's murderers, their capture, the dialogue
between the lame old woman and the Deer-mother, as well as the
depiction of the migration from Siberia to Issyk-kul, spring from the
author's imagination.[29] Yet despite the author's additions to and
omissions from the Bugu myth, he still preserves the totemistic connection between the tribe and the deer. Far more important, however, is the parabolic dimension Aitmatov gives the myth in relation
to the story of events at the deserted outpost.

The killing of the deer and the Bugu tribe's fall from grace stem
from human arrogance vis-à-vis the natural world and its own heritage. In a broader sense, Aitmatov's rendition of the myth represents
a condemnation of the creed of Might Makes Right. The resulting
loss of harmony with nature implicitly brings with it a destruction of
beauty—the deer leave the forests, and their human brothers sink
into depravity. Orozkul, the initiator of the deer hunt at the outpost,
is juxtaposed by the author with the Kirghiz of the myth, who forgot
their past and turned on their natural "brothers." Against the background of Momun's fairy tale, Orozkul's act of poaching, which takes

place in the central plot line, takes on a completely different connotation, "hyperbolized" into an apocalyptic attack on beauty and
harmony in the natural world. The boy's swimming away to his death
is tantamount to the Deer-mother's abandoning her ungrateful human children. Because of the parabolic dimension that the events at
the outpost thus acquire, the boy's death is no senseless suicide but
a defiant act of nonsubmission to an amoral world. The reader, therefore, is challenged to accept the logic of the parable and must view
the events and characters at the outpost in its light.

For the boy, there is no difference between the fairy-tale world
and the world he lives in. After seeing the deer for the first time, he
hopes that the doe, like the Deer-mother in the fairy tale, will bless
Orozkul with a son, symbolically bringing him a cradle on her horns.
Such a gift, in the boy's mind, would bring an end to the tyrant's
binge of violence and oppression. Momun's killing of the doe, therefore, destroys all hope for good in the boy's world and at the same
time robs him of his only ally at the outpost. Ironically, Orozkul is
directly responsible for the destruction of the very thing that, in the
boy's imagination, would have brought him respite.

Fairy tale and reality are united in *The White Ship* also through
an identity of moral purpose in the two major narrative voices in the
novella—Momun's, in the fairy tale of the Deer-mother, and the
author's, in the work as a whole.

Although Aitmatov is careful not to make too much use of "talk-
ing names" in his fiction, he chooses such a name for Momun. In
Kirghiz *momun* means "good" or "kind one."[30] Psychologically, Momun is the most complicated character in the novella. On the one
hand, he preserves and passes on the fairy tale, and on the other
hand, he is the murderer of the fairy tale, both for himself and for
his grandson. His keen sense of morality leads him to make comments on his narration of the fairy tale, just as the author intersperses
his narration of the events at the outpost with moral judgments. Momun, for example, interrupts his narration of events leading to the
Bugu tribe's betrayal of the Deer-mother with three asides: "Yes, my
son, it is bad when people take pride not in their knowledge, but in
their wealth! . . . Yes, my son, it is bad when bards compete in praise;
they cease to be bards and turn into enemies of song! . . . Yes, my

son, even in ancient times people said that wealth engenders arrogance, and arrogance—irresponsibility" (47).

The author's voice offers moral generalizations that are strikingly similar to Momun's. In his initial characterization of Momun, for example, he remarks: "Not in vain do they say that people do not forgive the man who is unable to demand respect. And he was unable" (13). When Orozkul forces Momun to help him haul a stolen tree from the forest reserve, the author's voice notes: "Yet not in vain is it said that in order to hide one's shame it is necessary to defame another" (50). In a sense, the author and Momun are doubles. Stylistically, the same number and color symbolism pervades both narrative voices.[31] Momun tells a story of how beauty, incarnated in the Deer-mother, abandons the world of greedy and arrogant men; the author, as morally attached to his narration as Momun is to his own, tells how beauty and spirituality, incarnated in the nameless boy, leave the dismal, evil world of Orozkul and his confederates.

Yet despite the sense of moral purpose they share, Momun is above all a character in the author's narration. The question thus arises as to why the author could have Momun, a character so sympathetic to him, go against his life's principles and kill the Deer-mother.

In *The White Ship*, Aitmatov is present as a moral absolutist. If the consequences of Momun's killing of the doe derive their gravity only from the parabolic context of the fairy tale, then his motivation for the deed lies purely in the context of the real world. Momun shoots the doe not to spare himself from Orozkul's violence but to save his daughter and grandson. He realizes that if Orozkul forces him to leave, the boy and his daughter will be left at his mercy. This dependence is powerfully expressed by Babka, who encourages him to appease Orozkul at all costs. Aitmatov adds to this economic pressure on the old man the threat of ideological repression, thus giving the conflict between Momun and his son-in-law a political dimension. Orozkul's yes-man, Seidakhmat, for example, threatens to inform the authorities of Momun's "anti-Soviet" views after he initially refuses to shoot the deer on the grounds that the deer are the children of the Deer-mother. Seidakhmat accuses Momun of propagating fairy tales from feudal times in order to "intimidate the people" (111), much as religious believers at that time were harassed by Soviet authorities for propagating religious views, a charge that could easily lead to criminal proceedings and imprisonment.

This political aspect in the novella, of course, did not go unnoticed by Soviet readers. They were fully aware that Orozkul's hostile attitude toward Momun's beliefs was in keeping with the ideology of the party, which encouraged the struggle against "religious survivals from the past." For example, in her ethnographic study of the Kirghiz, which appeared almost at the same time as *The White Ship*, Baialieva advocates taking a hard line toward people like Momun: "It is necessary to put an end to all backward national traditions and even more so religious survivals of the past that are hindering the complete socialist transformation of the people's lives and ideology."[32]

Aitmatov's novella speaks forcibly against such a senseless eradication of the past and intolerance of the spiritual heritage of his people. The result of such a policy, Aitmatov implies, is an Orozkul, a poor substitute for the beauty and harmony of the spiritual world that preceded Soviet life by many centuries.

Indeed, Orozkul's philosophy of absolute expediency in life—a woman who bears her husband no children may be beaten with impunity; fairy tales of the past are of no practical use in modern Soviet society and should be forgotten—is the predatory philosophy of the hunter Karagul in *Farewell, Gul'sary!* Later, in *The Day Lasts More than a Hundred Years*, Aitmatov would coin a term for men who have so wantonly turned their backs on their heritage—*mankurt*. As for Momun, critics have suggested that the old man's compromise in the face of Orozkul's tyranny can be seen as an allusion to the submissiveness of Soviet citizens during the Stalin era,[33] as a result of which they became unwilling accomplices in the crimes of the dictatorship.

Aitmatov contrasts the negative characters' antagonistic or apathetic attitudes toward the world of nature and tradition with their positive attitudes toward modern life in the city. Orozkul admires the modern Soviet city, with its automobiles, cinemas, handsomely dressed people, schools, and institutes. He is especially pleased that the children there speak exclusively Russian at home, having no need for the backward language of their fathers (49). Significantly, the boy's parents, who never figure directly in the novella, turn their backs on their moral obligation to their son by abandoning him and moving to the city. This rural bias would continue to be prominent throughout Aitmatov's fiction, where the city is associated with a certain rootlessness that manifests itself in the cynicism of power.

In this context it is important to note an allusion to the Kirghiz-Russian dimension of the conflict in *The White Ship*. A slight vowel change in the name of Aitmatov's villain from Orozkul to Oruzkul further reveals the negative in the character's portrayal. In Kirghiz, *oruzkul* means "Russian slave." Thus the character expresses the author's condemnation of those of his compatriots who rushed to worship everything Russian at the expense of their own culture.[34] In the minds of Kirghiz readers, the name immediately elicited the slavish implementation of Moscow's Russification policies in Kirghizstan by Turdakun Usubaliev, long-term Kirghiz party boss, who was in power throughout most of Aitmatov's career.

Momun shoots the doe primarily to save his loved ones from Orozkul's wrath, a compromise that ironically has the opposite effect, leading to the death of his grandson. Momun's self-betrayal and, on a deeper level, his violation of the tribal totem result in his symbolic death. This connotation becomes clear in the scene where the boy, just before making the decision to swim away, sees his grandfather for the last time. He discovers Momun lying on the ground in a drunken stupor: "He made his grandfather roll over and shuddered when he saw the old man's drunken face, spotted with mud and dust . . . and in that moment the boy imagined the head of the white doe, hacked up by Orozkul's axe" (113). Symbolic of Momun's spiritual death are the mutilated antlers that Orozkul lays at the old man's feet, an act reminiscent of the Bugu tribe's original sin of breaking the bond of gratitude with the Deer-mother. In Momun's fairy tale, the fallen Bugus use the antlers to adorn the tombs of their ancestors. With the spiritual fall of Momun, Aitmatov's tragedy is complete; the good at the outpost has been destroyed, and only Orozkul remains.

Yet in his dark parable of Soviet life, Aitmatov offers a glimmer of hope, albeit one exclusively in the realm of fantasy. It is found in the boy's delirious dream of freeing the outpost from Orozkul's tyr-

anny. In his imagination, his ally in driving away the tyrant is Kulubek, an episodic character whom he meets during a snowstorm. The
youthful Kulubek, as it turns out, appreciates the culture of his ancestors yet also feels at ease in the tough, everyday modern world.
Kulubek is the boy's grown-up double, Aitmatov's alternative to Momun. In the boy's dream, Kulubek calls Orozkul a fascist and drives
him away, threatening him with a machine gun and shouting at him
in German, "schnell, schnell! (get moving!)" Then he addresses the
people who witness the scene with the words, "How could you have
lived with such a man? Aren't you ashamed of yourselves?" (110).
Kulubek's last words in this dialogue can also be considered a universal appeal to the reader to resist the tyranny of men like Orozkul.

Soviet readers at the time could not help seeing in those words
a thinly veiled allusion to the plight of Soviet citizens living in conditions of increasing political oppression. Indeed, the isolated forest
preserve in *The White Ship* is portrayed by Aitmatov as a microcosm
reflecting the ills of Soviet society as a whole. Orozkul is clearly con-
ceived as a neo-Stalinist. With the fall of communism in the Soviet
Union some twenty years after Aitmatov published *The White Ship*,
Kulubek's rhetorical question has retained its explosiveness.

Kulubek thus combines reverence for the national heritage with
a strong, unyielding character. His way, Aitmatov suggests, is the
vykhod (way out) of the tragic dead end in the author's microcosm
of Soviet society. Although this intention was evident in the first
edition of the novella, in *Novyi mir*, Aitmatov decided to make it
even clearer in the book publication of *The White Ship*. Under pressure to compensate for the lack of the positive in the *Novyi mir*
conclusion to the novella, the author added a small paragraph to
further emphasize the idea of Kulubek as the boy's one potential
alternative to drowning in the river. Just as the boy imagines a happy
ending to Okozkul's reign of terror, in the new version of the conclusion it is the author himself who imagines a hypothetical happy
ending to the boy's misery:

> You swam away. You didn't wait for Kulubek. . . . If you had run along
> the road, you would have certainly seen him. . . . You would have had
> only to raise your hand, and he would have stopped. "Where are you

going?" Kulubek would have asked. "I'm coming to you," you would have answered. He would have taken you into his truck and you would have driven off. You and Kulubek. And ahead of you along the road, unseen by everyone else, would run the horned Deer-mother. But you would have seen her. (113)

This is all Aitmatov would add to mitigate the tragedy. He was, no doubt, under pressure to add more to assure that his novella would appear in a book edition. The hypothetical appendage was in a sense a bone thrown to appease the writer's orthodox critics. As if teasing the critics who would have preferred such an ending, Aitmatov then returns to the original plot, noting that the boy *did not* wait for Kulubek, but "swam away." This superfluous, belated intrusion of the author into his own work did not go unnoticed by careful readers. A Hungarian critic criticized Aitmatov's attempt to create a hypothetical deus ex machina just to satisfy Soviet critics who are afraid of real catharsis and who believe that in socialist conditions "real tragedies can no longer occur."[35] Yet, in essence, Aitmatov's sin against his work was a venial one; he had already eloquently defended his novella and his position on the tragic in his article "Neobkhodimye utochneniia" (Necessary observations for the sake of clarity) when *The White Ship* first appeared.

Aitmatov's later novellas—*Early Cranes* and *The Piebald Dog Running Along the Seashore*—also end tragically. Both works have boy heroes who derive strength from the heritage of their fathers. The boys are thus the spiritual brothers of the unnamed boy from *The White Ship*, yet they combine spiritual depth with the will to live by it.

The White Ship is a literary work with many dimensions. It expresses not only the age-old conflicts between good and evil and between man and nature, continuing and elaborating on Aitmatov's favorite theme of the danger of compromising with evil, but first and foremost it sounds a fervent plea for the preservation of the human spiritual heritage in a hostile, materialist environment. It is not by chance that Aitmatov makes Orozkul a Soviet official, albeit a minor one. His depraved weltanschauung stems not from the patriarchal past, as has been suggested,[36] but from postrevolutionary Soviet society, in which he was born and raised. Norman Shneidman tactfully points out that in Orozkul "the innate balance of evil and goodness has not been influenced in favor of the latter by his Soviet upbringing."[37] In *The White Ship*, Aitmatov protests vehemently against a system of socialization that deprives people of the spirituality of their ancestors. There are lessons to be learned from the past, and in all of Aitmatov's subsequent work his heroes' deep humanism is directly derived from their prerevolutionary cultural heritage.

5

Aitmatov in the 1970s
Confronting and Transcending Soviet Reality

During the years following the publication of *The White Ship*, Aitmatov went through a period of experimentation with different genres before eventually returning to the aesthetic principles that he had so successfully applied in his 1970 novella. In 1973, for the first and only time in his career, he tried his hand at drama, coauthoring with Kaltai Mukhamedzhanov, a Kazakh playwright, *The Ascent of Mount Fuji*. The work was first staged in 1973 at Moscow's Sovremennik Theater. In 1975, on the occasion of the thirtieth anniversary of the end of World War II, Aitmatov published an autobiographical novella, *Early Cranes*, depicting the harsh life of his family and friends in Sheker during the war years. Neither the play nor the novella relies on parabolic subplots in their depiction of Soviet reality. They are discussed briefly here as to their significance for the development of Aitmatov's career as a writer. A second novella written in the 1970s, *The Piebald Dog Running Along the Seashore*, represents Aitmatov's most daring attempt in the parabolic genre and is discussed more completely in this chapter.

The plot of *The Ascent of Mount Fuji* was originally intended by Aitmatov for a novella, but when his friends persuaded him to use the material for a stage production, he enlisted the help of Mukhamedzhanov, who wrote the first stage script of the play in Kazakh. Aitmatov then translated it into Russian.[1] The subject of the play is the collective guilt of Soviet citizens for the inhumanity of the Stalin era. Nowhere is Stalin directly mentioned, but his presence is felt throughout the drama. The play presents the taboo topic retrospectively and like *Farewell, Gul'sary!* reveals that the immorality of the Stalin era continues to cast its ominous shadow on contemporary Soviet society some twenty years after the tyrant's death. Typical of Aitmatov is the way in which the past is juxtaposed with the present and the morally decrepit are portrayed as those enjoying the greatest privileges in Soviet society.

The play opens with four former schoolmates, their wives, and their former schoolteacher meeting for a picnic on a mountain in Kirghizstan, humorously called Mount Fuji by one of the wives. They laugh at the strange Japanese name until one of the wives suggests they emulate Japanese Buddhists in confessing their sins to the "holy mountain."[2] The game, reminiscent of a similar soul-searching episode from Dostoevsky's *The Idiot*, turns sour at the mention of another schoolmate, who has refused to appear at the reunion. The missing classmate, Sabur, was once a talented poet, as well as the soul and conscience of the group. During the war, all five youths volunteered for the army and served at the front—the only Central Asians in their unit. Sabur's inspiring poetry was published in a wartime newspaper for Turkic-speaking soldiers, and he quickly became famous among his compatriots at the front. Near the end of the war, however, one of his four friends denounced him anonymously to the NKVD, after Sabur had read to them a pacifist poem he was working on at the time. The reading was private, and the poem existed only in the poet's notebook. Since the poem was in Turkic and had not been published, no one else in the unit could have known about it.

While only one of the four was directly responsible for the betrayal of trust and the subsequent incarceration of Sabur, the other three remained silent out of fear their protests would bring about their own arrests. Years went by, and when Sabur was eventually released, he returned home from the camps a broken man, while his former friends continued to suspect one another of the treachery. As the play unfolds, the audience is able to reduce the number of suspects to two. Through the dramatic dialogue on "Mount Fuji," the audience learns that after the war two of the men, Izabek and Osipbai, now a successful journalist and a director of a historical institute, respectively, made their careers through deceit and cowardice. These men later flee when the group discovers the next morning that they unwittingly killed a woman while playfully throwing rocks down the mountain the previous evening. The unwillingness of the two men to accept any responsibility for the arrest and suffering of Sabur, a crime committed twenty years earlier, is thus repeated in the present time frame, when they evade responsibility for the accidental death of the woman.

Like his prose fiction, Aitmatov's play expresses his concern that, by bringing to a halt the process of de-Stalinization and by disclaiming responsibility for the repressions under Stalin, the Soviet leadership was taking the country down a dangerous path where the crimes of the past were bound to be repeated. The play was produced with the stage set of "Mount Fuji" placed in the middle of the theater, thus spacially bringing the viewers closer to the soul-searching conversation taking place in their midst. Many of the lines justifying past crimes must have had a familiar ring to the audience: "Why stir up the past?";[3] "What is done in the interests of the general good can't possibly be called betrayal" (69); "I'm not going to beat my breast, as they say. I wasn't really involved. It has nothing to do with me. But I can tell you that Sabur was no lamb. There was something wrong somewhere. That's why they put him on trial and sent him into exile" (64); "He's not the only one who was exiled. Who do they blame? Who are they supposed to hold a grudge against? History? What great historical event ever took place without mistakes? . . . One has to rise above complications" (66).

These lines are spoken with the smug confidence of those in positions of power with something to hide.[4] One can imagine how uncomfortable the neo-Stalinists in the audience must have felt as the play exposed the immorality of those enjoying respect and authority in society at the cost of others. Indeed, after seeing the play in Moscow at the Sovremennik Theater, Hedrick Smith reported that "conservative-minded viewers complained about the play to the theater."[5]

Allusions made in the play seem to evoke Tvardovskii or Solzhenitsyn. Like Sabur, Tvardovskii became famous for his morale-boost-
ing poetry written as a soldier in the Soviet army during World War
II, and Solzhenitsyn was arrested at the front for his private correspondence, much like Sabur, who is arrested in the play for reading
from his personal notebook. Perhaps because of just such allusions,
the first Soviet review of *The Ascent of Mount Fuji*, a positive one
written by Konstantin Simonov for *Izvestiia*, makes virtually no reference to the plot of the play. Simonov speaks in generalities about
the need to perfect the "personal and social behavior" of Soviet citizens and the negative effects for Soviet society when "difficult problems" are evaded or relegated to "private discussion or chit-chat in
the lobby."[6] Readers of the review living in Soviet cities other than
Moscow, the only place where people could have either seen the play
or heard about it by word of mouth, were no doubt left guessing as
to its content.

A second positive review, published later in *Literaturnaia gazeta*,
was more specific, but still no mention was made of the fact that
Sabur was arrested. Instead, the author remarks that Sabur's poetry
brought him "misfortune, breaking him and ruining his life."[7] Such
reticence was perhaps in order. For almost twenty years, Aitmatov
and Mukhamedzhanov were unable to publish the play in the Soviet
Union. Hedrick Smith, who saw the play in Moscow, speaks of the
"electric silence" at the Sovremennik Theater and notes, "Not since
the Khrushchev era has the Soviet stage seen such searing social
criticism on such a painful issue."[8]

The Ascent of Mount Fuji brought Chingiz Aitmatov his first recognition in the United States. The play was successfully staged by
Arena Stage in Washington, D.C., with Aitmatov attending the premiere on June 4, 1975. Reviews were favorable. *Newsweek* evaluated
the play in the context of Solzhenitsyn's exile to the West, which had
occurred in the previous year: "The ultimate significance of Aitmatov
and his play may well be an ironic one. It is such official 'domesti-
cators,' rather than the Solzhenitsyns or Tsabours [Saburs], who are
the final expediters of change in their repressive societies."[9] Although
these words fail to do justice to Solzhenitsyn and many other prominent dissidents who paid with imprisonment and exile for their opin-

ions, they certainly ring true, from the perspective of the 1990s, for the way Aitmatov saw his literary mission in the 1970s and 1980s. Two of the play's major themes would surface again in his novel *The Day Lasts More than a Hundred Years*: the hypocrisy of Soviet citizens when confronted with the crimes perpetrated by their party and government, and the need to expiate their collective guilt, first through acknowledgment and repentance, then through greater tolerance and freedom. The latter idea is expressed poignantly in *The Ascent of Mount Fuji* when Aisha-apa, the old teacher of the four former schoolmates, declines their invitation to meet again until Sabur is able to join them.

Soviet literature in 1975 was dominated by numerous works dealing with the Soviet war effort in World War II, to mark the thirtieth anniversary of the Soviet victory. Entire issues of literary journals were devoted exclusively to the subject. Memoirs and interviews with prominent veterans appeared throughout the year, and the occasion was even used to resurrect the wartime memoirs of Il'ia Erenburg. Perhaps the best work on the war to appear in 1975 was Valentin Rasputin's classic novel *Zhivi i pomni* (Live and remember).[10] Like Rasputin's novel, which is set in a small village on the Angara River in Siberia, Aitmatov's *Early Cranes* depicts the gloom and deprivation of wartime life in a small Kirghiz *ail*, located thousands of miles from the front.

The depiction of the suffering women and children in the Soviet hinterland during World War II was a frequent topic of post-Thaw Soviet literature, and writers found it extremely difficult to break with the clichés associated with it. Rasputin breathed new life into the subject by portraying in a realistic way the relations of a wife and her deserter husband, who hides in his native village.[11] Aitmatov sought to break with tradition in *Early Cranes* by prefacing his realistic portrayal of the lives of five youths in the *ail* with three epigraphs designed to prefigure the plot and to add epic breadth to his novella. The first is from a love poem by a shepherd poet, who is also an episodic character in the work:

> Aksai, Koksai, Sarysai—the places I've been,
> But nowhere did I find a girl like you. . . .[12]

The lines are taken from a Kirghiz folk song and foreshadow the theme of love in the novella. The second quotation is from the Book of Job: "And there came a messenger unto Job, and said: 'They have slain the servants with the edge of the sword' "(514). Here the theme of innocent suffering and human perseverance is introduced. The suffering of the boy heroes and their Kirghiz village is thus cast as that of the righteous.

The third quotation alludes to hope and the cyclical continuity of human life. It is taken from the 233d psalm of the *Theragatha*, a collection of poems by Buddhist monks written in India around 80 B.C.:

> Again and again the plowmen plow the field,
> Again and again seed is thrown to the land,
> Again and again the heavens send rains . . .
> With hope men plow the field,
> With hope they sow the seed,
> With hope they go out into the sea. (514)

The image of the plowing evoked in the verse is central in *Early Cranes*; it represents the very activity the boy heroes must prepare for throughout the narrative. The theme of hope expressed in the psalm points to man's fragile position in the world, suggesting that the purest of motives and noblest of efforts do not automatically ensure success. Life is a never-ending struggle—hope aids humankind in its toil.

The time-effacing quality of the novella is further supported by allusions to the Kirghiz epic hero Manas. The setting of the story is an *ail* at the foot of Mount Manas. The epic hero is constantly on the mind of Aitmatov's boy hero, Sultanmurat, and the narrator frequently resorts to the imagery of the Kirghiz epic poem when depicting the boy's struggle. Thus while the plot of *Early Cranes* is classically realistic, generally characterized by metonymic style and an overall exactness of time and place, its allusions to ancient cultural monuments are constantly working at relativizing the effect of the realistic framework.

The plot of *Early Cranes* is highly autobiographical, based on Aitmatov's wartime experiences as a boy in his native *ail* of Sheker.

The five boy heroes, for example, are fictionalized variants of Aitmatov's boyhood friends: Baitik, Tairybek, Satar, Anatai, and Sultanmurat. During the war, the boys left school in the winter to help the kolkhoz in Sheker plow an additional two hundred hectares in the Koksai steppe. In a newspaper article, Aitmatov relates how the boys suffered a severe setback when horse thieves stole two of their best plow horses.[13]

In the novella, the five Kirghiz youths are requested by the kolkhoz chairman, Tynaliev, to leave school in the winter to make ready the kolkhoz's neglected plows, to groom and take care of the few half-starved horses, and to prepare themselves for the difficult task of plowing and sowing the vast Aksai steppe in the early spring.[14] In the boys' imagination, this is a military task. Uniting them is an intense yearning for their fathers, who are away at the distant front, and the desire to live up to their idealized images of them. Two of the boys' fathers have perished in the war, and the absence of letters from Sultanmurat's father hangs ominously over the whole narration. The boys are awkward teenagers groping to understand the adult world. Sultanmurat is thrust into that world, experiencing love and great suffering and nourished by the hope that his efforts will succeed and his father will return.

After four days' labor, the boys find themselves entirely alone and exhausted. They are heartened, however, by their sighting of cranes high above the steppe, which they interpret as a harbinger of a bountiful harvest. Yet their hopes are dashed when horse thieves attack and rob them of their best plow horses, an act that also threatens to deprive the *ail* of desperately needed grain. Sultanmurat pursues the armed thieves on one of the remaining horses (a horse that once belonged to his father). But the thieves shoot the horse from under him, and the novella closes with Sultanmurat left alone at the mercy of a wolf that has scented the blood of the dying horse.

Early Cranes is dedicated to Aitmatov's first son, Askar. The theme of mutual responsibility between father and son dominates the realistic plot line. Sultanmurat's initiation into the world of adults is made easier by the spiritual ideal he perceives in his father, Bekbai. In the opening three chapters of the novella, the boy hero remembers the prewar bliss he experienced when his father lived at home.

In particular he recalls accompanying his father on a trip to Dzham-bul (Aulie-Ata). During the trip, Bekbai allows his son to take the reins of the cart, an act that symbolizes the continuity of the gener-ations. The horses pulling the cart, Chabdar and Chontoru, are well cared for by Bekbai and function in the novella as a symbolic baton passed from father to son.[15] While Bekbai is away at the front, the horses, now weak and neglected, are returned to Sultanmurat to make up two of the four horses in the team with which he is to plow on the Aksai plain. In his father's absence, the horses become a con-stant reminder of Sultanmurat's image of his father, and the youth strives to return them to the condition they were in when Bekbai first gave him the reins on the road to Dzhambul.

The weltanschauung that emerges in *Early Cranes* views the val-ues of the preceding generation as the source of human inspiration and courage in times of crisis. Thus people are called upon to live in such a way that the following generation will also respect and derive strength from the spiritual values of their forebears. This idea of eternal continuity is a particularly important component of the Cen-tral Asian heritage. In his brief autobiographical essay, Aitmatov em-phasizes the veneration of ancestors in Kirghiz society:

> In our village it was considered absolutely obligatory to know one's ancestors to the seventh generation. The old men were very strict about this. . . . And if a boy happened not to know his genealogy, then rep-rimands would reach his parents' ears. People would say, "What kind of father is that who has neither clan nor forebears? Where is he look-ing? How can someone grow up without knowing his ancestors?" And the questions would go on and on. In this one finds a sense of continuity from generation to generation and a sense of mutual responsibility in one's clan.[16]

In *The White Ship*, the idea that people must learn the lessons from the past to avoid degradation into amorality is expressed in a dialogue between Kulubek and the boy hero:

> Really, they never taught you to remember the names of your seven ancestors? . . .
>   No they didn't. And what for? I don't know them, and am none the worse for it. Life goes on.

> Grandfather says that if people don't remember their fathers' fathers, they'll go bad.
> Who will go bad? People?
> Yes.
> But why?
> Grandfather says that no one will be ashamed of their evil deeds because their children won't learn about them anyway.[17]

The idea of eternal continuity finds expression in the author's evocation of the lessons and imagery of the Kirghiz national epos, *Manas*. Throughout the novella, Aitmatov's boy heroes see themselves as the epic hero's loyal lieutenants. Sultanmurat's first love is depicted against the background of the national epos. The hero's younger brother, Adzhimurat, refers to Sultanmurat and his girlfriend, Myrzagul', as Semetei and Aichurek (565), the legendary couple from *Manas*. Significant for the father-son theme of *Early Cranes* is the fact that Semetei is Manas's son, who avenges himself on his father's murderers and strives to restore the glory of his father's rule.[18] The parallel suggests that Sultanmurat's father will perish at the front, and the youth will persevere in his fight with the plunderers of his homeland. In *Manas*, Semetei must first prove himself worthy of Aichurek by eliminating her unwanted suitor, Toltoi, in battle. This he does, and nothing else stands in the way of their marriage.[19] Similarly, Sultanmurat must prove himself by overcoming his classmate and rival, Anatai, in a brawl (576–77).

The timeless frame intended by the author for *Early Cranes* is complemented by another of his favorite techniques—the shifting of the narrator's perspective to a vantage point somewhere far above the action. The resulting imagery is truly detached and timeless, reminiscent of the epigraph from the *Theragatha*:

> The snow continued to fall. The dark plows floated as ships in a white fog. And in that swirling snowy silence, swallowing all sounds, only the shouts of the plowmen could be heard:
> —Ana-ta-ai!
> —Erkin-be-ek!
> —Sultanmura-a-at! (586)

The appearance of the cranes, from which the novella receives its title, adds to the widening of the perspective: "The birds were high above. But the sky was even higher. It was an enormous, all-encompassing sky. And the cranes were but a floating, living island in that all-encompassing world" (591). The cranes are intended as a metaphor for the boys, for the purity of their aspirations and hopes. In the epic tradition of Turkic and Mongol peoples, the birds' color—white—has always been associated with the pure and the good; it was believed to have magical qualities capable of predetermining human fate.[20] Though the boys are defeated, the cranes symbolize the author's conviction and optimism that mankind's struggle will continue—the hope expressed in the epigraph from the *Theragatha*: "Again and again the plowmen plow the field. . . . In hope they sow the seed."

This promise of eternal hope is also implied in the epigraph from the Book of Job. Like Job, Sultanmurat at first has everything—the presence of his father represents a rich world to him—and, like Job, he loses everything, through no fault of his own. The words in the epigraph, "They have slain the servants with the edge of the sword," allude to the war. Sultanmurat suffers a second blow when the horse thieves attack. Yet although the novella concludes at the time of the boys' most bitter disappointment and Sultanmurat's fight for his life, the author suggests that, as in the Book of Job, righteousness will prevail and the boys will emerge stronger from their trial and encounter with evil in the world.

Unfortunately, however, Aitmatov's attempt at expanding the specific to the universal in *Early Cranes* fails aesthetically. Contrary to the author's intention, the epic and prefigurative devices serve more to confuse the theme than to clarify it. The associations are too diverse to give the work its needed unity. The martial and Buddhist imageries associated with the activity of plowing clash with one another. Traditionally, the imagery of plowing evokes the idea of peace; its description in military terms is a discomforting paradox. Moreover, the author juxtaposes the lofty martial allusions from *Manas* with military clichés and jargon from World War II. The resulting incongruity creates an effect that at times borders on the burlesque.

The general effect of combining biblical, Buddhist, and epic references in *Early Cranes* is confusing and hence self-defeating. It adds little depth to the characterization of the novella's heroes. When peppered with lines from *Manas*, the speech of the hero, Sultan-murat, becomes unconvincing and wooden. The use of folklore in Kirghiz literature was shunned for a long time precisely for this reason.[21] Beginning with *Farewell, Gul'sary!* Aitmatov's originality in interpreting and integrating folklore elements into his fiction led to a positive reassessment of folklore as a device and concept in Soviet literature. In *The White Ship*, for example, the mythic is presented predominantly in the form of interior monologue, which contributes greatly to the characters' realistic portrayal. Such depth is missing in *Early Cranes*. Since the publication of *Early Cranes*, Aitmatov has not returned to the prefiguration technique used in the novella. The work does reveal, however, that Aitmatov was seeking to attain universality—or, as Soviet critics would call it later, *global'nost'* (globality)—in the portrayal of the specific in his fiction. He would return to the parabolic technique of *The White Ship* in all of his subsequent literary work.

The year 1977 marked the sixtieth anniversary of the Russian Revolution, and writers were encouraged to devote their works to the principles of the revolution and to create exemplary heroes capable of inspiring Soviet readers in their efforts to build communism. Yet Aitmatov used the occasion to transcend Soviet reality by writing *The Piebald Dog Running Along the Seashore*, a mythic adventure story with a prerevolutionary setting. The novella first appeared in the April issue of *Znamia* and at the time attested to the widening gap between the official demands for socialist realism in belles lettres, on the one hand, and actual literary practice, on the other.[22]

Like *Early Cranes*, *The Piebald Dog* is a novella of initiation. In *The Piebald Dog*, however, the initiation is a literal one. The novella tells the story of a boy's first journey to sea. And the men who accompany the boy view the undertaking as a *rite de passage*. The three stages of the classical story of initiation—separation, initiation, and return—all find expression in Aitmatov's novella. Significantly, for the first time since "Newspaper Dzhuio," Aitmatov uses a setting outside his native Central Asia. The action in the novella takes place in northeastern Siberia and depicts the lives of the Nivkh people, who inhabit the coast along the Sea of Okhotsk. As in *The White Ship*, there is a convergence of the real and mythological worlds. But whereas the characters in *The White Ship* find themselves in opposing camps, based upon their belief or lack of belief in the central myth of their origin, in *The Piebald Dog* all characters are at home in both the real and the mythic worlds.

The plot of *The Piebald Dog* is dramatic. Three Nivkh hunters and their boy initiate, Kirisk, paddle out into the open sea beyond the sight of land in order to reach three rocky islands, where the boy's first hunt is to take place. The last land the men see before losing sight of the coast is their orientation point, a coastal mountain with spots of trees and snow that, from the distance, give it the appearance of a piebald dog.[23] The moment when the "piebald dog" disappears is an important one for Kirisk, for he now enters the world of men, who, in order to provide for their wives and children, must venture out to sea.

The three men accompanying Kirisk are his father, Emraiin, his uncle, Mylgun, and the clan elder, Organ, the most experienced fisherman-hunter in the hamlet, whose primitive, animistic understanding of the world is shared by all in the boat. Organ's thoughts and daydreaming during the course of the journey transport the reader into a mythical world. One dream that never leaves the elder is his dream of the great Fish-woman, the mythological mother of the Nivkh tribe, with whom he yearns to unite.[24] This longing finds expression in a number of erotic images. In his dreams, Organ follows her into the sea, swimming along with her until they reach a haven on land where, "overcome by passion," they would unite and partake of all "the sweetness and bitterness of the beginning and end of life."[25] Yet when they finally reach the haven in the old man's dream, their unification cannot be consummated, for the Fish-woman cannot leave her element and must return to the sea, where Organ can never reach her. This Tantalus dream in the novella also represents Organ's death wish, and as such it foreshadows the catastrophe that will befall the four men in the kayak.

After reaching the first island, where Kirisk fails to kill his first seal, the men set off for the second island. Immediately upon losing sight of land, they become engulfed in dense fog and must wrestle with a terrifying storm. They survive the storm yet lose their way in the fog. The fog settles down silently over the sea, and the little drinking water the men have brought with them is soon to run out. Realizing their plight might last for days, Organ steps into the icy water to his death in order to save drinking water for the others in the boat. As time goes on and the fog continues to hang low over the sea, the boy's uncle and father imitate the elder's act of self-sacrifice, leaving Kirisk the last remaining drops of water. Yet for Kirisk, the men never die; they live on in his animistic world—Organ as the wind, his uncle as the waves, his father as the guiding star that the boy, alone and exhausted, sees when the fog finally lifts. Kirisk is saved on the seventh day, as the winds drive the fragile kayak within sight of the "piebald dog."

The Piebald Dog is a masterpiece of Aitmatov's parabolic technique of integrating folklore elements into a realistic plot to express his philosophical ideas on humankind. More than in any other of his works, Aitmatov strives to free the novella from the confines of specific time and space. The only details the reader finds to determine the time of the events portrayed are references to bearded merchants from whom the Nivkh fishermen have bought their Winchester rifles and tobacco and who tell them of Christ—"the great man who walked on the sea" (171). The effacement of time and space, the extremely limited number of characters, and the dramatic situation all come together to make the novella as a whole a parable on humanity's plight in the closing decades of the twentieth century. Aitmatov's choice of a folklore so alien and distant to that of his Central Asian homeland was made not to satisfy a taste for the exotic but to find an appropriate metaphor for his cherished ideas and his concept of the contemporary human moral predicament.

In public statements made by Aitmatov in the 1970s and early 1980s, he resorts to boat metaphors to characterize humankind's condition in the age of rapid technological progress:

> The scientific and technological revolution gave modern man the possibility of instantaneous contact everywhere on the planet through the means of mass communication. Means of rapid transportation have

physically brought peoples closer together and, in doing so, made us much more dependent on each other than ever before. Today we are all in the same boat, and surrounding us outside is the infinity of space.[26]

These words appear in a wider context, in which the author expresses his fear that that same technology could some day destroy the world if people fail to work together to ensure its survival. The story of three men and a boy is the literary realization of the boat metaphor. Three generations are represented in the boat, and the survival of the boy is due to the efforts of the two preceding generations. The strength of Kirisk's father and uncle at the oars save the fragile boat during the violent storm, while the elder's skill at the helm, his wisdom, and his courageous example ensure that Kirisk will be given the utmost chance for survival. Thus by analogy, Aitmatov implies that in the face of impersonal destructive forces humankind must muster all its rational resources to ensure the survival of future generations. He presents solidarity as humankind's only hope in confronting such forces or in dealing with its own destructive irrationality.

These ideas are expressed not only in the resolution of the plot of *The Piebald Dog* but first and foremost in the imagery and mythic currents in the novella. The fog that engulfs the men is a powerful image of primeval darkness in the world, of death, of an indifferent and absurd universe. In the narration, it is called the "Great Fog" and likened to a threatening monster: "It approached as a living creature, as a monster intent on capturing and swallowing them along with their boat, together with the visible and invisible world" (150).[27] It moves like a "serpent," and when it blots out the sun the narrator speaks of it as "living darkness." One of the men, Mylgun, responds to the darkened world by rebelling against the Nivkh gods. He curses the wind-god, with the strongest of words, for deserting them. His blasphemy revolves around the idea of innocent suffering. Kirisk is an innocent boy, making his first trip to sea. Like Dostoevsky's Ivan Karamazov, Mylgun demands justice from his god before he is willing to show respect. And like Ivan Karamazov's call for justice, Mylgun's demands remain unanswered, his verbal rebellion senseless—the universe, like the fog, remains silent and indifferent: "No, the forces were too unequal: the darkness of eternity, existing before the sun appeared in the universe, and four condemned men in a fragile boat" (169). In such an uneven struggle, the human being must resist becoming the slave of circumstances. Aitmatov's novella suggests that its free spirit raises humankind above the impersonal forces of the universe. In response to threatening, uncontrollable events, humankind's true greatness is revealed in its capacity for love and sacrifice.

In the opening lines of the novella, the author depicts a universe of eternal struggle: "In the pitch-dark night, saturated with the spray and cold of the sea, along the whole coastal front of the Sea of Okhotsk the eternal battle of the two natural elements went on incessantly—the land sought to prevent the movement of the sea, and the sea tirelessly continued its assault on the land" (11). Humanity's position in this universe of conflict is portrayed as fragile: "Ever since the land came into being, the sea cannot find peace. Since then the sea and the land have been locked in struggle. And at times man is hard put between them. He is disliked by the sea because he belongs more to the land" (116).[28]

According to the novella's central myth, which Aitmatov borrows from Nivkh folklore, the world was originally covered by an unending ocean. The duck Luvr flew over the waters hoping to find land, where she could lay her egg. Realizing there was no place to build a nest, she landed on the water, pulled feathers from her breast, and made a nest. From this frail nest, the landmasses on earth began to grow. The biblical allusions in Aitmatov's parabolic rendition of the myth are obvious. In Genesis, for example, it is the spirit of God that wanders above the watery abyss. But in *The Piebald Dog*, the act of creation is seen not only as an act of love but as an act of sacrifice, as well. The duck must pull out its feathers to ensure the birth of life on the planet.

The myth of the duck Luvr is found on the first page of the novella. In light of the myth, the men's ultimate sacrifice assumes a different dimension. For like the duck, they too wander aimlessly about the darkened ocean until stepping into the sea. Their decision to leave the boat and perish is paradoxically a step for life—the stepping out into the water parallels the first act of creation. Through their sacrifice, the youngest in the boat survives, just as Luvr's sacrifice results in assuring life for her offspring. Although the men live in an animistic world, which seems to make their giving of life easier,[29] Aitmatov still shows their decision to be a difficult one, a giving of their own flesh, a painful experience reminiscent of Luvr's pulling of her feathers to build a nest on the water.[30]

Aitmatov's men in the boat face the awesome forces of nature and emerge triumphant in spirit through a display of love and human solidarity. Thus they refuse to let their fates be determined by the caprice of an unrelenting and hostile world, symbolized by the "Great Fog." Rather, they themselves choose the time of their departure. Their deaths, therefore, serve to affirm their humanity and are testimonies to the power of the human spirit. Curiously, Aitmatov seeks to tie the men's pagan self-sacrifice to that of Christ. In a brief episode in the novella, Kirisk's father recalls a story he had heard once from a red-haired trader: "He said that in a certain far away country there once lived a man who walked on the sea." Organ, who has decided to sacrifice himself that very day, replies: "That means he was a great man, the greatest of the great. . . . But for us the greatest of all is the Fish-woman" (171).

The Piebald Dog represents Aitmatov's attempt to find the common denominator between the shamanistic worldview of his ancestors and that of the Christian West. At the time Aitmatov wrote *The Piebald Dog*, it would have been difficult to extol Christ's sacrifice as exemplary, whereas censorship could and would accept the positive portrayal of the sacrificial deaths of representatives of a primitive people, especially if the plot were set in remote prerevolutionary Russia. Subsequently, some nine years later, when the political climate in the USSR was changing, the writer would return to the main idea of *The Piebald Dog* in his novel *The Place of the Skull*, in which the portrayal of Christ plays a central role in the composition of the work, and an effort would be made to unite elements of pagan and Christian worldviews.

Yet the world of *The Piebald Dog* is still pagan and animistic. In sacrificing themselves, the men hope to ensure the survival of their clan. If Kirisk survives, they know they too will live on, in his memory. After their "departure they continue to help the boy. Kirisk returns safely because he recalls their lessons. The veneration of the spirits of one's ancestors is shared by many cultures; among the Kirghiz, it corresponds to the cult of the *arbak* (revered fathers), whom the living call upon for help in times of great distress. Aitmatov brings that part of his cultural heritage to his novella about the Nivkh people. Thus from Organ, Kirisk remembers always to note the direction of the wind and recalls that the polar owl flies in straight lines over the sea from land to land. These lessons save his life. His respect for and reliance on the spirit of his ancestors find expression in their immortality in his animistic consciousness.

The manner in which Aitmatov transforms the folklore sources in *The Piebald Dog* substantiates again his contention that myths and legends are of literary value only to the degree that they are relevant to the problems facing modern humanity. The modifications to which he subjects the material reveal his stance as a moral absolutist and his intention to make the story a parable of the human condition in the second half of the twentieth century, in a world living with the fear of nuclear annihilation. The parable of the Nivkh fishermen in the boat calls upon humankind to see itself in a wider perspective, as part of an endless chain of humanity with responsibility to past, present, and future generations. Only through such a worldview will modern humanity, in Aitmatov's opinion, find the strength and wisdom to survive the perils of the future.

The plot of *The Piebald Dog* is based on an incident in the life of Vladimir Sangi, the contemporary Nivkh writer to whom Aitmatov dedicates the novella. At the time of the novella's publication, Aitmatov had neither visited the setting of the story nor done extensive research in preparation. Sangi's own experience is remarkably similar to that of the fictional Kirisk, with the significant exception, however, of the theme of self-sacrifice.

Sangi had been taken to sea by the village elders as a boy to learn the hunting skills of his people when, after they had successfully killed a seal on an island, an impenetrable fog suddenly descended on their boat as they were returning home. The men lost all orientation. To still their hunger, they began eating the raw meat of the seal. Suddenly the elder sharply turned the boat around—he had heard a polar owl fly by and knew that the birds, returning from the islands in the evening, always fly in a straight line to shore. Sangi and his people were saved.[31]

But the idea of sacrifice was important to Aitmatov, and he introduced the agony of thirst into the novella. Sangi notes:

> Thirst is the experience of a man who has grown up in hot regions, of a person who knows what thirst is like in the steppe under a blazing sun. The Nivkhs experience no thirst in the fog and cold of the Sea of Okhotsk, nor is there a keg of water under a seat in the boat. But without the motif of inhuman thirst, there would have been no problems of life and death to be resolved by the heroes and thus no novella.[32]

The incantation Aitmatov's boy hero repeats over and over throughout his ordeal to help himself fall asleep—"blue mouse, give me some water!"—stems from the author's own childhood experience of thirst. In Kirghiz, the incantation "chychkan ake suu ber" (uncle mouse, give me some water) is believed to calm sick children who want to drink but are not allowed to have water.[33] In the novella, however, the incantation passes easily for Nivkh folklore.

Most of the details in Aitmatov's novella that create the Nivkh atmosphere were borrowed by the writer from Sangi's historical novel *Zhenit'ba Kevongov* (The wedding of the Kevongs), 1975, whose plot bears little resemblance to that of *The Piebald Dog*.[34] Apparently, Aitmatov used *The Wedding of the Kevongs* primarily for its ethnographic information. Thus the names of Aitmatov's heroes Kirisk, Mylgun, Emraiin, and Organ, as well as the realia of the Winchester rifles, the dried fish (*iukola*), and the bearded Russian merchants, are all found in Sangi's work. Sangi's novel is clearly set in the years preceding the 1917 Russian Revolution, and Aitmatov's novella, despite its timeless quality, can also be placed in the same historical era because of the presence of the same realia in the plot. The theme of Sangi's novella—the threat of extinction of the Kevong tribe—also finds expression in Aitmatov's work, in the men's concern that Kirisk survive the ordeal. The Nivkh god Kurng, the evil spirits (*kingry*), and the men's feeding of the spirit of the hunting grounds are all transferred from Sangi's novel to give *The Piebald Dog* its unique shamanistic atmosphere. Of course, both Sangi's and Aitmatov's peoples share a not so distant shamanistic past.[35]

The appearance of *The Piebald Dog* in April 1977 brought to a head a new development in Soviet letters, one that Aitmatov himself had initiated and popularized with the publication of *The White Ship* in January 1970. The use of myth and folklore increased the aesthetic possibilities available to Soviet writers, and consequently, many sought to imitate Aitmatov's poetics. In the month following the appearance of the novella, Anatolii Bocharov, a leading Soviet critic, proposed to call the new trend in Soviet literature "synthetic realism." Bocharov clearly saw the parabolic dimension inherent in such prose and encouraged Soviet critics to accept it as a further enhancement of socialist realism: "Isn't it time for us to decide to quit employing the word parable to condemn or excuse, instead of using it to characterize a certain aesthetic quality?"[36] To support his plea for the legitimacy of the parabolic in Soviet letters, Bocharov offers an example from classical Russian literature, pointing to Dostoevsky's *Brothers Karamazov*. While its didactic nature made the parable popular among writers of the Age of Enlightenment, Dostoevsky may have preferred the parable form for his "Legend of the Grand Inquisitor" because "it enabled him to focus on the essence of his philosophical quest and served as a point of support for the dialogical structure of his novels."[37] Yet Bocharov's endorsement of the parabolic in contemporary Soviet prose soon found vocal opponents. A controversy arose in the pages of *Literaturnaia gazeta* between March and June 1978 that ended in an uneasy truce.

The polemics had their origin in an article by Lev Anninskii. If Bocharov saw the use of myth, allegory, and parable as having the potential of deepening the philosophical significance of a literary work, Anninskii perceived in the movement the threat of sacrificing reality for an abstract super-reality. The critic expressed the fear that the fascination of writers with allegory and parable would have a paralyzing effect on the narrative element in fiction and likened the presence of parables and allegories in a work to "bloodclots in the arteries of a narration."[38] Anninskii gives a number of examples of works he considers to have been ruined by excessive use of parable— "Ballada" (The ballad) by the Moldavian writer Nikolai Esinenku, *Rannie berega* (Early shores) by the Russian Nikolai Klimontovich, *Pervaia liubov' Khodzhi Nasreddina* (The first love of Khodzhi Nasreddin) by the Azerbaijani Timur Zul'fikarov. Discussing Aitmatov's *Piebald Dog*, Anninskii rejects its parabolic style outright, asserting that the novella's redeeming quality is found in the realistic portrayal of the fishermen's battle with the elements. Anninskii, considered at the time a liberal critic vis-à-vis the cultural establishment, saw in the movement, no doubt, an attempt by Soviet writers to escape the depiction of the pressing issues of the day by retreating into non-Soviet reality.

Anninskii's views are echoed by Aleksei Kondratovich, a conservative critic, in his article "Muza v tumane" (The muse in the fog), which, as the title reveals, concerns itself with *The Piebald Dog* more directly. Kondratovich juxtaposes passages from Aitmatov's novella concerning the eternal opposition of the sea and the land with a passage from an early story by Ivan Bunin, "Prazdnik" (Holiday), 1891, which also describes the sea in lyrical terms. The style of the two passages from Bunin and Aitmatov is labeled by Kondratovich as immature and mediocre, serving only to evade a realistic portrayal of life. To write "honest straightforward prose" is far more difficult, the critic concludes.[39] What Kondratovich, no doubt, had in mind when speaking of "honest straightforward prose" was fiction depicting Soviet reality in the mechanistic style of classic socialist realism.

The constraints on Soviet letters in the 1970s made it impossible for Aitmatov and other writers living in the USSR to depict the reality of Soviet life in a direct, "straightforward" way. As the title of his essay indicates, Kondratovich felt that Aitmatov was hiding behind his parabolic fiction, instead of revealing his attitude toward Soviet reality. Of course, the critic could deduce Aitmatov's attitude toward Soviet life by the very fact that, in the year of the sixtieth anniversary of the Russian Revolution, the author had forgone writing about Soviet workers or intellectuals "fighting" for world peace and instead had chosen to depict the lives and extol the values of an obscure people populating a remote region of prerevolutionary Siberia.

Aitmatov felt compelled to answer his critics publicly. In an interview with Vladimir Korkin, he replied to Anninskii's charge by asserting his loyalty to realism and criticizing the tendency among Soviet critics and readers to reduce realism to the strict chronological presentation of the everyday world.[40] Referring to Gogol's "magical realism," Aitmatov maintained that nothing should restrain a writer in his endeavor to express an idea. Pointing to other great writers from the past and present, he made a plea for artistic freedom:

> The true writer creates, discovers a new artistic reality by falling back on the experience of all mankind and his own personal spiritual experience—philosophical, ethical, and aesthetic—and using all the necessary and expressive means that are available to him to do this. . . . One could name writers from all times and nations for whom there never was a question as to how they should write, or what devices they should use in order to best express the idea exciting them.[41]

Aitmatov's works—all published under Soviet censorship—are a testimony to his efforts to take advantage of all the expressive means at his disposal. Myth, legend, and folklore have never been treated as canonical by the writer but as materials to be reinterpreted to produce a more poignant depiction of the plight of contemporary humanity.[42] Indeed, the writer's free interpretation and transformation of Nivkh folklore in *The Piebald Dog* demonstrates that his theme is not Nivkh civilization at the turn of the twentieth century, but modern humankind at the turn of the twenty-first century, caught in the paradoxes of the atomic age. In Aitmatov's following work, *The Day Lasts More than a Hundred Years*, his first full-length novel, he would add science fiction to his folklore repertoire, in an attempt to find ever more expressive means to portray the pressing problems of his time and country.

6

The Day Lasts More than a Hundred Years
Defining Soviet Mankurtization

"I kniga eta—vmesto moego tela, / I slovo eto vmesto dushi moei." (This book I offer instead of my body, / And this word instead of my soul). These lines, taken from Gregory Narekatzi's *Lamentations*, serve as the epigraph for *The Day Lasts More than a Hundred Years* and express the significance Aitmatov attaches to his first full-length novel. The epigraph also reveals the author's desire that his book be recognized as his personal statement to Soviet citizens in the 1980s. Appearing within a year of the Soviet invasion of Afghanistan, the forced exile of renowned human rights activist Andrei Sakharov to Gorky, and the boycott of the Moscow Olympics by the United States and other Western countries, the novel was for many Soviet readers a welcome cultural occurrence in the otherwise gloomy atmosphere of the final years of the Brezhnev gerontocracy. Since Aitmatov has always sought to express in his fiction the "body and pressure" of his time, there is no doubt that the events of 1980 were on Aitmatov's mind while he was writing his novel.[1] Although his novel alludes to those events with caution, such allusions were enough to make *The Day Lasts More than a Hundred Years* a literary sensation. The *Novyi mir* volume in which the novel was published became so scarce in Moscow that American journalists were reported to have made photocopies in the United States to give to dissident friends.[2]

Aitmatov's choice of epigraph from Narekatzi's tenth-century book of lamentations to God prefigures the novel's primary themes of memory, conscience, and responsibility. In his *Lamentations*, the Armenian monk and saint tirelessly recounts his sins and weaknesses, condemning himself as the most unworthy of God's creatures. For centuries the volume played a central role in Armenian culture; its mystical and cathartic qualities contributed to making it the most valued book—after the Bible—in Armenian homes.[3] The epigraph thus points to Aitmatov's hope that his portrayal of his country's sins—in particular, the repression of the national heritage of its peoples and attempts to exercise totalitarian control over their minds—might have a similar cathartic influence on the novel's Soviet readers.

Narekatzi's lamentations had a profound impact on Aitmatov, as is evident from a letter he wrote in 1978 to Levon Mkrtchian, a prominent poet from Soviet Armenia: "For us Narekatzi is 'terrifying' because of his incredible thoroughness, his inhuman ability to subject himself to the merciless judgment of the highest eternal court—the court of conscience and responsibility before God."[4] Precisely the manner in which Aitmatov's novel links the idea of conscience with the religious concept of God was highly significant for Soviet letters in 1980. In this spirit, *The Day Lasts More than a Hundred Years* calls upon readers to accept direct responsibility for their actions and for the world as a whole.

The original title of the novel was *Obruch* (Iron hoop), which alluded more directly to the prominent theme of political repression in the work. Soviet censors took exception to the title, however, and Aitmatov agreed to the present one, *I dol'she veka dlitsia den'* (The day lasts more than a hundred years), which was suggested to him by *Novyi mir*. The *Novyi mir* title proved to be a fortunate alternative. It captures lyrically the sense of time standing still, an idea that determines much of the novel's composition. Yet when the journal edition was submitted for publication in book form to Molodaia gvardiia publishing house, that title was also rejected and a new one given, probably because "the day lasts more than a hundred years" is taken from Boris Pasternak's poem "Edinstvennye dni" (Unique days), which was first published in 1959 by *tamizdat* in Munich (*Mosty* 2).

Instead of the line from Pasternak, Molodaia gvardiia proposed *Burannyi polustanok* (Snowstorm station), which directed attention to the hero's home and workplace, thereby emphasizing the novel's more prosaic labor theme. It is not the most important theme in the work, but it was one that literary conservatives and party officials at the time were constantly calling upon writers to resuscitate. In all subsequent book editions of the novel, however, Aitmatov has returned to the *Novyi mir* title.[5] The squabbles over the title are a good indication of just how much importance Soviet literary watchdogs of the time attached to the proper interpretation of a controversial novel.

Aitmatov's persistent efforts to universalize the moral conflicts of his characters continue in *The Day Lasts More than a Hundred Years*. To create the parabolic effect that had come to characterize his mature fiction, he incorporates myths and legends from the past and, for the first time, uses science fiction for the same purpose. As a result, a longer work was created, a novel, whose parabolic mode was sufficiently ambiguous to make it difficult for the censors to find much to fault. Aitmatov's own stature at the time and his inclusion of a pseudopositive hero also, no doubt, facilitated the novel's publication by the Soviet press. Nevertheless, the appearance in 1990 of *The White Cloud of Genghis Khan*, a chapter Aitmatov had excluded from the 1980 edition because of the "all-seeing censors,"[6] serves as an indication that the path of *The Day Lasts More than a Hundred Years* to the Soviet readership was far from smooth, and Aitmatov, like all other Soviet writers of the time, had to operate within the confines of the permissible.[7]

To give his novel a high degree of topicality, Aitmatov fills his work with allusions to the controversial milestones of Soviet history and juxtaposes them with the pressing issues facing Soviet society at the beginning of the 1980s. The novel thus touches upon the trauma of collectivization, the legacy of Stalin's nationalities policy, the harsh repatriation of Soviet prisoners of war, the arms race, and the polarized world of superpower confrontation. At the time of the novel's appearance, an honest discussion of those and similar themes was still taboo in Soviet letters. The issues were, however, on the minds of Soviet intellectuals, and they figured prominently at the time in the *samizdat* and *tamizdat* publications of Soviet dissidents.

Aside from the shift from novella to novel, aesthetically *The Day Lasts More than a Hundred Years* appears to be more a summation of positions taken and defended earlier in Aitmatov's work than a radical departure along a new path. The novel contains motifs and structures similar to those found in *Farewell, Gul'sary!*, *The White Ship*, and *The Piebald Dog*. As in these works, Aitmatov's novel integrates myth and folklore into a portrayal of contemporary reality. Similarly, the author closely identifies himself with the worldview of the main character. The central plot line includes a long exposition that gives way to a sudden crisis and climax. A degree of pessimism is omnipresent. The science fiction, which the author introduces for the first time in his work, represents his attempt to find new and more expressive means to impress upon the reader the gravity of the human dilemma in the last quarter of the twentieth century.

With the introduction of the science fiction subplot, *The Day Lasts More than a Hundred Years* became Aitmatov's most complex work structurally: the legendary past and the hypothetical future are combined in his depiction of Soviet reality in the Brezhnev era. The structure Aitmatov chose for his novel reflects the idea that, if the mistakes of the past are not corrected in the present, their consequences for the future will be graver. As in Aitmatov's novellas, strategically placed interlocking details tie the three temporal planes together, heightening the aesthetic formulation of the moral issues and increasing the reader's sense of urgency.

In the opening pages of the novel, the hero, Edigei Zhangel'din, learns of the death of his older friend and colleague, Kazangap Asanbaev, and resolutely decides to honor his friend's last request to be buried according to Moslem ritual at an ancient burial ground called Ana-Beiit. The preparations for the funeral and the procession into the steppe to Ana-Beiit make up the novel's "day." The slow movement of the funeral procession provides the frame for Edigei's reminiscences of his past life. The hero dwells upon memories of the crucial events in his life, which span a time period from the late 1930s until the present (implicitly, sometime in the 1980s).

The key junctures in Edigei's life are the repression of his family during collectivization; his service at the front in World War II; the infant death of his only son while he was fighting at the front; Edigei's concussion injury from an exploding artillery shell and his discharge from the army; his chance meeting with Kazangap, who persuades him to settle and work at Boranly-Burannyi, a small railroad hamlet in the Kazakh steppe; his confrontation with GPU (State Political Directorate) interrogators in the early 1950s, following the denunciation and arrest of Edigei's younger colleague, Abutalip Kuttybaev; Edigei's acquaintance with Elizarov, a Russian geologist, who takes an interest in Kazakh life and folklore, and who later helps Edigei attain the posthumous rehabilitation of Kuttybaev; and, finally, the death of Stalin and the gradual improvement of life at Boranly-Burannyi. On his way to the ancient steppe cemetery, Edigei also recalls two folklore legends associated with the history of the steppe: the ballad of Raimaly-aga and the legend of the *mankurt* (slave). The latter represents the genesis myth of the cemetery and tells of a matricide committed by a young warrior after being reduced to a slave by his sadistic captors, the Zhuan'zhuany. It is a gloomy tale and fits Edigei's mood as he progresses toward Ana-Beiit.

The pivotal event in the novel, the death of Kazangap, who had worked for over forty years at the isolated station, leads Edigei to reflect on his past and contemplate his own inevitable death. The solemnity of Edigei's mood, reflected in his elaborate plans for the procession and funeral, is ruined, however, by the arrival of Kazangap's son, Sabitzhan, from the city.

Sabitzhan turns out to be a petty party careerist who cares little about giving his father a proper burial.[8] He wants to get rid of the body as quickly as possible and suggests digging a grave somewhere next to the railroad tracks. Unlike Edigei, who greatly values Kazangap's spiritual heritage and views death as a solemn event, Sabitzhan's weltanschauung is narrowly and irreparably confined to the material world. In his unlimited faith in technological progress, he dreams of a world of human robots subserviently following orders from above. His ideas about the future of humankind unconsciously caricature communism's scientistic myth of a bright future. Thus he envisions a sort of universal Gosplan (State Planning Agency) and the total computerization of human actions. A supercomputer would instruct people when to work, when to dance, and, for the benefit of population control, when to engage in sexual relations. Theft, hooliganism, and other criminal activity would be programmed to disappear. Sabitzhan's ideal is the human "anthill," ridiculed by Dostoevsky's underground man more than a century earlier.

After quarreling with Edigei, however, Sabitzhan grudgingly agrees to join the funeral procession, which is to go deep into the steppe. Yet the procession never reaches the burial ground. Unbeknownst to Edigei, Ana-Beiit has been incorporated into the off-limits zone of a top-secret space center.[9] The young officer at the gate, a Kazakh lieutenant with the surname Tansykbaev, shows little concern for Edigei's sacred task. He brusquely informs the funeral party that Ana-Beiit will soon be liquidated to make room for a new housing project serving the space center. The lieutenant's total disregard for his own ancestry and for the sanctity of Ana-Beiit is symbolized by his refusal to speak to Edigei in his native Kazakh. Edigei has no choice but to leave, and with deep sorrow and anger he buries his friend in a ravine within sight of the barbed-wire fence that separates him from Ana-Beiit.

The third narrative plane of the novel, paralleling the drama at the funeral procession, depicts an unprecedented global crisis, of which Edigei is unaware. In the science fiction subplot, an American and a Soviet astronaut, part of a joint U.S.-Soviet mission to develop energy resources in space, have by chance discovered intelligent life on another planet, called Lesnaia grud' (Verdant Bosom) by its inhabitants. Purposely choosing not to inform their superiors on Earth, the astronauts accept an invitation by the aliens to visit Lesnaia grud'. The astronauts' act of insubordination stems from their fear that, given the Earth's political and ideological differences, the joint U.S.-Soviet Space Commission would bar them from undertaking such a trip because its consequences might affect the delicate balance of power between the two superpowers on Earth. When Mission Control is finally contacted by the maverick astronauts, it learns that the "new world" is a virtual utopia, free of disease, civil strife, and war.

As the astronauts had suspected, this discovery threatens to ignite a superpower confrontation. When the joint commission, functioning according to the principle of absolute parity, is requested by the two astronauts to allow well-wishing representatives from Lesnaia grud' to visit the Earth, it rejects the offer. Obsessed with maintaining the perfect balance of power on the Earth, the commission decides to secure the Earth's inviolability by initiating Project Iron Hoop. By cutting off all contact with the two astronauts, casting a cloak of secrecy over all aspects of the mission, and setting up an impenetrable ring of explosive orbiters around the Earth to ward off any attempted interference from outer space, the commission intends to erase all memory of the discovery of a better way of life.

Before the operation is put into action, the narrative returns to Edigei, who now stands alone at the barbed-wire fence of the space center, vowing to continue his fight for Ana-Beiit. Deserted by all who accompanied him in the procession, Edigei decides to go back to the gate of the space center, only to turn and flee in terror in the closing apocalyptic scene of the novel, as the Soviet Union commences its part of Project Iron Hoop and missile after missile thunders from the nearby launch site.

Soviet reviews of *The Day Lasts More than a Hundred Years* were generally favorable, lauding the author's success at creating a believable positive character and welcoming his shift from novella to novel. Some critics perceived in these factors an indication that Soviet literature was entering a new stage of development.[10] Others spoke of the work's *global'nost'* (having global significance) and *masshtabnost'* (epic breadth), as characteristics superior to the myopia of writers of Village Prose, who in short stories and novellas chose "remote and antiquated places" as settings and portrayed characters of "only marginal political and economical significance."[11] Although Aitmatov's novel is also set in a "remote and antiquated place," his worker protagonist is portrayed as playing an important role in Soviet society and is offered as an example for others to follow. While the proponents of socialist realism could certainly welcome such an upbeat portrayal of the labor theme, they failed to see that Aitmatov creates a positive hero whose ideology differs fundamentally from that of the prototypes of classic socialist realism. His hero, Edigei Zhangel'din, sees himself not as building socialism or subjugating his will to the progressive forces of history but as striving to preserve his Central Asian heritage and live with human dignity in a time of cultural and political repression.

Soviet critics at the time generally skirted the political implications of Aitmatov's novel. An exception to the rule was Vladimir Chubinskii's review in the Leningrad journal *Neva*. Chubinskii reminds readers that, although the party has corrected past mistakes, the scars still run deep. The posthumous rehabilitation of the denounced Abutalip Kuttybaev in Aitmatov's novel and that of thousands of people like him had, in the opinion of the critic, come too late: "That's why . . . memory should not be all-forgiving."[12] The political connotations of the science fiction parable in the novel did, however, provoke some controversy in the Soviet press. A number of reviewers curiously misread the message in the passages dealing with the Earth's decision to sequester itself from any contact with the newly discovered advanced civilization on Verdant Bosom. Alla Latynina, for example, remarked in the conservative *Oktiabr'* that the benevolent aliens might be a brand of "superhumanistic *Zhuan'zhuany* bent on enslaving the Earth."[13] Another review published later in the same journal viewed the new cosmic civilization as a sort of dangerous Trojan horse.[14] *Ogonek* characterizes the science fiction plot line as "unjustifiably pessimistic."[15]

The most weighty criticism, however, focused on Aitmatov's lack of differentiation in the roles of the Soviet Union and the United States in initiating Project Iron Hoop. Significantly, this criticism appeared in *Pravda*. The critic, A. Potapov, argues that one of the two superpowers (the USSR) should have been portrayed as qualitatively closer to achieving the ideal of a world community than the other power (the United States).[16] Other literary conservatives supported Potapov's advice. Implying that the United States, not the Soviet Union, was the cause of the Earth's fateful decision in the novel, Iurii Mel'vil' explains in an article published in *Voprosy literatury* that the Americans could never have permitted contact with an advanced civilization from outer space, unfamiliar with either war or violence, because "that would have threatened the pillars of the Western world." Moreover, in his opinion, "reactionary forces inevitably would have sought to use its [the newly discovered planet's] scientific and technological achievements in the world struggle, which in turn would have, in a fateful way, increased the threat of world war."[17]

It has been suggested that before the publication of *The Day Lasts More than a Hundred Years*, Aitmatov was pressured to make it clear that, in the fictional world of the novel, the Soviet Union could not be held responsible for implementing the operation to sequester the Earth. Unwilling to rewrite part of his novel, Aitmatov agreed to write a short introduction clarifying the narrative "vagueness" on the issue of superpower responsibility.[18] But in actuality, the introduction does nothing to clear up matters; the relations between the superpowers go virtually unmentioned. The author does call to mind the negative consequences of the lack of a "sense of history," yet in doing so he refers not to the USSR, the setting of the novel, but to China.[19] Elsewhere in the introduction, Aitmatov speaks of the tragedy of political, ideological, and racial barriers "engendered by imperialism" (197). Significantly, he focuses primary attention on his concept of the positive hero, a maneuver aimed at reassuring literary conservatives that his novel displayed the necessary degree of orthodoxy: "Edigei demonstrates my attitude to one of the basic principles of socialist realism, whose foremost thrust has always been directed to the laboring man" (196).

In the final analysis, Aitmatov's introduction increases the very "vagueness" his critics had wanted him to eliminate. Indeed, the introduction was generally viewed, even by Soviet critics, as superfluous and tending to severely limit the spectrum of the novel's meaning. Such a position was taken in an article in *Voprosy literatury*, in which the critic wrote that the introduction prepares readers to perceive the work in a predetermined framework, whereas the novel "will not fit in that framework. Its meaning is broader. It would have been better to say everything in an afterword, or perhaps not at all."[20]

The discussion of the controversial science fiction subplot continued long after the novel's first appearance in *Novyi mir*. Aitmatov's introduction did nothing to eliminate the novel's ambiguity. Indeed, the foreword seems designed more as doublespeak, and whereas the barrier mentality of imperialism referred to in it can be applied to either superpower, the relationship of the space subplot to the other parts of the novel suggests something quite different. Moreover, the Soviet Union's efforts to maintain a militarized iron curtain, its continued jamming of foreign radio broadcasts, and the forced isolation of Andrei Sakharov—making up the historical context in which *The Day Lasts More than a Hundred Years* appeared—support a parabolic reading of the cosmic subplot as pointing to Soviet responsibility for the Earth's isolation.

Such a parabolic reading is supported by the narrative's two folklore subplots as well. Both the legend of the *mankurt* and the ballad of Raimaly-aga, Edigei recalls, were recorded in the diaries of his repressed colleague, Abutalip Kuttybaev, and were later used by GPU interrogators in their case against him. Kuttybaev's arrest is depicted in the novel as occurring in January 1953 and accurately reflects the policy of cultural repression conducted in the Central Asian republics in the early 1950s.[21] In 1952 in Kirghizstan and throughout Central Asia, an official campaign was waged against the nation's oral epics. The controversy centered upon the subject matter of the national epics, purported to be "spoiled by alien stratification." The Kirghiz epic *Manas*, for example, was criticized for its "pan-Islamist and military-adventurist ideas."[22]

Moreover, at a time when the Soviet Union was cementing ties with the newly founded communist regime in China, the age-old anti-Chinese sentiments in *Manas* were also deemed contrary to Soviet policy. In the 1946 Russian translation of the epos, for example, most of the text was devoted to Manas's preparation and successful completion of a march of conquest against Beijing.[23] By 1952, the portrayal of the historical struggle of the Kirghiz hero against Chinese hegemony had clearly become unacceptable to Moscow. Several members of the Kirghiz Academy of Sciences working on *Manas* were arrested and sent to the camps. Although after Stalin's death in 1953 the attack on the epos was eased, subsequent editions continued to be purged of pan-Islamic and anti-Chinese content.

Such revisionism and falsification of the national cultural legacy at times bordered on the tragicomic. Revisionists substituted the Chinese in the epos with the Kalmyks, a conveniently repressed nation. Aitmatov recalls how people sought to build their careers on such "ideological speculation," noting that while "some made their careers on it, others died in prisons."[24] Aitmatov places Kuttybaev's investigation and arrest in *The Day Lasts More than a Hundred Years* in the months preceding Stalin's death and thus calls to mind the frontal attack by Soviet authorities on the Central Asian cultural heritage.

The legends' significance in the novel, however, goes far beyond the cultural context of the early 1950s. They create an atmosphere of "historical syncretism" and thereby call attention to the notion that, despite the passage of time, little had changed in Soviet nationalities policy and in the official attitude toward creative freedom at the time of the novel's appearance.[25]

The subject of creative freedom is addressed parabolically by the author in the ballad of Raimaly-aga. In all probability, the romantic subplot is the product of Aitmatov's imagination, although its lyricism and theme of the persecuted, love-sick bard betray some affinity with the Arabic legend of *Laila u Majnun*, which exists in many different versions in Central Asia. The legend was made popular throughout the region by Sufi poets, who sought to give it a mystical quality. The pain of the lovers' separation was portrayed as symbolic of the soul's yearning for God.[26] Aitmatov's ballad of a tragic love, which occupies all of chapter 10 in the novel, tells the story of an aging bard, Raimaly-aga, and his mad infatuation with a young girl singer, Begimai. Through the relationship, Raimaly-aga finds new inspiration and begins to sing of love with the spirit of his youth. The bard's brother, Abdil'khan, and other relatives, however, consider Raimaly-aga's new love and songs to be scandalous and connive to silence the bard.

While on the surface the ballad models Edigei's passionate love of Kuttybaev's widow, Zaripa, and the inevitable scandal their love would create if allowed to develop, in the greater context of the novel it can be read as a plea for freedom of expression. It mentions "powerful, well-off people" (431) who disapprove of Raimaly-aga's songs and his nonconformist behavior. Raimaly-aga is thus condemned by the leaders of his clan, the *barakbai* (in Kirghiz and Kazakh, lords of the barracks), though the people admire the bard and come from miles to hear him. After the *barakbai* pronounce the bard insane, they proceed to make it impossible for him to perform, smashing his *dombra*, killing his horse, and finally tying him to a birch tree and leaving him to die.[27]

The treatment of Raimaly-aga parallels the fate of Abutalip Kuttybaev in the novel and thus evokes the political persecution of Soviet
scholars and writers during the early 1950s. The charge of insanity
used to justify the harsh treatment of Raimaly-aga seems also to allude to Soviet authorities' widespread use of psychiatry in dealing
with dissidents during the 1970s and 1980s. Significantly, the very
fact of Kuttybaev's possession of the ballad of Raimaly-aga among his
writings makes up part of the GPU's case against him. The price he
must pay for his literary activities is the same price Raimaly-aga pays,
and thus by inference his persecutors are linked parabolically to the
barakbai of the legend. Just as Raimaly-aga's *dombra* is silenced, so
is Kuttybaev's collection of Kazakh legends confiscated and lost forever. Moreover, decades after the Twentieth Party Congress, Edigei,
recalling that his Russian friend Elizarov, an ethnographer, wrote
down one of the legends in 1957 (the legend of the *mankurt*), is
skeptical that Elizarov's copy would ever be published in the present
time, the 1980s. In this manner, Aitmatov reveals the extent to which
the persecution of the late Stalin era has perpetuated itself in contemporary Soviet society.

The most important parable from the past, however, is that of
the *mankurt*. Significantly, the legend's organizing role in the composition and its parabolic function are emphasized by its central position in the novel, appearing in the sixth of twelve chapters. The
legend of the *mankurt* depicts the mistreatment by the Zhuan'zhuany
of prisoners taken during their raids. One of the methods used by
the tribe to torture captives was to shave their victims' heads and to
stretch taut caps (*shiri*) of fresh camel hide over their skulls. As the
hide dried and contracted in the intense heat of the steppes, most
of the prisoners died in agony. The few who survived the torture
suffered a complete loss of memory and thus became submissive
slaves of the Zhuan'zhuany.[28] Their captors refered to them as *mankurt* and placed a price on them many times that of normal slaves.[29]

In Aitmatov's version of the legend, one such *mankurt*, following
the orders of his masters, kills his own mother, Naiman-Ana, when
she desperately seeks to revive his lost memory by repeating his name
to him and by constantly begging him to repeat his father's name—
Donenbai. According to the legend, as Naiman-Ana fell, pierced by

her son's arrow, her scarf turned into a white bird that even today flies over the steppe crying, "Whose son are you? Donenbai, Donenbai . . ." The place where Naiman-Ana fell became known to the inhabitants of the harsh Kazakh steppes as Ana-Beiit (Mother's Repose). Through the centuries, the legend-veiled site became the sacred burial ground for generations of nomadic peoples populating the vast steppes.[30] Ana-Beiit figures in all three temporal planes in the novel: the legendary past, the recent past and present, and the near, yet hypothetical, future.

In order to shed some light on the parabolic intent of his legends, Aitmatov often ties them to the other narrative planes through the transfer of key words and phrases. In *The Day Lasts More than a Hundred Years*, the legend of the *mankurt* resonates through a system of interlocking details throughout the narration. Foremost among such elements is the place name, Ana-Beiit. In the legend, it is the place of Naiman-Ana's death; in the present time frame, it is the name of the cemetery and goal of Edigei's journey; and in the science fiction plane, it is part of the space center. Another important word is *obruch* (iron hoop), which Aitmatov originally chose as the title of his novel. It appears twice, inconspicuously, in the legend of the *mankurt*—"Mercilessly contracting in the burning sun, the *shiri* pressed and crushed the shaven head of the slave like an iron hoop" (301)—yet figures prominently in the science fiction plot as the designation of the operation to isolate the Earth. The attempt to cut the Earth off from all external influence is thus portrayed by the author as tantamount to placing a *shiri* around the planet. The deprivation of memory is further symbolized by the premeditated stranding of the two astronauts, whose desperate cries over the radio echo unanswered, reminiscent of the call of the mythical bird Donenbai.

At the very beginning of the Soviet part of the operation, when Edigei flees amidst the fire and roar of the missiles, the cry of the white bird Donenbai is heard. It will be recalled that in the legend of the *mankurt*, the mythic bird comes into being as Naiman-Ana falls to the ground. The appearance of the bird at the conclusion of Aitmatov's novel is a multivalent symbol. It not only warns man to resist those bent on depriving him of his cultural legacy (forcing him, like the *mankurt*, "to kill his mother")[31] but alludes in more universal terms to the apocalyptic tragedy that awaits all of humankind if *man-kurt*ization is permitted to develop to its logical conclusion. The term *mankurt* also serves to tie the legend to Edigei's time frame. The link is Kazangap's worthless son, Sabitzhan. Like the *mankurt* in the legend, Sabitzhan refuses to question orders from above, readily submitting to the planned destruction of Ana-Beiit. His people's heritage means nothing to him; he is willing to turn his back on everything to please his superiors. When Sabitzhan is unwilling to go with Edigei to complain about the space center's encroachment on the Kazakh heritage, Edigei exclaims in frustration, "You are a *mankurt*! A real *mankurt*!" (485).

The key word *pamiat'* (memory) and its derivatives figure prominently in all three narrative planes, symbolized by the bird Donenbai: first in the legend, then as the title of a chapter in Abutalip Kuttybaev's diary, and finally in the thunder and fire of Project Iron Hoop: "A white bird quickly soared past the man, calling to him in that roar and terrifying chaos: 'Whose son are you? What is your name? Remember your name! Your father is Donenbai, Donenbai, Donenbai' " (488).

Thus, true to his technique, Aitmatov projects the moral lesson and values from the legend of the *mankurt* into narrative planes that seemingly have little in common with it. Only through the legend's prism can the other narrative planes be fully understood and appreciated. Seen in its light, for example, the Stalinist interrogators who confiscate Kuttybaev's memoirs become modern Zhuan'zhuany, trying to deprive him of the memory of his cultural heritage. The analogy becomes clear when the chief GPU interrogator, Tansykbaev, rejects Edigei's contention that a person's memoirs are apolitical, remarking that "it is important to recall and speak of the past—but even more so when we write about it—in a manner that can be useful for us right now. And whatever doesn't help us, should not be remembered. And if you don't want to abide by this, then you are engaging in subversive action" (352).

By analogy, Kuttybaev's death en route to the camps reveals that he is destined to share the fate not of the *mankurt* but of the prisoners in the legend who die from torture: "Most of those condemned to die an agonizing death in the field perished in the hot sun of the

Sarozek steppe. Only one or two *mankurt* from five or six victims survived" (301). This aspect of Abutalip Kuttybaev's death gains special significance in view of the fact that he survived a Nazi concentration camp during the war. Alla Latynina notes in her review of *The Day Lasts More than a Hundred Years* that the Nazis violated only Kuttybaev's body, while the Stalinists' crime was greater, aiming at the destruction of his soul.[32] Thus, just as the seven khans attempt to turn the future Kirghiz national hero Manas into a *mankurt*, Soviet authorities under Stalin are depicted as seeking to rob the peoples of the Soviet Union of their memory, historical heritage, and national destiny. Parabolically, the moralizing words of the narrator in the legend clearly refer to the excesses of Stalin and his henchmen: "They had discovered the means to deprive slaves of their memory. By doing so they inflicted upon human nature the most horrific of all imaginable and unimaginable crimes" (302).

Although in *Oktiabr'* it was suggested that Project Iron Hoop could be considered necessary to protect the Earth from a potential danger emanating from outer space, the interlocking details connecting the science fiction plot to the legend of the *mankurt* allow for an altogether different reading. The space center is replete with negative imagery and associations. First of all, the secret community serving the space center has no name, a detail linking it directly to the *mankurt*, who has been deprived of his real name and can refer to himself only by the generic term *mankurt*. A similar procedure has occurred with respect to Ana-Beiit. The cemetery has been forgotten by the local Kazakhs, and they refer to the facility built on its territory as *pochtovyi iashchik* (the mailbox), a term used throughout the Soviet Union to denote secret facilities. The barbed wire fence around the compound functions as a *mankurt*'s cap, depriving the site of its real name and Edigei and his people of access to the past and the memory (heritage) of their ancestors.

These associations, of course, extend the Zhuan'zhuany-Stalinist line to include the abuses of Soviet leaders at the time of the novel's publication. It is well known that prior to the disintegration of the Soviet Union, the Kazakhs had no control over the top secret military sites within their republic's territory. Only ten years after the appearance of Aitmatov's novel the Kazakhs were able to put a stop to nuclear testing on their territory near Semipalatinsk. Leading the

Kazakhs' struggle with the Soviet Ministry of Defense was Olzhas Suleimenov, a prominent Kazakh writer. Contributing to the strong support in the republic for Suleimenov's efforts were revelations about "the destruction of Kazakh historical sites and the use of Kazakh villagers as human guinea pigs during above-ground nuclear tests in the 1950s."[33] In 1980, however, Aitmatov's novel shows that some Kazakhs made themselves the willing tools of a policy conducted against their republic's better interests. Thus the author casts the Kazakh lieutenant, who turns Edigei's burial procession away, in the role of *mankurt*. Significantly, the lieutenant refuses to speak with Edigei in Kazakh, the language of his fathers, and his surname, Tansykbaev, is identical to that of the GPU interrogator who arrested Kuttybaev a quarter of a century earlier. Aside from his blind respect for orders from above, his *mankurt* character is brought out by Edigei's seemingly irrelevant question: "Hey, who is your father?" (471). Edigei's question is identical to the one Naiman-Ana puts to her *mankurt* son in the legend.

In light of these interlocking details, the use of the site to launch robot orbiters to protect the Earth reveals that the ambitious space project is only another form of *mankurt*'s cap, with an identical sadistic function. The fact that the orbiters have atomic weapons on board (171) and the narrator's reference to their launch as *svetoprestavlenie* (the end of the world) evoke the image of the catastrophe of nuclear war on our planet, a fear Aitmatov consistently expressed in his journalistic work during the 1970s and 1980s. Significantly enough, the novel reveals that this danger proceeds directly from the xenophobic attitude toward other peoples and their "different ideas" characteristic of Soviet policies in the Brezhnev era. Although Aitmatov's introduction to the work refers to the Cultural Revolution in China as illustrating the dangers of falsifying history, the novel as a whole speaks out primarily against Soviet xenophobia and chauvinistic attitudes toward the past.[34] By implication, the responsibility for Project Iron Hoop must be seen as resting at least partially on the shoulders of Soviet decision makers. This was recognized by more than one Soviet critic and can explain Potapov's suggestion in his *Pravda* review of the novel that Aitmatov do more to stress the negative role of the United States in the cosmic plot line.

Any allusions to the attitudes and failings of the Soviet Union during the Brezhnev years, however, are made cautiously in the novel. Katerina Clark remarks that the novel has a certain "now-you-see-it-now-you-don't" quality,[35] and some readers can choose to overlook the profound criticism of Soviet society that to others may be quite obvious.[36] Clark believes Aitmatov's years as a *Pravda* correspondent contributed to the protean quality of his work, remarking that "he knows the ropes" and is a "superb bricolleur."[37] Aitmatov indeed draws upon many literary and nonliterary sources—including the socialist realist tradition—to put together *The Day Lasts More than a Hundred Years*. The novel tests the reader's attentiveness to detail. Once the reader recognizes the parabolic currents in the novel, the author's intentions become clearer.

The issue of the national delimitation of Central Asia as well as Soviet language policy is evoked through the same legend of the *mankurt*. The depiction of a Kazakh lieutenant who guards the cosmodrome as unwilling or unable to speak Kazakh calls to mind the specter of Russification, as well as the politically motivated linguistic reforms carried out throughout Central Asia in the 1920s and 1930s. Aitmatov had to be careful in broaching the subject of Russification in his fiction, because it was still a taboo topic in the early 1980s.[38] In a number of newspaper articles written after the advent of glasnost, he reveals his views on Russification in Kirghizstan, which, to a large degree, was typical of many Soviet national republics at the time. In 1986 he decries as outrageous the fact that Kirghiz is not taught in the schools of Frunze, the capital of Soviet Kirghizstan, and calls upon the authorities to open up Kirghiz kindergartens in the city. He especially condemns Kirghiz officials who, like the *mankurt*, praise everything Russian and denigrate their own language.[39] In 1989, Aitmatov warns of the "monopolization of Soviet spiritual life" through excessive Russification in the national republics and notes that the lauded phenomenon of Soviet bilingualism often means "one-directional bilingualism," with limited use of Kirghiz even at the republic's universities.[40]

Aitmatov, of course, is not advocating the suppression of the Russian language in Central Asia; indeed, Russian has been the medium through which he has reached his readers for the past quarter of a

century. Yet he expresses his fear at the time that Russian could eventually swallow up Kirghiz or the Soviet Union's other minority languages. Here it should be noted that the author has translated his major works back into Kirghiz, and experts consider the language of the Kirghiz versions of his works to represent a high linguistic standard for Kirghiz literati. It is to the author's credit that *The Day Lasts More than a Hundred Years* broached the issue of linguistic injustice at a time when the subject had been taboo for many years.

But the imagery of *mankurt*ism in the novel calls to mind not only Russification but also the Soviet manipulation of the various Turkic languages in Central Asia after the revolution. Before 1924, important articles and documents written by Central Asian intellectuals appeared in the regional papers in Arabic script, which has since become unintelligible for the vast majority of today's Central Asians. They are thus cut off from the cultural and political legacy of their fathers. The manner in which Moscow introduced alphabet reform throughout Central Asia was exceedingly heavy-handed, reminiscent of the callousness of the Zhuan'zhuany of Aitmatov's legend. First, to counter the influence of Islam in the region, the Latin alphabet was introduced to replace the Arabic in the late 1920s. Although latinization met with strong resistance in Central Asia, its introduction was largely complete by 1935. Then came a sudden volte-face. The fear of pan-Turkic nationalism in Central Asia, heightened perhaps by the fact that Turkey was also using the Latin alphabet, caused Moscow to hastily abolish the Latin alphabet in the region and introduce the Cyrillic. Supporters of the Latin alphabet in the republics were liquidated.[41]

Evidence of just how important the switch was considered in Moscow can be found in the fact that Kirghiz was officially "Cyrillized" on September 12, 1941, at the height of the Nazi offensive on the Soviet capital! The introduction of the Cyrillic alphabet was aimed at strengthening Moscow's control over the region. It facilitated, of course, the teaching of Russian, which had become compulsory in 1937, and precluded the development of strong cultural and political ties with Turkey, which was beginning to assume a sense of responsibility for the Turkic peoples inside the Soviet Union. The imagery in Aitmatov's novel casts the consequences of the policy in

a particularly pernicious light. Perhaps for this reason, as late as 1986 a play based on *The Day Lasts More than a Hundred Years* was banned from the theaters of the Kirghiz capital.[42] No doubt, the cultural watchdogs in the republic recognized themselves in the *mankurt* of the novel.

Closely related to the question of Moscow's linguistic policies in Central Asia is the question of the national delimitation of the region in 1924. Dividing up an essentially homogenous Turkic territory into five "independent" Central Asian republics and then seeking to ex-aggerate the cultural and linguistic differences of each republic has been seen by scholars as part and parcel of Moscow's policy to coun-teract the centripetal forces operating in Central Asia in the 1920s and 1930s. The decision proved expedient for its time, but in the early 1980s there was strong indication that the sense of national identity of Central Asians transcended the borders of their respective native republics. Indeed, throughout Aitmatov's novel all "dividers" are cast in a negative light—similar to the *shiri* that constrain the memory of the *mankurt*—and are depicted as alien to the natural life of the Kazakh steppe. The railroad tracks, for example, cut the steppe in two. Their unnaturalness is emphasized in the opening pages of the novel, as a fox in search of food is repelled by the roar of the trains and the garbage scattered along the tracks. The fences around the cosmodrome are a threatening hindrance to the members of the funeral party, cordoning off their ancestral burial ground.

While Aitmatov's novel does not seek to turn back the clock, it does make clear the unnatural implications of the delimitation through the frequent use of images of fences and barriers. Aitmatov wants to tear down barriers, to remove the *mankurt*'s cap from the memories of Central Asians. The fact that Aitmatov, a Kirghiz, uses a different Central Asian republic for his novel's setting is an indi-cation of the importance the author attached to these issues in 1980. When it finally became possible to discuss such issues in the Soviet Union with a degree of openness, Aitmatov expressed the desire that centripetal forces in Central Asia be encouraged again and specifi-cally mentioned in that context the issue of language. In an interview in 1988, he remarked that the "mutual exchange of terms and words between them [the various Turkic languages] should be intensified."

He notes, however, that the older denationalized generation resists such efforts, even with respect to Kazakh and Kirghiz, the most closely related of the Turkic languages.[43] He believes the schools and colleges of the region should help rectify the damage of successive waves of *mankurt*ization through the teaching of the Runic and Arabic alphabets, thus allowing Central Asians access to their common culture.[44]

The important theme of responsibility in *The Day Lasts More than a Hundred Years* flows from the novel's concern with memory. By recalling past failures and injustices, Aitmatov hopes to inspire people to rectify the wrongs of the past and display a willingness to shoulder responsibility in bettering society. Without memory, people are pliable tools in the hands of villains.[45] Aitmatov's concept of responsibility finds its primary expression in his characterization of Edigei and other important figures in the novel.

The hero-mentor relationship, characteristic of classic socialist realism, is central to Aitmatov's novel. Edigei's character as a man of memory and responsibility is revealed in the narrative primarily through his relationship to three "double figures": his longtime friend and countryman, Kazangap; the Russian geologist and admirer of Kazakh life, Elizarov; and Edigei's majestic camel, Karanar. Karanar fulfills a role similar to that of Gul'sary in *Farewell, Gul'sary!*, paralleling Edigei's emotions and ever present during the critical stages of the hero's life at Boranly-Burannyi. Kazangap and Elizarov function as mentors, aiding the hero in overcoming his resignation in difficult times.[46]. Both, in turn, are juxtaposed with auxiliary figures, whose depraved characters serve to heighten the moral qualifications of the mentors. Thus Kazangap appears almost as a mystical *starets* (holy elder) when contrasted with his modern yet morally decrepit son, Sabitzhan. Similarly, Elizarov, by his positive attitude toward Kazakh traditions and folklore, shines brightly as an ideal for Russians to emulate in Soviet Central Asia. His proper attitude is contrasted with that of the GPU interrogator, Tansykbaev.

Kazangap is an unusual mentor figure for Soviet literature. He is a simple, uneducated worker, devoid of political consciousness, and represents "what used to be called *mrakobesie*—he stands for the

old traditions and [Muslim] religiosity."[47] His apolitical nature stems from the unjust arrest of his father as a kulak during the 1930s. Kazangap leaves his native village on the Aral Sea and never returns, while those responsible for the death of his father hold their positions of power into the 1950s. During the long years of his voluntary exile in the Sarozek steppes, he never forgets the past and instills in Edigei the conviction that people bear absolute responsibility for each and all of their actions. Mistakes and crimes of the past should not be forgotten. In response to Sabitzhan's heartless ridicule of the millions of Kazakh and Kirghiz forced to flee their native lands to China during the revolution, Kazangap reminds his son that Soviet authorities must accept moral responsibility for the calamity: "Only God is beyond criticism; if he sends death, well then say goodbye to life, that's why you were born. But for everything else on earth, someone must answer" (259). The philosophy of absolute responsibility professed by Kazangap stems not from his Soviet experience but from prerevolutionary Kazakh culture. In the novel, Kazangap is the repository for the ancient legends of the Sarozek steppes. His gift of Karanar, whom he believes to be a direct descendant of Naiman-Ana's legendary white camel, Akmai, is symbolic of his passing on to the younger Edigei the treasures and wisdom of the Sarozek past.

Edigei also inherits from Kazangap his conscientious attitude toward work, which finds expression in the novel in a scene depicting Kazangap's and Edigei's superhuman efforts to clear the tracks of snow after a blizzard. Aitmatov's novel reveals the sore lack of such virtues in modern Soviet society. The novel opens with Kazangap's death, and although Edigei continues in the steps of his mentor, no one among the younger generation is depicted as fully sharing his sense of responsibility. Significantly, Edigei himself has no son, while Kazangap's son has been turned into a *mankurt* by his Soviet upbringing. Edigei's final thoughts over Kazangap's grave, when he expresses his hope that the young men with him would return to the site to bury him next to Kazangap, are a powerful condemnation of the younger generation: "But I don't see anyone here who could pray for me. They don't believe in God and don't know any prayers. . . . What will they be able to say to themselves and others in the solemn hour of death? I pity them" (480). The younger generation's disbelief

cuts them off from the world and the virtues of their fathers. Sabit-zhan, the only party member among them, is depicted as the most cowardly and as the one least concerned with the fate of others.

Edigei's second mentor figure in the novel is the Russian geologist and communist, Elizarov. If Kazangap is a complete reversal of the mentor figure from the classic socialist realist novel, Elizarov fits very much the old pattern. According to that pattern, the mentor was usually an old Bolshevik or a high party official. He possessed superior wisdom and could see the overall political and social picture.[48] His function was to explain the complicated situation to the positive hero. As such, Elizarov is the public complement to Kazangap's function in the private sphere.

Aitmatov depicts Elizarov as well qualified for his role in the novel. His party membership goes back to the 1920s, when he fought in the Red Army against Central Asian counterrevolutionaries. Moreover, Elizarov is a successful geologist and scholar. The outward signs of his public stature are his private ZIM (automobile) and his home overlooking the capital of Soviet Kazakhstan, Alma-Ata (459). Like Kazangap and Edigei, Elizarov highly respects the folklore of Kazakhstan. He is one of two people to have ever written down the legend of the *mankurt*, Edigei recalls. He represents the author's concept of the ideal Russian attitude toward Central Asian culture, an attitude that can hardly be considered typical. At the time of the novel's publication, Soviet census data revealed that fewer than one percent of all Russians living in the republic could speak Kazakh.[49]

Unfortunately for the novel, Elizarov's characterization appears to be stereotyped and flat. Although his name is evoked from time to time in the narration, only in the final chapter does the reader learn much about him. His dialogue with Edigei seems contrived to make him function as the author's mouthpiece. One gets the impression that the character was hastily added to the novel to counterbalance the forceful criticism of Soviet reality in *The Day Lasts More than a Hundred Years*. Thus it is Elizarov, a Russian, who plays the major role in helping Edigei attain the posthumous rehabilitation of Kuttybaev after the Twentieth Party Congress in 1956. It is Elizarov who lectures Edigei on the importance of the party's new sense of responsibility for the mistakes of the past. He speaks of *samois-*

pravlenie (self-correction) and *samoochishchenie* (self-purification) of Soviet society as guarantees that such mistakes would be rectified.

Yet Aitmatov's novel is written from the perspective of twenty-four years after the Twentieth Party Congress. He is fully aware of the triumphs and limits of *samoochishchenie*. His narrative juxtaposes in the final chapter Elizarov's encouraging words with events occurring many years later—the threatened liquidation of Ana-Beiit and the arrogance of the lieutenant barring Edigei's path to the ancient cemetery. Like the optimistic words of Kerimbekov, the young party leader in *Farewell Gul'sary!*, Elizarov's remarks reflect the hopes of the late 1950s rather than the reality of the 1980s. Significantly, nowhere in Aitmatov's mature fiction are such hopes expressed in a contemporary time frame. Aitmatov's reminder of an optimistic past challenges readers to question the extent to which the party has really accepted the responsibility Kazangap demands from all people of conscience. No doubt most readers at the time had few illusions about the party's history of whitewashing its grievous failures. Even after the demise of the Soviet state and the banning of the party in 1991, the question of responsibility looms unanswered in many quarters of the former Soviet Union.

As was noted earlier, the introduction of folklore parables into the narrative serves to heighten the social criticism in Aitmatov's fiction and to further emotionalize the tragic twists of the central plot. For obvious reasons, when *The Day Lasts More than a Hundred Years* first appeared, Soviet critics did not dwell on the sharper edges of that social criticism, opting instead to discuss Aitmatov's Edigei and welcoming his advent as the new positive hero, capable of breathing new life into the anemic Soviet novel. Edigei does indeed occupy a central place in the novel; almost all of the narrative (with the exception of the cosmic plot line) flows through his consciousness. As Aitmatov admits in the introduction to this novel, he closely identifies himself with the hero's worldview. Although Soviet critics were quick to point to the affinity between Aitmatov's positive hero and those of classic socialist realism, the way in which Edigei differs from such apparent prototypes is far more significant.[50]

Similar to classic positive heroes, Edigei is extremely conscientious about his work. He seems to belong to an elect few, who possess the *vyderzhka* (endurance) to work in the Sarozek steppes and "to withstand the onslaughts of the elements, a common criterion for the truly positive hero in Stalinist fiction."[51] Edigei has seen countless railroad workers come and go, but only he and Kazangap have been able to handle the extreme heat and cold of Boranly-Burannyi. Moreover, like the positive heroes of industrial novels, Edigei is employed in a technical capacity as a switchman. As such he is a throwback to socialist realist models that preceded Village Prose, whose heroes are portrayed in nontechnological settings. Finally, the role of Edigei in Aitmatov's novel parallels structurally that of the classic positive hero. Like his classic prototype, Edigei is faced with a difficult task, which he resolves to complete. The hero encounters obstacles and overcomes them through great willpower. Inspiring him on his way are two mentor figures, whose wisdom is beyond question and who encourage him in his time of greatest doubt.[52] Thus it is easy to see why Edigei could be so appealing to the Soviet literary establishment. In his speech at the Seventh Writers' Congress, the head of the Writers' Union, Georgii Markov, praised the novel, focusing exclusively on Edigei as a positive hero with working class credentials.[53] Party and literary officials at the time could praise Edigei's conscientious attitude toward his work and point to his determination and exceptional endurance as ideals for Soviet youth to emulate.

Yet, socialist realism was already a terminally ill patient in 1980. Those who yearned for its resuscitation were to be disappointed. The differences between Aitmatov's hero and the positive heroes from classic socialist realism clearly indicate that the author was not trying to breathe new life into a wooden aesthetic system. In her study of the Soviet novel, Katerina Clark points out that the classic positive hero subjugates his spontaneity, in a sense his individuality, to a higher form of consciousness, namely, to that embodied in party doctrine.[54] Aitmatov's Edigei is neither a party activist nor a man willing to subjugate himself to its "greater wisdom." Unlike Sabitzhan, who as a party member never questions party decisions, Edigei accepts nothing and questions everything. Significantly, Aitmatov links such a critical attitude to Edigei's work ethic, maintaining that "an energetic industrious man will ask himself questions which others might think have been answered a long time ago."[55] Aitmatov's positive hero stands for the author's conviction that Soviet society needed not compliant, albeit productive, robotic *mankurt*like workers but critically thinking ones. In the novel, this thought is expressed by Kazangap's words: "For everything . . . on earth, someone must answer" (259). Accordingly, Aitmatov's hero claims for himself the right to hold the decision makers of his country directly responsible for their mistakes. No one is above criticism; responsibility is absolute.

The emphasis Aitmatov places on the rights of the individual as opposed to those of an all powerful state is also reflected in the nature of the task Edigei feels compelled to accomplish. In classic socialist realism, the hero was faced with a "public task"—for example, building or restoring a factory, organizing resistance to fascists or counterrevolutionaries, overfulfilling a production contract, and so on. In *The Day Lasts More than a Hundred Years*, Edigei's is a private task, and a religious one at that: to bury Kazangap according to Moslem customs and to reclaim his people's cultural heritage.[56] The obstacles on his way to fulfilling the task ironically seem to be caused by the party, rather than resolved by its superior wisdom. Thus Sabitzhan, a party careerist, must be persuaded to go along with Edigei's plan to bury Kazangap at Ana-Beiit, and the barbed-wire fence enclosing the cemetery is a barrier that ultimately prevents Edigei from completing his solemn task.

Yet another important reversal of the classic concept of socialist realist hero is found in Edigei's attitude toward technological progress. While Edigei is aware that his work at Boranly-Burannyi has been made easier by technology (snow drifts no longer must be removed by shovel), he harbors a deep mistrust of grandiose technological projects. Such an attitude would be clearly out of place in the classic socialist realist novel. In this, Aitmatov shares the spirit of Village Prose, perhaps best expressed in Valentin Rasputin's *Farewell to Matyora* (1976). Thus when Edigei witnesses the launch of a missile on the night of Kazangap's death, he watches the fireball disappear in the sky with emotions devoid of pride in his country or technological progress. Instead, he is left with a feeling of fear and apathy—"He understood that it was something that was none of his concern" (216)—and his thoughts turn to the fox he had seen earlier fleeing in terror from a passing train.

This scene, occurring in the opening chapter of the novel, has its complement in the closing chapter. The missile launch Edigei observes in this chapter intensifies the hero's previous feelings, and once again Aitmatov shows the terrifying side of technology for both man and beast:

> The sky came crushing down on their heads, ripped asunder into clouds of ferocious flame and smoke. A man, camel, and a dog—those simple beings, out of their minds from fear, fled headlong. Overcome by fright, they ran together, afraid of losing each other. They ran through the steppe, their forms standing out mercilessly against the background of gigantic columns of fire. (488)

This is an ominous scene indeed, pointing not to a bright technological future but to a dark and frightening one. It is an apocalyptic scene, evoking the specter of nuclear war.

Edigei's mistrust of technology is also evident in his thoughts upon seeing the Aral Sea, which, as he discovers, is slowly drying up due to its ill-conceived exploitation for large-scale irrigation projects.[57] He recalls that he and Kazangap once drove ten kilometers on the dried bottom of the sea. Seeing the sea, Kazangap remarks: "The Aral Sea is as old as the Earth. Now that it is drying up, what is there to say about human life?" (234).

Kazangap, who grew up on the shores of the Aral Sea, asks Edigei to bury him miles away in the steppe at Ana-Beiit. But that wish is frustrated as well, and the novel implies that technology has taken away one's basic right to be buried alongside one's ancestors, an idea that is likewise present in Rasputin's *Farewell to Matyora*. The ecological disaster caused by the desiccation of the Aral Sea is evoked parabolically in two of the novel's subplots.[58] In the science fiction line, the theme appears in the image of the planet Lesnaia grud' (Verdant Bosom). The name Aitmatov chooses for the planet reveals its function in the novel as the Earth's double in the realistic narrative plane. In the pre-Islamic Kirghiz cult of nature, the Earth is referred to as *toshu tuktuu zher*, which is rendered in Russian as *zemlia s pokrytoi rastitel'nost'iu grud'iu* (the earth with its verdant bosom).[59] On Verdant Bosom, the inhabitants are facing the eventual death of their planet as desert areas continue to devour more and more of the planet's inhabitable land. Significantly, in this parable the inhabitants unite to battle the onslaught of the desert, whereas in the realistic plot line of *The Day Lasts More than a Hundred Years*, set in modern Central Asia, only despair reigns as the main characters view the shrinking sea. Indeed, today in the areas surrounding the Aral Sea, windblown salt from the exposed bottom has led to a process of devegetation, turning pastures and wetlands into deserts. The inhabitants are deathly ill from the disaster, with infant mortality at an all-time high. Aitmatov's novel equates the situation with that of a dying planet.

The Aral Sea is likewise tied to the legendary plot line of the novel by the rich folk culture it evokes. Edigei's recollection of catching a golden carp and its importance as an expression of his wife's hope and aspirations during her first pregnancy are cast in mythic form and written in the same lyrical style as the legend of the *mankurt*. The child's death during Edigei's absence at the front, the couple's inability after the war to renew their lives in their native village by the sea, and their decision to abandon it forever are suggestive of the cheerless fate that awaits the sea itself. The destruction of the Aral Sea is thus portrayed as an irreversible catastrophe for the peoples of Soviet Central Asia and serves as a warning of the danger inherent in scientistic myths and a utilitarian approach to life and nature.

Finally, although Edigei is a hard and conscientious worker whose endurance is not unlike the Stakhanovites' populating Stalinist socialist realism, his philosophy of labor is quite distinct from their all-sacrificing, masochistic faith in the righteousness of their cause.[60] Unlike the traditional positive hero in Soviet letters, Edigei's conscientiousness is not motivated by the vision of a bright future. He works not for tomorrow or for the new Soviet man to come but for the simple satisfaction that such work affords, for a sense of solidarity with people like himself. Nor is Edigei totally preoccupied with his work: his family and private life are equally important to him. The author places his labor in a realistic context; the glorification of labor so often found in Soviet letters is conspicuously absent in the novel. Instead, Edigei's work ethic resembles that of another well-known hero from Soviet literature—Solzhenitsyn's Ivan Denisovich. In *A*

Day in the Life of Ivan Denisovich, the hero diligently lays brick at a prison construction site. He works to the best of his ability, but he is motivated not by the idea of contributing to the construction of the Soviet future by building a power station for the town of Sots-gorodok but by "pride at doing a job properly."[61]

Like Solzhenitsyn's hero, Aitmatov's Edigei finds meaning in his life and labor in and of themselves; the teleological thrust that motivated the classic socialist realist positive hero is markedly missing in *The Day Lasts More than a Hundred Years*. This distinction was critical for Soviet letters at the time of the novel's appearance. Aitmatov's concept of humankind, along with that of other Soviet and ex-Soviet authors writing in the 1970s and 1980s—Vasil' Bykau, Iurii Trifonov, Fazil' Iskander, Vasilii Shukshin, Georgii Vladimov, Valentin Rasputin, to name only a few—was instrumental in undermining the scientistic myth propagated by Soviet officialdom. The meaning that the word *mankurt* gains in the course of *The Day Lasts More than a Hundred Years* is an accurate characterization of Soviet citizens who failed to question the state's ideology. Geoffrey Hosking's characterization of Marxism-Leninism in the final years of the Brezhnev gerontocracy is eloquent on that score:

> Articles in the Soviet press, government pronouncements and party resolutions are still underlain by the image of human beings as cogs in a social mechanism directed by the expert few who are in a position to rise above it and control it. The image is a powerful determinant of the way most Soviet citizens see themselves and understand their own lives. Especially this is so for intellectuals, who have the most intensive regular contact with official propaganda.[62]

In Aitmatov's novel, this official image of humanity is caricatured in Sabitzhan's vision of remote-controlled human beings. The same negative image is found in the tragedy of the cosmic subplot, when a handful of experts secretly decide the fate of the world without consulting the rest of mankind.

Aitmatov's Edigei is aware that he is part of a universal whole and that Boranly-Burannyi is only a minuscule station in a gigantic railroad system that unites it with the whole world. Yet if he considers himself a cog in a larger machine, he sees himself as a priceless one.

He emerges in the novel as an individual who feels immediately responsible for the many other individuals in his hamlet, homeland, and country. His sense of responsibility for everyone prevents him from subjugating his consciousness to some higher or abstract purpose. Edigei is portrayed as basing his humanism on the individual. He inevitably questions all projects for the common good that are detrimental to the individual.

One of the most remarkable aspects of the appearance of *The Day Lasts More than a Hundred Years* is that it represented "one of those relatively rare instances when a Soviet novel excites simultaneously the imagination of the powers that be, dissidents, and Western commentators."[63] Such a reception testifies to the pervasive ambiguity in the work. The reader's right to subjectivity is not negated by the overwhelming narrative voice of the author. The tangible presence of an evaluating author is further reduced in the text by the use of Edigei's subjective consciousness as the organizing principle of the narration. The reduction of the narrator's voice and the resulting personalization of the narration were two means by which contemporary Soviet writers at the time sought to change the authoritarian and "monological" narrative forms of classic socialist realism.[64] Aitmatov's novel demands the active creative participation of the reader. And since readers differ in their experience of art and life, their readings of *The Day Lasts More than a Hundred Years* can vary greatly. Nevertheless, as this discussion shows, the author does provide signposts leading the reader to a more perceptive reading of the work. And those signposts emerge first and foremost from the folklore legends in the novel—his parables from the past.

At this point, the discussion of *The Day Lasts More than a Hundred Years* might have ended. But nine years after the novel first appeared, Aitmatov decided to take full advantage of the new possibilities engendered by glasnost. In August 1990, he published for the first time an important chapter, *The White Cloud of Genghis Khan*, which he had been unable to include in the original 1980 text. All subsequent editions of the novel will appear with the *The White Cloud of Genghis Khan* inserted as chapter 9. In the short introduction to the new "old" chapter, the author does not elaborate on reasons for the exclusion of the chapter in 1980 but refers to the "era of ideological *diktat* (demands)" and "opinions from above that decided the fate of a literary work in an administrative manner." Aitmatov speaks metaphorically about the necessity, which writers faced at the time, of sacrificing a part to save the whole, or, in his words, "of not overloading the ship, which would face a violent storm on its way to the readers' shores."[65] Indeed, it would have been inconceivable in 1980 for Soviet censorship to permit the publication of a chapter whose allusions to the country's political ills were all too transparent.

The chapter's major departure from the original 1980 version of the novel is the suicide of Abutalip Kuttybaev. In the original text, Kuttybaev's wife receives a telegram informing her of his death from a heart attack in the camps. The belated chapter portrays his incarceration and interrogation by the GPU. Reminiscent of scenes from Solzhenitsyn's *The First Circle*, the chapter depicts Kuttybaev's torture in the Alma-Ata Lubianka, where he is beaten and kept awake for days by a bright light in his cell. In his hopeless dreams and longing for his family, he recalls the Kazakh legend, "The Sarozek Hangings," which he had written down at Boranly-Burannyi.

The legend, written in the same lyrical style as the other two legend-parables in the novel, tells the story of Genghis Khan's campaign to subdue and occupy the West. In writing the chapter, Aitmatov could draw from a wealth of Central Asian legends about the Mongol warlord. The man who had subdued Central Asia in the thirteenth century with such violence, cunning, and cruelty was not forgotten in Turkic folklore and histories. As in his other literary legends, in the legend of the Sarozek hangings Aitmatov combines commonly held beliefs with fiction to create a parable for contemporary readers. The author's portrayal of the Mongol despot brings to life the known facts of his biography. The reader learns of the khan's boyhood murder of his brother, Begter; his lifelong suspicion that his first wife, Börte, had betrayed him while she was a captive of the Merkits; and his belief that he was the sky-god Tengri's representative on Earth, which he used to justify his cruelty toward all who opposed him.

In his portrayal of megalomania and totalitarian thinking, Aitmatov takes the well-known accounts of the iron discipline in Genghis Khan's armies and reduces the concept of total obedience to the absurd. Thus, to maintain discipline among his men during the great westward march, Genghis Khan in Aitmatov's legend issues a decree forbidding the wives of his soldiers, who follow the massive army, to bear children until the campaign has been successfully completed. At the outset of the march, a white cloud appears on the horizon and accompanies the army's westward movement.[66] Genghis Khan deems the cloud a sign of favor from the sky-god, Tengri. A soothsayer warns the khan that he must protect the cloud, or else he will lose all power. For days the khan is pleased to see the cloud, but in the end he is punished for his arrogance and violation of natural law: "He wanted even God to serve him, for the conception of a child is a sign from God" (20). Genghis Khan would have God wait until he would permit childbirth; all must be sacrificed to the greater goal of conquest.

When the khan discovers that a child has been born by one of the women in the wagons following his mighty army, he becomes the hostage of his own absurd order. To his surprise, the father of the child is Erdene, one of the khan's closest lieutenants, and the mother, Dogulang, is an embroiderer of the army's banners. But Genghis Khan makes the decision to punish the couple anyway, believing that "a public execution is necessary to ensure that people obey the authority which has been established for all of them by their supreme leader" (40). The couple's son is taken away from them, and Erdene and Dogulang are hanged together according to nomadic custom— ropes are attached across the back of a camel, and when the beast is forced to rise the nooses tighten around the victims.[67] After the senseless execution, Genghis Khan continues his westward march. Yet he realizes that something has changed. Looking upward at the sky, he notices to his horror that the white cloud has disappeared. Realizing that the sky-god has turned his back on him, he leaves his armies at the Volga and returns home "to die and be buried in some unknown place" (45).

In the "new" chapter, Tansykbaev, the GPU prosecutor, is further delineated, and an attempt is made to depict the circumstances that form his character and that of the repressive organization he represents. His ruthlessness is grounded in personal ambition and thirst for power: "To reach the god of power one must constantly serve him in dark deeds, in exposing well-masked enemies" (13). The reader learns of executions of "bourgeois nationalists" in Alma-Ata in the winter of 1952. Tansykbaev relishes the news that among those repressed were scholars who wrote in Kazakh "idealizing the cursed patriarchal past at the expense of the new reality" (11). All of this reinforces the *mankurt* imagery in the novel. Aitmatov, through the consciousness of the prosecutor, reveals explicity what the parable of the *mankurt* implied—that the text can be interpreted as a veiled call to "oppose the assimilation of nations" (46).

Tansykbaev also seeks to tie Kuttybaev to a conspiracy of former Soviet POWs, working for Great Britain against the Soviet state. For this reason, Tansykbaev transports Kuttybaev by train to Orenburg for confrontation with other "suspects." In an emotionally explosive episode, Kuttybaev presses his face to the barred window of his wagon in a desperate effort to catch sight of his wife and children as the train carrying him to Orenburg rolls through Boranly-Burannyi.[68] In the seconds he sees his family flash by, he realizes that he has been forcibly deprived of everything that had given his life meaning. Upon arrival in Orenburg, he takes advantage of the inattentiveness of one of the GPU guards and throws himself to his death under a passing locomotive. It should be noted that Kuttybaev's suicide in *The White Cloud of Genghis Khan* is clearly foreshadowed in the 1980 version of Aitmatov's novel, in the scene in which Kuttybaev is seen walking on the tracks in a trance, as if longing for death from a rapidly approaching train (294).

The White Cloud of Genghis Khan represents an unrelentingly dark parable of Soviet totalitarianism. Genghis Khan's subordination of everything (even the Supreme Being) to his ambition of conquering the West clearly evokes the increasing militarization of the Soviet economy and society in the postwar era. The legend mentions the khan's demands for "iron discipline" (19), which calls to mind both Stalin and the military. His "ban on childbearing" appears ridiculous and unnatural, recalling a number of Soviet ideas and projects aimed at suspending the laws of nature, such as the genetics of Trofim Lysenko or the more recent efforts aimed at reversing the flow of Siberian rivers. The *dobulbasy* (drums) the khan beats incessantly after killing his brother, as well as in other key parts of the legend, become a symbol of the stupefying propaganda that poisoned the minds of many in Soviet society for decades. In the chapter, the narrator links the drums with the propaganda of hate: "The merciless trial by gossip was the continuation of the vicious roll of the *dobulbasy*. The roar of the oxen hide drums was so insistent and deafening precisely in order to overwhelm and to instill hate toward those whom the khan had decided to hate" (39).

It is unfortunate that the chapter did not appear with the rest of the novel in 1980. Yet if Aitmatov had insisted on the inclusion of *The White Cloud of Genghis Khan*, *The Day Lasts More than a Hundred Years* would certainly have never appeared in the Soviet Union. Aside from the chapter's scathing portrayal of totalitarianism, Aitmatov suggests another reason why the material was deemed unpalatable by the censors. "Someone," he believes, "saw Genghis Khan's ban on childbirth as an allusion to the fate of Zoya Fedorova," a Soviet movie star who was arrested in 1946 for her love affair with an American naval attaché assigned to Moscow.[69] When the NKVD discovered that Fedorova had violated Soviet laws banning intimate relations with foreigners, the American was immediately expelled from the USSR, while Fedorova was sentenced to twenty-five years of hard labor in the gulag. Before her incarceration, Zoya gave birth to the American's daughter, Viktoria, who throughout her childhood knew nothing about her real parents. Viktoria was reunited with her mother after Zoya was released from the camps in 1954, having served eight years of her sentence. In 1975, Viktoria was eventually allowed to come to the United States to see her father. She subsequently published a book in the United States on her family's ordeal.[70] Because the book was published in 1979, just before the appearance of Aitmatov's novel, the censors, in Aitmatov's opinion, could not have overlooked the parallels between the Fedorova affair and the subject matter of *The White Cloud of Genghis Khan*.

Aitmatov never entertained thoughts about publishing the material of *The White Cloud of Genghis Khan* by *samizdat* or *tamizdat*, which at the time were very active.[71] The epic view of life and time so prominent in the author's fiction serves him as a strategy for real life as well. Aitmatov sought to play by the rules and, when he deemed it possible, was willing to compromise a part for the sake of the whole. Keenly aware of the advantages afforded by his official stature, the writer was seeking to widen the realm of the permissible in Soviet literature. His novel therefore did not aim at defying the powers-that-be in a frontal attack. Although compromises were made—the writing of the tendentious introduction, the penning of two slightly upbeat paragraphs after the real conclusion of the novel in Edigei's apocalyptic flight from the cosmodrome, and the sacrifice of *The White Cloud of Genghis Khan*—Aitmatov was able to *probit'* (get through the various levels of censorship) a very powerful novel, which provides a vivid illustration of Soviet mind control. It is to his credit that the word *mankurt*ization quickly entered the political idiom of his day as a term designating ideological brainwashing and cultural denationalization.

7

Soviet Society at the Crossroads
"New Thinking" and The Place of the Skull

"You are advocating a monopoly on truth, but at the very least that is self-deception, for there can be no teaching, not even a God-given one, which has come to know all the truth once and for all. Indeed, if that were the case, then such a doctrine would be lifeless, a dead teaching."[1] This defiant yet self-evident passage captures the central idea of Aitmatov's provocative glasnost novel. It is delivered to a representative of the Moscow patriarchate by the novel's main hero, Avdii Kallistratov, an iconoclastic young seminarian, on the eve of his expulsion from the Orthodox church.

While *The Place of the Skull* has been hailed for its unprecedented discussion of religious and spiritual life, the author casts the debate on Orthodox dogma in a broader context, implicitly attacking the high priests of Communist party ideology, which by the 1980s had become increasingly untenable and uninspiring. Political and ideological paralysis was reaching the crisis stage, best symbolized by a wheezing, mumbling Konstantin Chernenko addressing the party faithful. Cynicism was rife in all quarters of society, and Soviet intellectuals were becoming more and more alarmed by the decline of morals, perceived by many as stemming from a widening spiritual vacuum.[2] While the theological ideas expressed by Avdii to a representative of an established Christian church can stand on their own merits—indeed, the thoroughness with which Aitmatov breaks the religious taboo seemed to fascinate both Soviet and Western critics more than anything else in the novel,—the historical context in which the novel appeared, when traditional ideological rigidity in the Soviet Union was crumbling, makes the parabolic reading natural and at best thinly veiled.

Aitmatov's *The Place of the Skull* calls upon readers to question the lifeless, oppressive dogmas of their time. The novel suggests that failing to challenge such doctrines or, worse, submitting to them engenders pernicious cynicism, which in turn makes society vulnerable to a host of dangerous social ills. Taking advantage of the first real relaxation of Soviet censorship, Aitmatov rushed to portray the corruptive influence of state-sponsored idolatry—the blind adherence to dead words and authorities—and presents in *The Place of the Skull* a powerful portrayal of a whole gamut of social ills, from narcotics abuse, alcoholism, and economic corruption to Soviet militarism and political hypocrisy.

The Place of the Skull reflects the state of Soviet society and the events transforming it from 1982 to 1986.[3] Its somewhat disjointed structure reflects the author's attempt to capture the complexity of the rapid and astounding changes occurring in Soviet society precisely in those years. The year 1982 saw the passing of Mikhail Suslov, longstanding Politburo member and chief party ideologue, who for decades played a central role in the straitjacketing of Soviet letters. Chief among his achievements was the dismissal of Aleksandr Tvardovskii, liberal editor of *Novyi mir*, for "anti-Soviet activities."[4] Suslov's rigidity in protecting the party's ideological interests is perhaps best reflected in his boast in 1961 that Vasilii Grossman's anti-Stalinist novel, *Life and Fate*, would have to wait two hundred years before it could appear in the Soviet Union. Fortunately for Soviet letters, Suslov's prediction was off by 173 years. The year 1982 also saw the death of party boss Leonid Brezhnev, and while the Soviet intelligentsia had hopes for relief from the cultural stagnation in the post-Brezhnev era, these were soon dashed with the ascent to power of KGB chief Iurii Andropov and, subsequently, the lackluster Konstantin Chernenko.

Although in the words of one observer, Andropov and Chernenko "were in many respects at odds with one another, they were united in the conviction that the most desirable form of literature for the CPSU . . . was that of the agitational-propagandist type."[5] The aging party hierarchy wanted to make it clear that it would not tolerate any questioning of the ideological principles of Soviet life. The following two years, 1983 and 1984, witnessed further repressions against dissident writers and human rights activists. The Andropov regime quickly showed its dour disposition in the arrest and sentencing of the poet Irina Ratushinskaia in March 1983, as well as in the forced exile of novelist Georgii Vladimov and the incarceration of the writer Leonid Borodin in May of the same year. The death of Andropov in February 1984 did little to improve the dismal picture. His successor, Konstantin Chernenko, continued the attempts to preserve the repressive legacy of the Soviet leadership. During his placeholder regime, Elena Bonner was arrested and sentenced to five years' exile.

Speaking in his capacity as chief party ideologue in 1983, Konstantin Chernenko called upon communists to increase their influence in writers' organizations to ensure that the proper ideological principles were upheld. Indicating that there were some truths that have been established once and for all, he condemned "subjectivism" and "nonstandard" interpretations of Soviet history and reality, which, in his opinion, regrettably had found their way into a number of works of Soviet literature.[6] It is easy to see how many Soviet readers, with such events and appeals fresh on their minds, would associate rigid church dogma with the equally zealous manner in which the party sought to protect the inviolability of its monopoly on ideology.

The Andropov-Chernenko years also saw the dramatic worsening of U.S.-Soviet relations over issues of arms control. In response to the Soviet deployment in Eastern Europe of SS-20 nuclear missiles during the 1970s, NATO began to install on European soil highly accurate Pershing missiles, capable of reaching Soviet cities in a matter of minutes. Particularly threatening to the Soviet leadership was the Reagan administration's March 1983 announcement of its intention to develop a space-based defense against Soviet intercontinental missiles (the strategic defense initiative), which, in the Soviet view, had clear offensive capabilities. After the downing of Korean Airline flight 007 in September 1983, the already soured relationship degenerated even further. Two months later, the Soviet Union walked out of the Geneva arms talks, making the prospect of superpower confrontation seem more likely.

As the rhetoric of accusation and counteraccusation intensified, so did the specter of nuclear apocalypse. Indeed, a world smoldering in atomic ash became one of the prevailing images of the time. Revelations made by KGB defector Oleg Gordievskii in 1990 indicate a high degree of paranoia in the Soviet political hierarchy of the time and suggest that Andropov expected a NATO attack in 1983.[7] The fear of nuclear holocaust was on the minds of many in those years; it pervades Aitmatov's journalistic work throughout the 1980s and expresses itself in the apocalyptic imagery of the opening and closing pages of *The Place of the Skull*.[8] Significantly, the events in parts 1 and 2 of the novel take place in the summer and late fall of 1983.

After the death of Chernenko in March 1985, his successor, Mikhail Gorbachev, initiated efforts to defuse the dangerous superpower standoff and sought to bring about rapid changes in domestic policies as well. An important gesture was made to the intelligentsia at the Sixth Congress of the Russian Republic's Writers' Union (December 1985), when Gorbachev's chief of ideology, Aleksandr Yakovlev, indicated that he planned to introduce glasnost to Soviet letters through a reform of the nation's creative unions.[9] Although not without opposition, the movement for glasnost continued to find broad support in the months to come; the appearance of Aitmatov's *The Place of the Skull* in June 1986—no doubt written with little direct interference from the censors—helped usher in a new thaw in Soviet literature.[10]

In an interview following the appearance of *The Place of the Skull*, Aitmatov noted that his original idea was to write a novella on Jesus Christ and Pontius Pilate.[11] During the Andropov-Chernenko years, the biblical material would have lent itself well to a parabolic commentary on the repressive nature of Soviet reality, exposing the arrogance of worldly power and the place of the free individual in a world that denies the primacy of the spiritual over the material.

Moreover, biblical motifs were becoming very topical at the time, with orthodox believers in the Soviet Union preparing for the millennium of Christianity in Russia.[12] Seeking to expand the impact of the novella, Aitmatov then added the story of a family of wolves to organize the plot and to introduce the theme of ecological disaster.

Finally, under the influence of budding glasnost, he introduced Avdii and the taboo theme of narcotics trafficking in the Soviet Union. Part 3 of the novel was written last, perhaps as late as 1986.[13] Although the author continues his attack on lifeless dogma in part 3 as well, its chapters read more like an endorsement of Gorbachev's antialcohol campaign and calls for perestroika of the Soviet economy. It even accurately prophesies the kind and source of opposition to economic reform the leadership could expect. Thus, within the composition of *The Place of the Skull* one encounters the parabolic approach Aitmatov had developed over the years of literary censorship and, with the advent of glasnost, a shift to an increased use of another mode—artistic journalism—through which the author presents the topical social and political issues of his day in an immediate, forthright manner.

The novel's publication created a sensation in the Soviet Union. The ground swell of public attention can be attributed primarily to its treatment of questions that for decades the Soviet media was unable or unwilling to tackle. The depiction of the narcotics trade in the USSR, for example, was highly journalistic and, in a manner similar to that used in popular American novels and exemplified by Arthur Hailey's *Airport*, satisfied a demand for information on the workings of a criminal underground whose existence had been denied for so long by the Soviet media. Interestingly, Aitmatov introduces the narcotics trade plot line as the journalistic work of his defrocked hero, Avdii Kallistratov, who, upon leaving the seminary, takes up the profession of freelance reporter. Avdii's portrayed inability to publish, in a Komsomol newspaper, his muckraking material on the youthful narcotics runners is a clear reflection of the state of Soviet journalism before 1986.

In his review of *The Place of the Skull*, Vladimir Lakshin notes the difficulties facing Soviet writers after being "surprised" by glasnost.[14] While he praises *The Day Lasts More than a Hundred Years* as a major novel in Soviet literature, a *roman-vekha* (a milestone-novel), he characterizes *The Place of the Skull* as disappointing, attributing the novel's aesthetic shortcomings to the author's "chasing clumsily after the fleeting day." In taking up the burden of journalism and writing on Soviet narcotics abuse, Aitmatov, in Lakshin's view, had shown courage. Yet, now that the taboo had fallen, "what was the gain for art?"[15] The same can be said about Aitmatov's treatment of the formerly taboo religious theme. Avdii's characterization of Soviet values as "inflated and vulgarized" (88) and his conviction that religion can play a positive role in Soviet society lost much of its shock effect rather quickly in the following years. But realizing the door of glasnost had been thrown open, Aitmatov rushed in, perhaps fearing that it might again be closed. The result is a provocative literary "monument to the moment," whose mere fact of publication and emotional effect on the reader, in the opinion of Lev Anninskii, will be difficult for future literary historians to understand.[16] Indeed, many of the author's ideas on taboo themes are expressed no longer organically, in subtle extended metaphors or parables, but bluntly in the soliloquies of his main characters.[17]

Aitmatov's attempt to capture contemporaneity results in a loose collage of plots and genres,[18] or, in the words of two French critics, a "soupe-à-la hache."[19] Indeed, the work virtually defies attempts at summarizing. Of the novel's three parts, the first two deal with the life of Avdii Kallistratov, who represents the author's first attempt to portray a Russian as the central hero in a work of fiction. Like Aitmatov's previous works, *The Place of the Skull* has several inserted parables. The most important of these occur in parts 1 and 2: the legend of the six and the seventh and Avdii's dream of the interrogation of Jesus Christ by Pontius Pilate. Part 3 of the novel is essentially an autonomous tale, having no characters in common with parts 1 and 2, and to some extent recalls the plot of *Farewell, Gul'sary!* The author seeks to overcome the disjointedness of the three parts by weaving through all of them the story of a family of steppe wolves struggling to survive vis-à-vis the increasingly violent encroachments of man into their natural habitat. Inspiration for the animal tale—which represents a third parabolic subplot in the novel—springs from the ancient Kirghiz epos *Kodzhodzhash*, whose philosophy found expression earlier in Aitmatov's rendition of the legend of Karagul in *Farewell, Gul'sary!*

The name of Aitmatov's hero, Avdii Kallistratov, is significant. The narrator calls attention to the fact that the strange name is mentioned in the Third Book of Kings (Douay) in the Old Testament. The biblical Avdii (in English, Obadiah) was King Ahab's righteous vizier, who saved a hundred prophets from execution after Ahab had led the people of Israel away from the true God, inducing them to worship the pagan gods of Baal.[20] Blood sacrifice was an integral part of the cult of Baal. Obadiah finds and brings to King Ahab the prophet Elijah, who calls down fire from heaven to convince Ahab of the power of Yahweh. Aitmatov's conception of his hero is similar—Avdii wants to save true religiosity from the new paganism of his time. He serves as a warning to modern humanity, and to Soviet people in particular, calling upon all to reject the pagan idols of materialism and hedonism and to seek meaning in life through an increased awareness of the spiritual side of being.

The narrative represents the account of the *khozhdeniia po mukam* (trials and tribulations) Avdii must endure when trying to put his theological ideas into practice. The reader's first acquaintance with Aitmatov's hero occurs near the beginning of the novel, on the eve of his death. Retrospectively, through Avdii's consciousness, the reader learns of the hero's heresy of *immanent messianism*—the belief that God is not transcendent but exists and reveals himself in the words and deeds of men. When interrogated by Father Dimitrii from the Moscow patriarchate, whom the seminarians call "father coordinator," Avdii rejects out of hand the primacy of dogma and demands that the human spirit be given "the freedom to know God as the highest essence of its own being" (85).

After his excommunication, Avdii applies his spiritual zeal to journalism, seeking to publish material on the evil of narcotics in the Soviet Union. At first, the editors of a regional Komsomol newspaper encourage his plan to infiltrate and gather information on a group of *anasha* (wild cannabis) runners traveling to and from Central Asia. Avdii's real agenda, however, is to make a personal contribution in the battle against worldly evil by appealing to the young dealers to repent of their ways and to "seek peace with themselves and with

Him who bears the name of God" (122). Aitmatov depicts the group's ringleader, Grishan, as a cynical Stalin-like figure who would substitute religion with the *kaif* (high) derived from drugs. For the most part, Avdii's sermons about spiritual life fall on deaf ears, and the youths throw him off a train when he begins to toss the *anasha* they have gathered onto the tracks. Lying half-dead in a delirious state near the railroad track, Avdii experiences in dream the biblical encounter of Jesus Christ and Pontius Pilate, whose debate on the nature of God mirrors many of Avdii's own ideas on theology. Avdii survives his fall, however, and while convalescing in a hospital, he meets and falls in love with a botanist, Inga Fedorovna, who is likewise concerned with the *anasha* problem in Central Asia.

After his return to Russia, Avdii begins to correspond with Inga, hoping to marry her. With that idea in mind, he leaves again for Central Asia. While awaiting Inga's return from a trip, Avdii unwittingly gets involved with a group of thugs hired by local party bosses to fulfill the region's plan for meat production. The plan calls for the secret slaughter of the wild antelope in the Moiunkum steppe and passing the meat off as kolkhoz and *sovkhoz* production. When Avdii tries to stop the insane project by appealing to the men's conscience, they beat him and string him up by his arms and feet to a saxaul tree, leaving him to die. Aitmatov's first Russian hero is thus "crucified" in the middle of the novel.

Part 3 of *The Place of the Skull* introduces a totally different plot, which is tied to Avdii's story only by the common Central Asian setting and by the story of the steppe wolves that serves as the frame for the novel as a whole. The hero of part 3 is a hardworking shepherd, Boston Urkunchiev (*urkun*, rebel, a term used to designate Kirghiz participants in the 1916 uprising), who is very reminiscent of Tanabai Bakasov from *Farewell, Gul'sary!*[21] Like Tanabai, Boston rebels against the economic mismanagement he sees about him. He rejects the party's economic and political dogma as incapable of bringing prosperity to the area, arguing instead for a form of privatization of land as the means to interest people in their labor and increase the productivity of livestock breeding at the *sovkhoz*. Attempting to nip such perestroika ideas in the bud is the shepherd's ideological opponent, Kochkorbaev, the party representative at the *sovkhoz*, who condemns Boston for attempting to violate the long established truths of Marxism-Leninism.[22]

Jealousy also motivates the good shepherd's enemies. Chief among them is Bazarbai Noigutov, a lazy worker and an alcoholic. Boston hates Bazarbai for stealing a litter of wolf pups in the mountains and then fleeing to Boston's homestead when the pups' mother and her mate follow in hot pursuit. After Bazarbai's departure, the wolves return again and again to Boston's homestead in search of their stolen pups. Despite Boston's pleas to return the pups, Bazarbai refuses. Instead, he responds by slandering the prosperous Boston as a kulak seeking to subvert the kolkhoz's higher interests. Aitmatov's novel thus illustrates prophetically how the new ideas of economic perestroika would soon be opposed by a powerful alliance: party bureaucrats and lazy, incompetent workers envious of the industrious.[23] The consequences he suggests are tragic—the demise of conscientious, hardworking people, like Boston Urkunchiev. In the end, the mother wolf, yearning for her offspring, carries off Boston's two-year-old son. When the shepherd sees the wolf fleeing with his child, he shoots, killing with the same bullet both the wolf and his son. Boston then seeks out Bazarbai, whom he now holds responsible for the loss of his son, and shoots him down.[24] *The Place of the Skull* concludes with the hero's "righteous" revenge and his bitter realization that by murdering his enemy he has destroyed his own world as well. His suicide is hinted at in the closing lines of the novel:

> "The end of the world has come," Boston uttered aloud, and a frightening truth revealed itself to him: until this time the whole world had incorporated itself within him, and that world had come to an end. . . . Everything that he had seen and experienced in his life had been his universe, had lived in him and for him, and now, although all would continue to exist as it had for centuries, it would be without him—it would be a different world, whereas his world, unique and incapable of rebirth, had been lost and would not be resurrected in anyone or anything. (300–01)

Compositionally, Aitmatov ties together the two main, yet dissimilar, plots, which depict Avdii's and Boston's paths to their individual Golgothas, through the lyrical story of the steppe wolves. The wolves' saga is woven in and out of the narration and, like almost all of the author's animal stories, has a parabolic dimension.

The novel opens with an apocalyptic scene of a helicopter flying low over the mountains where the she-wolf, Akbara, and her mate, Tashchainar, have found a new home. Akbara is expecting her third litter of pups. The roar of the helicopter is likened to a horrible earthquake. It causes a landslide whose flow is compared to that of blood (14). Frightened, in a panic, the wolves howl at the "iron monster," seeking to make it go away. In a number of flashbacks throughout the novel, the reader learns that the wolves have sought refuge in the mountains, having been twice driven from their home in the steppe by reckless human attacks on the natural world. The wolves lose their first home and first three pups in the Moiunkum steppe, when they inadvertently become the victims of the antelope slaughter depicted in part 1 of the novel. The depiction of the mechanized and aerial assault on the antelope is one of the most powerful in the novel. Aitmatov shows a world turned upside down, with both wolves and antelope fleeing together before the human threat. In Akbara's view, even the sun itself has become humanity's victim, silently trying to escape the "mad roundup" (36).

After their offspring perish in the stampede of death, under the hooves of their traditional prey, Akbara and Tashchainar flee to the wetlands near Lake Aldash. Finding a safe haven there, Akbara gives birth to a litter of five. But the wolves' sense of security is a false one, and they must again take flight when men set fire to thousands of hectares of reeds surrounding the lake, in order to clear the area for the establishment of a gigantic defense facility. For such a project, the narrator remarks pointedly, "men are permitted to gut the earth like a melon" (206). All their pups perish in the resulting inferno. The mountain home near Lake Issyk-kul is their third and last chance to survive and perpetuate themselves. The helicopter overflight at the beginning of the novel is a sign that here, too, they can expect no mercy. Several weeks later, Bazarbai accidentally stumbles upon their last litter of four pups and thus sets into motion the tragedy of part 3 of the novel. In the end, it is the innocent who suffer, symbolized by the violent death of Boston's child.

The chain of violence reaches an apocalyptic crescendo in the closing pages of the novel. The world of nature avenges itself on the unsuspecting Boston for the wanton abuse visited upon it by others. In shooting Akbara, Boston brings to an end his own biological line—his son Kendzhesh (*kendzhesh*, the last-born) is killed by the same bullet—and sets the scene for the subsequent murder of Bazarbai, as well as his own probable suicide. The violent conclusion of the novel makes it Aitmatov's darkest work. Humanity's moral degeneracy is shown as presaging doom for all of society, both the iniquitous and the innocent.[25]

The appearance of *The Place of the Skull* was the most important literary event of 1986 in the Soviet Union. Long waiting lists of people wanting to read the novel formed at Soviet libraries, and not until the end of 1987 had most of those people received the opportunity to do so.[26] The novel was discussed in the press and on television throughout the Soviet Union[27] and received more reviews in the West than any of Aitmatov's previous novels. Positive responses—primarily to the novel's breaking of the religious taboo—were published in Russian emigré journals. Mikhail Nazarov, for example, comments in *Veche*, the organ of the Russian National Union (Munich), that Aitmatov's work proposes for the first time in Soviet history to "shift the official point of view from militant atheism to agnosticism," and in an article in *Posev*, he correctly predicts that in the Soviet Union "Aitmatov's *The Place of the Skull* would, no doubt, help propagate a normal attitude toward religion."[28] While Western and Soviet critics agreed that the novel lacked the cohesiveness characteristic of Aitmatov's previous works, almost all concurred that for official Soviet letters the novel marked the crossing of a major ideological boundary.

Soviet critics of all persuasions were thus compelled to react to the novel's appearance. The conservative reaction to the open religiosity in the novel came swiftly, even before its serial publication in *Novyi mir* was completed. A strongly worded antireligious article appeared in *Komsomolskaia pravda* under the title of "Petty Playing with God." The author, Iosif Kryvelev, condemns religiosity in the latest works of prominent Soviet writers Vasil' Bykau and Viktor Astav'ev and singles out Aitmatov's *The Place of the Skull*:

His hero, Avdii Kallistratov, an expelled seminarian, is searching for god. He is not satisfied with the traditional "archaic" image of supreme being, but at the same time he does not like atheism. He has to seek a way between the two, a certain "god-contemporary," who corresponds to the "needs of the time." . . . As far as the "missionary" task that Avdii takes upon himself is concerned, it is apparently used to express the same idea of the author . . . that with the help of religious tenets it is possible and even necessary to improve the behavior and morality of man.[29]

Other Soviet defenders of atheism continued the attack against the positive portrayal of religious values or sought to reverse the meaning of their depiction in the novel. In the Communist party organ *Pravda*, for example, Evgenii Surkov argues that Aitmatov's novel shows the social inadequacy of Christian ideas,[30] and Suren Kaltakhchian in *Komsomolskaia pravda* calls for a strengthening of atheistic instruction among Soviet youth: "Our younger generation has the right to hope that cultural figures will make a worthy contribution toward improving atheistic education, in developing new Soviet customs and traditions, as well as strengthening Communist morality, which is free of the falsehood and hypocrisy characteristic of religious morality."[31]

But it was clear that times were changing in the Soviet Union. Kryvelev, for example, sought to lend authority to his antireligious attack on Aitmatov's novel by quoting from Lenin's famous letter to Gorky, in which the future founder of the Soviet state condemns the "god-building" theme in Gorky's novel *Ispoved'* (Confession, 1908). The letter, a lengthy tirade of crude epithets, chides Gorky for his "petty playing with god," the very words Kryvelev uses for the title of his article. Lenin characterizes the "god-searching" or "god-building" (in his mind the concepts are synonomous) of Gorky's hero as "ideological necrophilia," "inexpressible filth," and "the worst form of self-humiliation."[32] Kryvelev, no doubt, detects the affinity between Gorky's and Aitmatov's novels and, emulating the militancy of Lenin in the letter to Gorky, demands that Aitmatov return to the proper ideological path.

Such criticism would have had ominous consequences only a few years earlier. Now, Aitmatov saw no need to distance himself from his hero or from his portrayal of Christ. He publicly rejected Kryvelev's primitive approach to literature and states that "Jesus Christ enables me to say something to modern man which to me is very important."[33] In condemning the primitive atheism of Kryvelev, Aitmatov indirectly questions the virulent dogma of the very authority with which his accuser had cloaked himself, that of Lenin himself. In the past, such presumption would have been unimaginable for a Soviet writer. But at the end of 1986, even Lenin was beginning to become mortal, and his utility in silencing Soviet writers was rapidly diminishing.[34]

Recognizing that the time for greater spiritual freedom in the Soviet Union had finally come, Georgii Gachev, in his review of *The Place of the Skull*, made an eloquent appeal to Soviet officials to expand what he called "the space of the soul": "It would cost society so little, yet bring people tremendous joy. Regimentation, on the other hand, demands great effort: placing in the space of the soul obstacles in the form of walls and corridors, locks and prohibitions; like a pharmacist one must constantly weigh what is allowed and what is not."[35] Indeed, "the space of the soul" continued to expand dramatically in the months following the appearance of Kryvelev's article, and eventually his name came to be characterized in the Soviet press in the most negative terms, becoming an embarassing symbol for the ideological intolerance of the past.[36]

Although other critics cautiously continued to play down the association of morality and religiosity implicit throughout *The Place of the Skull*, they were fighting a rearguard action. In the years following 1986, the idea that religious values could be beneficial to Soviet society gained widespread support, and churches rapidly expanded their activities. For Aitmatov, the positive portrayal of spirituality in *The Place of the Skull* culminated a process begun much earlier, with his depiction of the Kirghiz cult of the earth (Umai-ene) in *Mother's Field* (1963), the worship of nature by the positive characters in *The White Ship* (1970), the central relationship between humanity and its deities in *The Spotted Dog* (1977), and the respect for religious ideas and traditions displayed by Edigei in *The Day Lasts More than a Hundred Years* (1980).

Aitmatov's depiction of religiosity so dominated the critical response to the novel in the Soviet Union that the highly topical themes of narcotics trafficking and ecological destruction received little attention. No serious attempt was made to discuss the work from the viewpoint of its place in socialist realism, although, without doubt,

Avdii Kallistratov represented a highly undesirable positive hero for the proponents of the discredited literary doctrine. Nor was an effort made to criticize Aitmatov for unduly blackening Soviet reality, an approach used in the past with particular effectiveness in respect to *The White Ship*. By 1986, there was a strong consensus among Soviet critics of all persuasions that a serious moral vacuum did indeed exist in the Soviet Union, and narcotics abuse, political corruption, and alcoholism were undeniable social evils. Critics now decried the fact that in the past, due to a false understanding of national prestige, materials on such issues had been repressed. In his discussion of the novel, for example, Valentin Oskotskii reveals to readers that, in 1962, *Literaturnaia gazeta* intended to publish an article on Soviet narcotics abuse but was prevented from doing so by the censors.[37] Another critic points out that in 1975, a Georgian writer, Temur Abulashvili, published a realistic novella, *Zheleznye sandali* (The iron sandals), on the same subject in a university almanac appearing in Georgian, but the story was later banned from print.[38]

Commenting on the aesthetics of Aitmatov's novel, most Soviet and Western critics agreed that the composition was disjointed and that Aitmatov had attempted the impossible: to unite within the work paganism and Christianity, the worlds of animals and that of human beings, the languages of fiction and journalism, the call to nonviolence (Avdii) and Boston's bloody revenge. Alla Latynina expresses amazement at the inconsistent quality of the novel, noting that well-written passages seemed to be strangely interconnected with less-convincing parts of the work. She suggests that perhaps Soviet critics do not possess the proper criteria to assess the novel and that perhaps it is "some kind of different art form."[39] The best description of the novel is provided by Lev Anninskii, who expresses his frustration in trying to understand both Aitmatov's ideas and the way those ideas are realized in the text. Referring to the strange parallelism between Avdii Kallistratov and the she-wolf Akbara, Anninskii labeled the work "a strange centaur," which, despite all its apparent contradictions, somehow was able to gallop.[40]

The question naturally arises whether there is indeed a common denominator that can bring together the disparate themes to produce the novel's central idea. In previous works, Aitmatov had employed folklore parables to tie together the numerous subplots in his works. Those parables, as we have seen, also reinterpret the specific and topical into more universal terms. Therefore, the search for artistic *tselostnost'* (integrity) in *The Place of the Skull* should begin with an examination of the parabolic subplots in the novel.

The first of such subplots is the legend of the six and the seventh, which Aitmatov introduces early in the novel, on the eve of Avdii's departure to Central Asia with the *anasha* runners. To give the lyrical story a religious aura, Aitmatov depicts Avdii as recalling it while listening to a Bulgarian choir singing liturgical music at the Pushkin Museum in Moscow. The idea that music and song can unite people and "transcend the dogmas of all ages" (74) inspires Avdii as he sets out on his mission of brotherly love. The Georgian ballad, which Aitmatov has since admitted to be the product of his imagination— a fact confirmed by a Georgian poet[41]—tells how in the final days of the bloody civil war in Georgia a brave chekist, Sandro, infiltrates a band of counterrevolutionaries headed by Guram Dzhokhadze, a famed partisan hero. Gaining Dzhokhadze's confidence, Sandro manages to lead the unit into a devastating ambush and then flees with the surviving six men into the mountains. Realizing the futility of further struggle, Dzokhadze tells the men that their fight is over and advises them to continue their flight to Turkey or Iran. The night before the departure, the men form a circle around a campfire, drinking wine and singing Georgian songs. The songs transcend the class warfare of the revolution, and though Sandro plans to kill the six counterrevolutionaries, he becomes one with them in singing the songs of the past.

As the last songs are sung, Sandro rises and leaves the circle to get more wood for the fire. When he returns, however, he quickly pulls out his heavy Mauser and kills point-blank Dzhokhadze and the other five men. He drives all the horses away and circles the dead men as if bidding them farewell; then, stepping to the side, he puts the pistol to his own head and kills himself. While listening to the singing of the Bulgarian choir, Avdii experiences an uncanny sense of seeing himself reincarnated in one of the members of the choir. Avdii concludes that the reason Sandro chooses not to return and reap the rewards for his bloody deed is that, in singing the songs that "contained the faith of all seven men,"(73) he had become one with them. His sharing in the spirituality of his six enemies made it impossible for him not to share in their fate. In killing them, he in effect kills himself.

This rather enigmatic parable with the apocalyptic number seven in its title prefigures the outcome of the lives of the two main characters in the novel, Avdii Kallistratov and Boston Urkunchiev.[42] Just as Sandro chooses death because he is unable to deny the common spirituality that binds him to the "class enemies" he murders, so Avdii's demise at the hands of the antelope hunters is effectively accomplished by his refusal to deny his belief in God and the spirituality he shares with all human beings. Yet Sandro's suicide models more closely that of Boston, who, after killing his oppressor, Bazarbai, contemplates putting an end to his own life as well. Like Sandro, Boston sends his horse (*zhanybar*, having a soul) away before committing the act. He realizes that in murdering Bazarbai he has extinguished his own humanity.

Interestingly, in the legend of the six and the seventh, Sandro seeks to justify the murders of Dzhokhadze and his men by dehumanizing them as class enemies; in the events of part 3 of *The Place of the Skull*, which take place some sixty years after the Russian Civil War, the villain Bazarbai resorts to the same lethal relativism when he declares Boston a kulak and class enemy (244). But this time, the tables are turned, and Boston does the killing. The bloody deed can thus be seen as the perpetuation of the excesses committed at the beginning of Soviet history, symbolized by Sandro's murders and suicide. The cycle of violence engendered by class warfare comes around full circle in *The Place of the Skull*, with little hope of an end in sight. It is notable in this context that the original title Aitmatov envisioned for his novel was *Krugovrashchenie* (The turn of the circle).[43] Although the worldviews and motives of Sandro and Boston are portrayed as quite different, Boston's transgression being viewed as more justified than Sandro's, the parabolic dimension of the legend suggests the author's condemnation of both killings as unwarranted, indeed counterproductive. In this light, the legend of the six and the seventh can be seen as an appeal to stop the cycle of violence in the world by refusing to perpetuate it.

The imagery of the legend suggests the treachery of Sandro's act. Dzhokhadze's final evening evokes the Last Supper. His disciples gather around him, as the apostles did at Christ's bidding, on the eve of the Crucifixion. As Judas betrayed Christ, so Sandro betrays Dzhokhadze, and, like Judas, when he realizes the treachery of his deed, he kills himself.[44] This is certainly how Avdii understands the legend, for he concludes tautologically: "And so blood was shed for blood shed, again and again in the vicious cycle of murder" (72). Thus the futility of Sandro's "righteous" violence, and, by analogy, Boston's, is contrasted with the nonviolent selflessness of Christ and Avdii, who readily take upon themselves the guilt of their contemporaries.

Aitmatov shares Avdii's view of the perils inherent in violence, especially if attempts are made to justify it as instances of class or revolutionary warfare, as is the case with Sandro's murders of the six men. *The Place of the Skull* reveals that Sandro's act of violence and those of many others like him continue to reverberate in different places and times. It is not by chance that the revolutionary slogan— "If the enemy doesn't give up, he must be killed" (66)—from the legend of the six and the seventh resounds again at the end of the novel, when party boss Kochkorbaev accuses Boston of being "a new brand of kulak and counterrevolutionary" (273), labels used earlier in Soviet history to justify the liquidation of millions of people. Aitmatov's novel seeks to discredit forever the dogma of class struggle or "class approach" to human society by revealing its murderous results. This attitude is expressed in unequivocal terms in one of Aitmatov's newspaper interviews, appearing several years after the publication of his novel: "The class approach inevitably brings forth violence, therein lies the lesson of our history. The people who are calling upon society to introduce all kinds of 'workers' control' shouldn't forget this. Any desirable benefit which is achieved through violence is no longer a benefit, but fundamentally immoral."[45]

The second parable in *The Place of the Skull*—Avdii's dream of Pontius Pilate's interrogation of Christ on the eve of the Crucifixion—is the central one in the novel. It departs significantly from Bulgakov's depiction of the Passion scene in *Master and Margarita*, although both share a number of narrative details.[46] Bulgakov's rewriting of the Gospel passage was undertaken to fulfill an aesthetic function in the portrayal of his hero. Also, the psychological realism of the Bulgakov episode focuses more attention on Pilate and the motives for his cowardice. Aitmatov's rendition shifts the emphasis from Pilate back to Christ and, at the same time, offers a new interpretion of the tragic character of the Roman procurator.

While Bulgakov's Christ says very little in the Jerusalem chapters of *Master and Margarita*, in *The Place of the Skull* Christ expounds his ideas on God, worldly power, life after death, and the end of the world. His function is to delineate further Avdii's nontraditional theology. Aitmatov's Pilate is portrayed as arrogantly sure of himself and his role in Judea. Bulgakov's Pilate is a tragic figure, suffering under the burden of his decision; in Avdii's dream, Pilate is depicted as a tyrant with a materialist philosophy of worldly power reminiscent of Aitmatov's conception of Genghis Khan in *The Day Lasts More than a Hundred Years*.

Although one can criticize Aitmatov for the intrusion of journalistic style into Avdii's dream—Lev Anninskii remarks that the scene gave his aesthetic feelings convulsions,[47]—both Christ's theological lecture and the portrayal of Pilate as unrelenting villain flow naturally from Avdii's personality and iconoclastic worldview. Avdii is portrayed as an aspiring journalist possessed by a sense of mission. Moreover, his dream of Christ and Pilate occurs after he is thrown from a train by the *anasha* runners. Presenting the novel's theological discussion indirectly through the character of Avdii, who is disoriented after his fall, formally distances the author from the ideas expressed in the dream, which can be seen as a precautionary maneuver by the author at a time when calls for intensifying the antireligious struggle still echoed in the ears of Soviet citizens.[48]

Significantly, Aitmatov's version of the interrogation of Christ constitutes a separate chapter and is placed at the exact center of the novel. Christianity has fascinated Aitmatov for some time; in an interview given in 1982, he admitted publicly that he had read the Bible and continued to read it with "great interest and benefit."[49] After publishing *The Place of the Skull*, he explained that, although his Central Asian background might be expected to orient him more toward Islam, he had become fascinated by Christ and was drawn toward Christianity because of its teachings on repentance. Of all the major religious figures in the world, he found Jesus Christ to be the most "striking and dramatic." In his view, the spirit of Christianity was very much needed in today's world.[50] He noted that Soviet society is oriented more toward Europe than the Middle East, and that Eurocentricity, about which he had no regrets, made his literary use of biblical materials legitimate.[51]

The Christ figure in the dream embodies Avdii's concept of immanent messianism, which he expresses to the Grand Coordinator on the eve of his expulsion from the seminary. The God Avdii hopes will be able to pull the Soviet people from the jaws of depravity is not above the world (God as Pantocrator), but in it, and as dependent on humanity as it is on him. Avdii's "new faith," although clumsily expressed and simplified, is remarkably similar to the ideas propagated by the Russian religious philosopher Nikolai Berdiaev (1874–1948).[52] It is interesting that the term *bogoiskatel'* (god-seeker), commonly used to refer to the religious thinkers of the silver age and in particular to Berdiaev, appears several times in the narrative in connection with Avdii. Significantly, Aitmatov's hero remarks to the Grand Coordinator: "Excuse me, Father, but it is better to call things by their names. There is no God outside of our consciousness" (82). This key idea, it should be noted, was chosen by Berdiaev for the epigraph to his *Smysl tvorchestva* (The meaning of the creative act), 1916: "I know that without me God cannot live a moment; did I not exist, he must of necessity give up the spirit." When Avdii realizes that his excommunication is imminent, he defiantly declares, like Leo Tolstoy before him, "My church will always be within me. . . . I myself am my church. I recognize neither temples nor priests, especially in their present forms" (87).

The Christ in Avdii's dreams demands that humankind take an active role in ushering in the new age, the Second Coming, the kingdom of God on Earth:

> Not I, for whom remains to live only the distance to be walked through the city to Golgotha, will come, rising from the dead, but you, people, will come to live in Christ, in the highest righteousness; you will come to me in yet unknown future generations. And that will be my Second

> Coming. In other words, I will return to myself in mankind through
> suffering; in people I will return to people. (153)

The giving of oneself in love for others will create the glorious "God-Tomorrow," Christ tells Pilate. Each individual is called upon to come to Christ "through suffering, through the struggle with evil, and by rejecting vice, violence, and bloodthirstiness" (153). Avdii's radical adherence to such ideas predetermines his fate in the novel.

His death on the tree is thus the logical outcome of his faith. Avdii moves with determination toward his Golgotha, despite the fact that worldly wisdom would prompt him to behave differently. The apparent lack of motivation for Avdii's actions in *The Place of the Skull* can be explained only by his role as the literary embodiment of an idea, that of sacrifice—his "crucifixion" is more important to the author than the road he takes to get there. The idea that selfless love is humanity's creative act inspires Avdii to try to change the lives of the young *anasha* runners, who have chosen the path of evil. Yet those whom he would save beat him mercilessly. When Avdii implores the antelope hunters to stop the carnage and pray to God for forgiveness, they simply kill him by stringing him up on the tree. But in Avdii's conception of the cosmos, he has helped bring closer the Second Coming of Christ through his selfless example and his appeals for repentance, "one of the greatest achievements in the history of the human soul" (189). Christ in Avdii's dream tells Pilate that, even though he may choose not to believe, Pilate will be unable to deny having heard his words and will "not be able to stop himself from thinking about what was said" (159). Aitmatov thus implies that humankind will be able to change for the better only slowly and painfully. Although Avdii does nothing tangible to change the world for the better, one of the boys of the *anasha* ring, Lenka, appears to be not without remorse after witnessing Avdii's selfless sacrifice on his behalf.

Another important idea expressed by the Christ in Avdii's dream is the freedom of human beings to determine their spiritual fate: "Man is both the judge and creator of each of his days" (154). The act of faith is free and without coercion. In his argument with Father Dimitrii, Avdii demands that "the human spirit be given the freedom to know God as the highest essence of one's own existence" (85).

Faith through coercion deprives humanity of the divine in its nature. Aitmatov's hero recognizes, as did Berdiaev, that not believing in humanity goes hand in hand with not believing in God. In his study of Dostoevsky, Berdiaev writes:

> Not believing in God, the Grand Inquisitor also ceases to believe in man, for they are two aspects of the same faith; Christianity is the religion of the God-man and therefore demands belief in both God and man. But the idea of the God-man, the uniting of the divine and human principles in one freedom, is precisely the idea that the Grand Inquisitor will not have; it is asking too much of man to saddle him with the spiritual responsibility, he must escape from Christian freedom and its burden of discriminating and choosing between good and evil.[53]

The Place of the Skull speaks out eloquently against the coercion of faith from free human beings, whether in the religious or secular spheres. Just as the father coordinator takes upon himself the role of intermediary between a transcendental God and Avdii, the party organizer in part 3 of the novel, Kochkorbaev, demands the right to be the sole arbiter of Marxism-Leninism among the Kirghiz shepherds. He kills any initiative Boston Urkunchiev may have with the words "We don't have the right to distort the principles of socialism" (248) and "We will not allow anyone to question the foundations of socialism" (249). Avdii's and Boston's rebellions are both for the dignity of humankind, for freedom from oppressive dogma.

The Christ-Pilate story discusses parabolically the apocalyptic danger of striving for absolute worldly power. Unlike Bulgakov's rendition of the Christ-Pilate encounter in *Master and Margarita*, in which Pilate is depicted as suffering from his cowardice, Aitmatov's Pilate is arrogantly sure of his faith in the power of Rome. His depiction is reminiscent of Nikolai Ge's portrait of Pilate, "Chto est' istina?" (What is the truth?) 1890, which shows Pilate haughtily ridiculing his battered victim. Pilate's philosophy of power in *The Place of the Skull* does not permit him to respect the weak—neither Christ nor the rest of humankind. Like Dostoevsky's Grand Inquisitor, he tells Christ that people "will always follow the caesars of the world as sheep do their shepherds" (156).

Continuing, Pilate asserts that men will always bow to power and wealth and "will sing praises to those who lead regiments into battle, where blood flows in rivers in the name of conquest, submission, and humiliation of others" (156). In such martial deeds—conquering and enslaving other peoples and depriving them of their land—Pilate also sees the meaning of human existence and the immortality of the soul. Christ warns Pilate that his philosophy of Might Makes Right will inevitably lead to the end of humankind, "as a scorpion kills itself with its own venom" (158). He completes his condemnation with an apocalyptic vision of nuclear holocaust: "Everything was dead, all was covered in black ash from the raging fires, the earth lay totally in ruins—there were no forests, fields or ships in the seas" (156).

The danger of apocalypse inherent in the pursuit of a weltanschauung based on the primacy of military conquest finds expression in other parts of the novel as well. Thus the opening scene of the antelope slaughter is depicted as a military operation complete with helicopters and military transport vehicles. The attack on the flora and fauna near Lake Aldash, where Akbara and Tashchainar have found a new home, is likewise described as an aerial assault with incendiary materials. Significantly, when everything is engulfed in flames, the narrator uses the word *svetoprestavlenie* (the end of the world) to characterize the operation.

In his dialogue with Pilate, Christ calls upon human beings to recognize the "power of good" (157) within them, the spirituality that links them to their creator. Pilate's view of humanity as sheep following their shepherds is condemned not only for its potential for enslavement, but also because such a philosophy will inevitably lead to global conflict and extinction. Aitmatov's novel articulates those fears and captures the zeitgeist of his age. In the years following the publication of Aitmatov's novel, as glasnost became ever bolder in the USSR, the Soviet press began to devote more and more attention to the danger of the Soviet totalitarian legacy and the excessive militarization of the Soviet economy and society. Major shifts in Soviet foreign and domestic policy followed, leading to a reduction of Soviet armaments through arms agreements with the West and *konversiia* (retooling military plants to produce consumer goods) at home.

Unlike the parabolic myths and legends of Aitmatov's previous novels, which are narrated in a solemn, lyrical style, the central "parable from the past" in *The Place of the Skull*, the Christ story, is cast in the clichéd idiom of Soviet journalism. As a result, the important subplot is bereft of the beauty and enigmatic quality of parable. Yet Aitmatov wanted to impress on the reader the topical nature of the themes of sacrifice and naked power. His Christ speaks like a political dissident and his Pilate like a member of the Soviet *nomenklatura*. A degree of immediacy is achieved, and readers recognize the reality of their world in the portrayal, but only at the cost of trivializing a venerable cultural text. Soviet critics were quick to recognize the aesthetic "miscalculation," decrying Aitmatov's irreverent treatment of such a beautiful legend.[54] He nevertheless felt as free to tailor the Christ-Pilate story to his artistic needs as he had when adapting the legend of the Deer-mother in *The White Ship*.

The story of Tashchainar and Akbara, which runs as a gray thread throughout the narration, constitutes a third parabolic subplot in the novel. In presenting the lyrical story of the steppe wolves, Aitmatov draws on the pre-Islamic oral tradition of his people. Critics have noted that the wolves seem more human than the people in the novel, and the author's reversal of the negative connotation of a predator animal supports his portrayal in *The Place of the Skull* of a world gone awry. Yet in Turkic folklore, the wolf has positive connotations. Indeed, it is one of the totem animals of Central Asia, and in numerous passages from *Manas* it stands as the symbol of proud Kirghiz ethnicity. For centuries, the wolf graced the banners of many Central Asian armies, and one of the frequent epithets for Manas is *kok dzhal* (the gray-maned).[55] In modern Central Asian letters, the wolf has continued to have positive connotations, standing for pride and tenacity. The mistreatment of wolves and their association with Central Asians represent a major theme in *The Immortal Cliffs*, an important novel by the contemporary Uzbek writer Mämädäli Mähmudov.[56]

For Central Asian readers of *The Place of the Skull*, therefore, the incessant persecution of Akbara and Tashchainar, as well as the deaths of all of their offspring, can evoke the attacks by Soviet authorities on Turkic culture and ethnicity over many years, as well as the rape of the Central Asian ecology in the name of dubious military and industrial projects. Aitmatov's wolf story thus invites a number of readings, including such a narrow nationalistic one. Adequate evidence exists elsewhere in the novel supporting such a reading; particularly telling is the scene in which Ernazar complains to Boston about party authorities' attempts to eradicate Kirghiz customs. Ernazar laments that the party organizer, Kochkorbaev, "condemns all the old ways," from Kirghiz wedding customs to the old-fashioned names (implied are Turkic and Islamic names) Kirghiz couples give their children. Even funeral traditions are attacked by Kochkorbaev, who ridicules the Kirghiz custom of loud lamenting over the deceased (255).

In a more universal reading, however, Akbara and Tashchainar appear as symbols for the good of the natural world, the expression of meaning and harmony in Creation, which is in keeping with the pre-Islamic worldview still surviving in parts of today's northern Kirghizstan. The story of the wolves' life of suffering represents Aitmatov's free rendition of the ancient Kirghiz epos *Kodzhodzhash*, which can be traced back far into the shamanistic past of the Kirghiz, a time, in the words of the author, "in which man, nature, and the animal world were still perceived as a whole."[57] Aitmatov had used the folklore material earlier in *Farewell, Gul'sary!* in the legend of Karagul. *Kodzhodzhash* calls upon man to preserve the natural balance in the world, warning of nature's revenge if humankind should be so arrogant as to disturb that holy balance. In the legend of Karagul, the attempt to exterminate all mountain goats backfires on the hunter, who is left to die at the hands of his own father.

In *The Place of the Skull*, unnamed Soviet authorities and their criminal supporters are cast by the author in the role of Karagul. Akbara's first litter is destroyed in the antelope slaughter organized by the local party authorities. In the massacre of the antelope, no effort is made to spare the females. The violation of nature's balance is symbolized by the fact that both wolves and antelope flee together in a single herd pursued by a common foe—humanity. Akbara's second litter is killed, again by human beings, in a massive assault on the flora and fauna at Lake Aldash. Bazarbai steals the third and final litter, hoping to sell the pups for vodka.[58]

Retribution for this wanton assault on nature, however, is exacted not from Soviet Karaguls but from the innocent family of Boston (*bos*, gray, and *ton*, coat) Urkunchiev. That is the essence of Aitmatov's new variation on the ancient legend. Akbara, like the she-goat that Karagul pursues, has lost all her offspring and her mate through the senseless violence of humankind; Boston, like Karagul's father, tragically kills his own son. The parabolic dimension of the wolves' story presents a strong warning to human beings to respect the natural world. Aitmatov portrays that world as imbued with human spirituality—Akbara, whose very name evokes *Allahu Akbar* (God is great!), is portrayed as praying to a moon deity. Interestingly, Akbara is depicted as having blue eyes (certainly unusual for wolves!), the same color as those of Avdii's Christ.[59]

Aitmatov shows the animal's boundless love for the world through Akbara's "human" care for her pups; indeed, her carrying off Boston's son is depicted by the narrator as motivated not by revenge but by her desire to nurture the boy. In the final minutes of Avdii's life, the blue-eyed wolf appears at his "cross," pitying him as if moved by his sacrifice. And Avdii's last words, "You have come" (205), are a recognition of the goodness and love in the natural world that Akbara, "the great one," represents. An assault on the natural world, Aitmatov suggests in his novel, is an attack on God and the preordained order of the universe. The novel presents a unique blending of the shamanistic worldview and the nontraditional Christian idea of immanent messianism. Akbara is the Christ of the natural world; like the Savior, she suffers for the sins of the human world and perishes at her own Golgotha.

To find unity in the apparent disharmony of the many different ideas, themes, and styles in *The Place of the Skull*, the reader must assume the author's vantage point, from which unrelated phenomena suddenly become interconnected. This invitation to the reader is suggested in Aitmatov's fiction by images of birds hovering high above the narrated events. For example, a hawk or an eagle circles high overhead throughout the entire dialogue between Christ and Pilate. The same high point of observation is suggested at the beginning of the novel, as the antelope hunt ends: "If there had been a watchful eye looking down on the earth from the heavenly heights above, it probably would have seen how the roundup had taken place and what it had done to the Moiunkum savannah" (37).[60] From such a height, it is suggested, the hypothetical eye would be able to see the seemingly disconnected links in a chain of action and reaction. It would be able to see simultaneously the dead antelope, the wolves fleeing their homeland, Avdii beaten and left to die, and even the *anasha* runners, who might be gathering the plant on a distant part of the same plain.

But continuing the analogy, the narrator notes that even had there been such an eye, it would not have been able to know the consequences of the events below nor what was "yet to come" (37). It is left to the reader not only to see the disparate links, but to join them together imaginatively in a chain of causality. Aitmatov calls upon the reader to become aware of the causal unity of all things and thus to accept the idea that the unnamed authorities who issued the order to slaughter the steppe antelope bear indirect responsibility for the death of Kendzhesh, Boston's son, as well as for the bloodshed at the novel's conclusion.

Aitmatov's *The Place of the Skull* reads as an appeal to Soviet readers to question established authority. In part 3 of the novel, the need to liberate independent-thinking Soviet citizens from the oppressive control of party ideology is addressed directly, with Boston likening the ideologues to an unnecessary "fifth wheel" on a wagon (251). Parts 1 and 2 deal with the same issues in a more parabolic manner through the characters of Avdii, Christ, and Pilate, as well as through their discussions of theology. But in all parts of the work, there is a prevailing mood of gloom and impending apocalypse that give the author's appeal a sense of utmost urgency.

The Chernobyl nuclear disaster of April 1986, occurring just two months prior to the novel's appearance in *Novyi mir*, provided the real-world context for the apocalyptic mood in *The Place of the Skull* and no doubt gave it added poignancy. The calamity served as an overwhelming illustration of one of the novel's major themes—the possibility of the natural environment avenging itself on innocent people for the sins of the arrogant few. In the wake of Chernobyl, the consensus for political reform began to grow rapidly. Perhaps the first real signal of a willingness to tolerate dissent was the return, at the end of the same year, of Andrei Sakharov and Elena Bonner from their forced exile in Gorky. In the minds of many, the event presaged an end to the ideological tyranny of Stalin's heirs. Those hopes were to be fulfilled in the following years, with the blossoming of glasnost and the revelation in the Soviet press of crimes perpetrated by the Soviet state against its own people. The title of Aitmatov's novel, *Plakha* (literally, the execution block), is a fitting image to describe the fates of millions of Soviet citizens who, like Aitmatov's father, found themselves at odds with the ideology of their time.

Although published at a time of increasing optimism that the party's monopoly on ideology would soon be broken, Aitmatov's *The Place of the Skull* warns that the path to reason, tolerance, and respect for the individual in the Soviet Union would be difficult. Only in the second half of 1987, two years after Mikhail Gorbachev came to power, did the idea begin to find official acceptance that a plurality of opinions best served the interests of society. A new ideological concept was soon formulated—"socialist pluralism"—by which the party would seek to channel support for perestroika.[61] Although written in support of ideas destined to fall under the rubrics of "new thinking" and "socialist pluralism," Aitmatov paints a dark picture of the fate of those opposing the dominant ideology. In all the narrative planes of his glasnost novel, the *inakomysliashchie* (those who think differently)--Avdii, Christ, Boston Urkunchiev—are crushed by the powers that be.

As in Aitmatov's previous novels, *The Place of the Skull* invites its readers to overcome the unrelenting tragedy through a process of catharsis, which the writer hopes will motivate them to fight for his characters' ideals in real life. Part of this strategy in the novel is the elicitation of the readers' active hatred for the vestiges of Stalinism in Soviet behavior and attitudes. Those who carry the germs of the disease are depicted as particularly petty and depraved. Perhaps the most vicious of such figures in *The Place of the Skull* is Ober-Kandalov,[62] who uses the rhetoric of Stalinism to justify all his actions. Seeking his reinstatement in the Communist party after his expulsion for extorting sexual favors from recruits while serving in the army (193), Ober-Kandalov aims to ingratiate himself with local party officials by aiding them in the project "to realize" the natural meat reserves in the steppe. The same Ober-Kandalov presides over Avdii's murder by "crucifixion," when the latter demands that the slaughter of nature's creatures be stopped.

Another neo-Stalinist in the novel, Bazarbai Noigutov, is portrayed as equally despicable. A brutal alcoholic, he beats his wife, Tursun, so often that people in the community call her *Kok* (blue) Tursun because of her bruises (210). In the end, the reader is emotionally set up by the author to relish Boston's murder of Bazarbai and to applaud it as righteous. But, whereas Aitmatov has no intention of calling for violent reprisals against neo-Stalinists—Boston's demise and the legend of the six and the seventh make that clear—he certainly aims at engaging the readers' emotions to make all efforts to neutralize the grip of such people on Soviet society. In short, the spirit of Stalin as a modern anti-Christ pervades much of the novel. The negative characters in the work are possessed by it as if by demons.

The most powerful hypostasis of the tyrant is found in Aitmatov's portrayal of Pontius Pilate. In professing his faith in military hegemony, Pilate speaks of a world controlled by *vlasti* (the authorities) and sees "enslaving nations" and "taking away their land" as the *smysl bytiia*, the very "meaning of existence" (156). Granted, Aitmatov stresses the universality of Pilate's mentality and that of other themes, such as the ecological issue; yet as in all of his fiction, the issues raised in *The Place of the Skull* must be seen in the context of Soviet history and contemporaneity.

Avdii's religiosity and his crusade against the moral vacuum wrought by decades of dogmatic materialist ideology can be seen as Aitmatov's appeal to his compatriots to cease deluding themselves and face up to the inhumanity and moral relativism pervasive in their society as a result of the Stalinist legacy. In an interview published soon after the appearance of his novel, Aitmatov spoke of absolute moral values, passed down by generations of human civilization: "The lessons of the past offer us the means to purge the present day of mistakes so that we can see more clearly in it the fresh sprouts and signs of our tomorrow."[63] Only by tapping the moral wisdom of centuries of human civilization, including religious experience, would it be possible, in Aitmatov's view, to achieve real political and social improvements in the Soviet Union. Avdii's words on the need for repentance are to be understood precisely in this light. The fourfold tragedy in the novel—Christ's, Avdii's, Boston's, and the wolves'— show that Aitmatov had no illusions about the difficulty the Soviet Union would face in attempting to fill the moral vacuum with a new sense of responsibility for humanity and the natural world.

Conclusion

The failed coup of August 1991 represented the dying gasp of an ideology that, despite its utopian pretensions, represented a contemptuous view of humankind. The inability of KGB chief Vladimir Kriuchkov, Defense Minister Dmitrii Yazov, and their fellow plotters to crush the fledgling Soviet democracy and take the seat of the Russian parliament building—labeled Yeltsin's "White House" by Muscovites because of its white marble facade—bore eloquent testimony to the deep psychological changes in the attitudes of Soviet citizens toward their country's despotic legacy. Commenting on the victory of the democratic forces in an article in *Literaturnaia gazeta*, Alla Latynina lauds the successful defense of the parliament building by the populace of the Soviet capital with the words: "The attack on the Winter Palace has finally been repelled," implying that seventy-four years of Bolshevik rule have finally come to an end.[1] Noting the lackluster characters of the would-be dictators, she reminds her readers that for more than seven decades similarly undistinguished men have held the country in an iron grip.[2]

In the wake of the democratic victory at the Russian White House, steps were immediately taken to dismantle the powerful repressive organs of a one-party regime. Party cells were expelled from the army, the KGB, and other government organs. The powerful Writers' Union, whose complicity in the repression of Soviet writers is well documented, has for all intents and purposes ceased to exist. Its demise was hastened by evidence that some of its leading members worked to prepare the ground for the attempted August coup and then openly supported it.[3]

Economic and administrative failures are not the only reasons for the demise of the Communist party dictatorship throughout the vast Soviet state. The psychological dimension is equally important, if not fundamental, in explaining why totalitarianism disintegrated so rapidly after its final agony began. Soviet writers—I use the term *Soviet* loosely to include those who published their work abroad (*tamizdat*), those who circulated their work in *samizdat*, and writers who ran the full gauntlet of censorship to see their works appear in the official Soviet press—certainly deserve much credit for preparing the ground for the collapse of the one-party state. For uniting all these different groups was a strong rejection of the moral relativism of Soviet socialism.[4] Writers were quick to see that precisely such amorality constituted the clay feet of the seemingly all-powerful state. Throughout the 1970s and the early 1980s, Chingiz Aitmatov and other Soviet writers like Vasil' Bykau, Iurii Trifonov, Valentin Rasputin, Fazil' Iskander, Boris Mozhaev, Ion Drutse, and others hammered away at that vulnerable point. *Moral prose* (*nravstvennaia proza*) was the name given to their works by progressive Soviet critics, while "party-minded" (*ideinye*) commentators twisted and turned in efforts to co-opt the movement for socialist realism.

People of conscience raised their voices in opposition to incipient totalitarianism almost immediately following the establishment of Bolshevik rule. Some of the most important works written in the early years of the regime attacked the very essence of the utopian illusion of the revolution: Evgenii Zamiatin's novel *My* (We), Mikhail Bulgakov's *Sobachee serdtse* (Heart of a dog), and Andrei Platonov's *Kotlovan* (The foundation pit). Yet the broader struggle with the one-party state began only in 1956, the year of the Twentieth Party Congress. In that year of protest, writers increasingly demanded to know the truth about the abuses of the Stalin era and fought for the right to publish works dealing with the sensitive issues of Soviet history and contemporary life.

The same year was notable for an important literary event—the first Soviet publication of Dostoevsky's *Besy* (The possessed). While the appearance of this prophetic novel was overshadowed by Vladimir Dudintsev's celebrated *Ne khlebom edinym* (Not by bread alone), in the final analysis the nineteenth-century classic had a far greater impact on the liberation of Soviet letters from the myths of the revolution. In the words of Soviet critic Natal'ia Ivanova, the "rehabilitation" of Dostoevsky represented "a new stage in the spiritual life of [Soviet] society."[5] In *The Possessed*, Dostoevsky points to the dangers latent in social experimentation and in "the bright hopes" of nineteenth-century Russian socialists. Shigalev's dream of a harmonious future society composed of 10 percent masters and 90 percent happy slaves and Peter Verkhovenskii's idea that the cause of socialism justified the suspension of the existing moral order represent concepts that were destined to bring great tragedy to Russian society. Some forty years before the Russian Revolution, Dostoevsky foresaw what many Soviet citizens chose not to see forty years after the events of 1917. While many writers of the 1960s recognized the truth of Dostoevsky and began to delve into the roots of the ideology that led to the Russian "apocalypse,"[6] Ivanova notes that they "took fright, and backed off aghast at their newly won insights, retreating to positions that had become obsolete long ago. And in doing so they returned to their own blindness."[7]

Ivanova believes that Aleksandr Tvardovskii's *Novyi mir*, while spearheading the efforts of the Soviet intelligentsia to overcome the Stalinist legacy, ironically did much to "rehabilitate" Marxism in the Soviet Union.[8] Many of the writers who became prominent after 1956 and whose careers were closely tied to the journal were united by the hope and illusion that socialism in the Soviet Union could be democratic and have a human face. Throughout the 1960s, *Novyi mir* featured numerous pieces calling for the return to true Marxist-Leninist norms and principles. While for some writers such calls might have been merely a tactic, the majority expressed them sincerely. Their awakening came a decade later, through *samizdat* and *tamizdat* editions of the works of Aleksandr Solzhenitsyn and others. Most recently, the idea that the very ideological foundation of the revolution was immoral has found expression in the candid essay of the Soviet philosopher and publicist Aleksandr Tsipko: "Khoroshi li nashi printsipy?" (Are our principles good?). In the piece, Tsipko advocates a "shock therapy" of truth for Soviet society, because

> no one in the history of mankind has been so enslaved by myths as our people in the twentieth century. We thought that we had tied our fates to a great truth, but it turned out that we had put our faith in an intellectual fantasy that could never be incorporated into real life. We thought that we were pioneers, leading the rest of mankind to the kingdom of freedom and spiritual bliss, but it turned out that our way was the road to nowhere.[9]

Tsipko's way out of the dead end is to return to basic human values:

> Overcoming Marxist dogmatics, we must learn to love and respect not some future man, but man as he is. The impossible is impossible. That which is dead cannot come to life. There is and can be no alternative to being civilized or to the principles of civil society. There is and can be no alternative to universal human morality, to the ideals of kindness, justice, and respect for each human personality.[10]

Aitmatov's career is representative of the psychological liberation of his generation and the movement from Gorky to Dostoevsky. As a child, he was deprived of his father during the bloodletting of the 1930s, and like his peers he was subjected to the crude ideological indoctrination practiced in Soviet schools. He suffered the hardships of the war years and, after the revelations of Stalin's crimes, pinned his hopes on the restoration of "Leninist norms." As a young adult, he quickly came to condemn Stalinism. Knowledge that his father and uncles had been unjustly executed under Stalin helped Aitmatov to liberate himself psychologically from the myths surrounding the *Velikii Kormchii* (Great Helmsman), which lived on tenaciously in the minds of many Soviet citizens decades after the dictator's death. Yet moving beyond Stalin and freeing himself from the myths of the revolution was a far more difficult task. It was, no doubt, painful for Aitmatov to realize that the cause to which his father had devoted his life might somehow be tainted. In many ways, his attitude toward his father was similar to that of Iurii Trifonov, whose father, a prominent Bolshevik, was arrested and executed in the purges of 1937. Trifonov, who died in 1981, never rejected the ideals of the revolution. Instead, "he came to understand that the Bolsheviks, blurring ends and means in their quest for power, were in a large part responsible for the destruction of those ideals."[11]

Such a characterization accurately describes Aitmatov's own ambivalent feelings throughout the 1960s and 1970s. *Farewell, Gul'sary!*, written in 1966, epitomizes that state of mind. It is embodied in his hero Tanabai Bakasov, an impatient and fiery child of the revolution, whose sense of justice leads to his expulsion from the party. At the end of his life, he comes to realize that the wholesale rejection of tradition and custom, epitomized by collectivized husbandry, was immoral and foolish. The novella closes without his acceptance of an offer to be reinstated in a "reformed" Communist party. This theme—the reexamination of prerevolutionary values—would become more prominent in Aitmatov's fiction published after 1968. In *The White Ship*, for example, those who mouth Soviet values are portrayed as either rootless people or sadistic cynics, while the ancient myths and legends of the Kirghiz uplift the reader and reflect a deeply humanistic view of the world. Even in the war novella, *Early Cranes*, Aitmatov's boy heroes find inspiration not in the heroic deeds of the Red Army but in the legendary exploits of the Kirghiz epic hero Manas and his lieutenants.

The realization that the roots of Stalinism lay in the ideology of the Russian Revolution came late for Aitmatov and most of his generation, the children of the Twentieth Party Congress. In the words of Natal'ia Ivanova, "The liberation from utopianism would become the most arduous spiritual task of the generation."[12] Aitmatov joined the Communist party in 1956, the very year of the crucial party congress. For years to come, he served the party in numerous official roles, and in frequent public interviews and essays, appearing prominently in *Literaturnaia gazeta*, *Izvestiia*, and *Pravda*, he spoke out in support of Soviet policies and party resolutions. He endorsed Soviet positions in the arms control arena, justified the presence of Soviet troops in Afghanistan, and lauded the party's role in the cultural and creative life of Soviet society.[13] Aitmatov's loyalty as a party member was never questioned and in part accounts for his ability to overcome the hurdles of official censorship more successfully than many of his colleagues. His ascendency in the reform-minded Gor-

bachev regime was a natural consequence of his being a highly respected liberal writer and a good party member.

After the fall of the Soviet Union, one might question the integrity of a man so involved in the official life of the Soviet state, one
who had demonstrated willingness to make compromises, albeit
small ones, with the censors, as was the case with *The White Ship*
and *The Day Lasts More than a Hundred Years*.[14] Yet virtually no
one in the Soviet Union was immune to compromise. Moreover, it
is very likely that writers like Aitmatov saw themselves as playing the
role of Trojan horse or, to borrow an image from Kirghiz folklore,
chypalak, the Tom Thumb in *The White Ship* who, though swallowed
by a wolf, cries out from within the beast, warning the shepherds of
the predator's approach.

Arthur Miller's play *The Archbishop's Ceiling*, depicting the dilemma of writers and intellectuals living under a totalitarian regime
in an unnamed Eastern European country, exposes the naiveté of a
visiting American writer who wants perfect clarity in knowing who
occupies the moral high ground, a quick answer to the question,
Who's who? An official liberal writer in the play argues with conviction that his compromises are justified because he is keeping literature alive and preventing the country from falling even further into
darkness. A dissident writer is portrayed as unable to live without his
persecutors and must hear the bitter truth that "they are your theme,
your life, your partner in this dance that cannot stop or you will die
of silence!"[15] There may be no simple answer to the question: Who's
who? Ideas and convictions evolve and change. The ease with which
numerous prominent Soviet communists have become democrats,
may of course give rise to suspicion. Yet, for many, that transformation is sincere, being the result of inner stuggle over a long period
of time.

Like many Soviet writers of his generation, Aitmatov's awakening
and overcoming (*preodolenie*) of the mystique and myth of revolutionary utopianism occurred with the aid of Dostoevsky and, later,
Solzhenitsyn. In his discussions with Daisaku Ikeda in *Begegnung am
Fudschijama*, Aitmatov speaks of Dostoevsky's prophesies in *The
Possessed* and *Notes from the Underground* and concurs with the
author's conviction that "under no circumstances can a normal man

agree to live according to someone else's will, to be a tool in someone else's hands, a means to achieve a goal which others force upon him."[16]

Aitmatov's 1986 novel, *The Place of the Skull*, represents a watershed in the author's changing attitude toward the revolution. It soundly rejects materialist philosophy, class warfare, and the state's monopoly on thinking. As James Woodward puts it, Aitmatov is no longer disposed "to attribute the ills of Soviet society to the Stalinist perversions of a noble ideology. He now attributes them directly to the ideology itself, making no distinction between past and present and even criticizing 'new thinking' in the limited sense of economic reform."[17]

The ideology of the Bolshevik Revolution is rejected even more fundamentally in *The White Cloud of Ghengis Khan* (1990). Here, the arrogance of totalitarian thinking is exposed by exaggerating it to its logical extremes. Aitmatov shows how despotism attempts to deify itself, deludes itself into believing that it can harness all of the natural world to its will, and inevitably becomes militant and expansionistic. Like many of the cultural elite in the Soviet Union, Aitmatov has come to embrace ideas and positions arrived at earlier by Aleksandr Solzhenitsyn. *Begegnung am Fudschijama* contains praise of Solzhenitsyn's courage and recognizes his contribution to freeing Soviet thought. Aitmatov extols the Nobel laureate as an "irreconcilable opponent" to the "all-encompassing evil in the Soviet Empire."[18] Those words, no doubt, did not come easily for Aitmatov, who in 1973 had signed a petition denouncing Solzhenitsyn and Sakharov for their "attempts to cast suspicion on the peaceful policies of the Soviet state."[19]

Like Solzhenitsyn, Aitmatov expresses the belief that the October Revolution put an end to democracy in Russia and was a tragedy for the peoples of the Soviet Union. He speaks of the value of evolution over revolution:

> Revolution is mutiny, a disease of the masses, mass violence and total catastrophe for a nation, people, and society. We have learned that lesson well. Look for the way leading to democratic changes, the path of bloodless evolution. . . . Evolution requires more time, patience, and compromises. . . . I pray to God that coming generations will learn from our mistakes![20]

Like Solzhenitsyn, he speaks of the need for personal responsibility for the sins of one's age and nation and calls for the unity (*sobornost'*) of not only the Russian nation but all the nations of the world on the basis of shared spiritual values: "Today there is a need for a new world faith or new religious-cultural teaching. Throughout the long history of mankind the souls and hearts of people were divided. One needs to bring them together in common harmony. We need to do that now, or mankind will perish."[21]

The central themes in Aitmatov's fiction—the struggle with despotism, concern for the ecology, and the idea of the combined uniqueness and universality of the human experience—can be found in the works of other prominent Soviet writers of the 1960s, 1970s, and 1980s. Yet there is a pronounced and consistent apocalyptic quality in Aitmatov's vision and his expression of such issues. In his fictional world, there is a striking distinction between good and evil, and moral failings lead to the abyss. To use Ales' Adamovich's words, Aitmatov's fiction is *sverkh"literatura*, designed to shock readers out of their complacency. The author's statement quoted above, "We need to do that now, or mankind will perish," epitomizes the extremes in his world. There is no middle ground between good and evil. His despots and henchmen are thus unrelenting in their ruthlessness and arrogance. Even the petty Orozkul in *The White Ship* takes on epic proportions when his actions lead to the demise of a microcosm. On the ecological front, the killing of a doe in the same novella is likened to humankind's betrayal of a holy covenant; the dessication of the Aral Sea in *The Day Lasts More than a Hundred Years* is juxtaposed against the slow dying of a planet, and the poignant images of the mass slaughter of the steppe antelope in *The Place of the Skull* are presented in human terms and remain with the reader long after the book is closed.

Moreover, Aitmatov closely connects the ecology theme with the theme of totalitarianism's attack on humanity. In *Begegnung am Fudschijama*, Aitmatov writes that, before inciting people against people, the founders of the Soviet state first incited them against the natural world.[22] People bereft of a sense of marvel and reverence for the natural world are, in his view, destined to fall easy prey to attacks on their cultural heritage as well. This notion is embodied in a whole array of Aitmatov's Sovietized villains, beginning with Orozkul in *The White Ship*, continuing with Sabitzhan and Tansykbaev in *The Day Lasts More than a Hundred Years*, and culminating in Ober-Kandalov, the leader of a band of sadists in *The Place of the Skull*.

Opposing such villains in the cosmos of Aitmatov's fiction are heroes with rich spiritual worlds engendered by the experience of previous generations. Their concern for their national heritage is depicted not as serving shortsighted nationalistic goals but as the link tying them to values transcending the Soviet experience, that is, to *obshchechelovecheskie tsennosti* (universal human values).

Aitmatov's respect for the national heritages of the world's many peoples leads us to the most important theme in Aitmatov's mature fiction—the dream of a world recognizing the sanctity and spiritual autonomy of the individual, based on the universality of the human experience. The great ethnic diversity of the heroes in Aitmatov's fiction, which makes it unique among that of other contemporary Soviet writers, springs from just such a vision. Tanabai Bakasov is Kirghiz, Edigei Zhangel'din is an Aral Kazakh, Kiriisk and Organ are Nivkhs, and Avdii Kalistratov is Russian. Through diversity, the human condition transcends the temporal and ethnic boundaries that appear to divide people. It is the human condition, therefore, that is Aitmatov's hero: human beings struggling to find meaning in life and keenly aware of their finitude in the world.

While the portrayal of ethnic diversity is in keeping with the slogan of *druzhba narodov* (friendship of peoples), a cliché so abused by Soviet propaganda, the virtue and inspiration of Aitmatov's heroes emanate not so much from Soviet internationalism as from the pre-revolutionary values of their peoples. Aitmatov's folklore parables portray his heroes as rooted in cultures that are timeless and imbued with wisdom and beauty. While such parables give the author a useful screen for dealing with the censors and are thus part of a greater strategy designed to ensure that his fiction would become accessible to the broad Soviet readership, they are particularly representative of Aitmatov's own thinking and worldview.

In discussing Aitmatov's *The Place of the Skull*, one Soviet critic notes that the novel fails aesthetically because the writer tries to encompass the unencompassable (*ob"iat' neob"iatnoe*).[23] Although one could argue about the aesthetic merits or defects of *The Place of the Skull*, the critic accurately characterizes what Aitmatov was trying to do in the novel. Aside from uniting the human and animal worlds and merging past, present, and future in one existential time, Aitmatov seeks to bring together the worldviews of East and West. Yet the Eastern weltanschauung appears to dominate. The Eastern, cyclical view of time seems to have greater influence on the structure of the novel than the Western, linear understanding of time. Aitmatov's attitude toward the natural world is also strongly oriental, revealing a conviction that "man is an integral part of nature or the universe, and that he should not strive to set himself over and against it as having a unique form of being or destiny."[24] Nowhere is that worldview more poignantly expressed than in the ancient Kirghiz legend of *Kodzhodzhash*, a work that has continually inspired Aitmatov's fiction since *Farewell, Gul'sary!*

There is also a clear predilection for Eastern didacticism in the novel, reminiscent of that of the Kirghiz *manashchi*. As in the recitations of the epic singers of *Manas*, an air of improvisation seems to pervade Aitmatov's work, with style and composition clearly subjugated to the compelling moral message the author wants to convey to his readers.[25] Aitmatov, a Kirghiz, has come to think of himself as a bridge between East and West. In the future, he will no doubt seek to expand that role. His recent collection of essays with Daisaku Ikeda, president of the Japanese Buddhist society Soko Gakkai, testifies to that mission and to his desire to "unite the souls and hearts of people in common harmony."[26] He reports that his visit to Japan "taught him to think as an oriental" and dream of "a new world religion or a religious-cultural theology."[27]

With the end of the Soviet Union as the world has known it for the past seventy years, it will be difficult for Aitmatov to adjust his craft to the new circumstances brought about by the passing of communist rule in the Soviet Union. While he no longer has to contend with a repressive regime and its ubiquitous censors, events since 1985 continue to change his attitudes and those of his readers. He writes that "all those years of perestroika have made me view differently all which we call the literary process, including my own work. I feel as if my readers have moved to some other planet, to some other dimension. The people, as well as the milieu in which I was accustomed to work, have changed, and our criteria are now different."[28] Freedom has made the world far more unpredictable, and Aitmatov has compared his feelings to those of a man standing "in confusion before a vast plain."[29] Yet if the publication of *Begegnung am Fudschijama* is any indication, Aitmatov will work to fulfill his role as a writer as he understands it: trying to unite people on the basis of shared spiritual values, seeking the common denominators of seemingly diverse civilizations and worldviews: "The unification of people and nations, which Leo Tolstoy saw as the mission of literature, is only possible on the basis of values common to all mankind. Standing before the face of history, an artist can know no greater responsibility."[30]

Afterword

Much in the world changed during the time I was completing this study of Chingiz Aitmatov. The Soviet Union ceased to exist. As a result, the literary scene throughout its former territories changed radically. Now, writers no longer see themselves as civic-minded standard bearers seeking to correct or ameliorate malevolent government policies. The term "non-Russian Soviet writer" is no longer applicable to writers from the national republics of the former Soviet Union. No longer do those writers lead the struggle for recognition of their respective nationality's rights in a vast multinational state. Nolens volens, non-Russian writers now find themselves back in their national literatures. Aitmatov is no exception. Critics have begun to refer to him as a Kirghiz writer, although the author, who enjoys a worldwide readership, has long since outgrown that definition and sees himself as a supranational writer.

Chingiz Aitmatov has just published (November 1994), in Germany, his first novel in the post-Soviet era, *Das Kassandramal* (The Mark of Cassandra), which could not be discussed in the framework of this monograph. The new novel contains many of Aitmatov's prominent themes, reveals the author's continuing fascination with the natural world and science fiction, and reflects the deep pessimism that characterized *The Place of the Skull*.

The Mark of Cassandra is pervaded by the author's fears that humanity's noble causes and eternal drive for moral perfection seem destined to fail in the face of irrational evil, embodied in dishonest and shallow people who are easily seduced by fame and privilege and who place personal power and ambition above the good of society as a whole.

Aitmatov's readers will miss in the novel the folkloric and parabolic *podtekst* (subtext) that was so critical for his work as a Soviet writer. Indeed, one cannot escape the impression of a writer still seeking to define his role under the new conditions of freedom and market realities, and, at the same time, to inspire readers sharing his concerns for human civilization. *The Mark of Cassandra* represents an important first step into the "vast steppe" of freedom challenging the author and will, no doubt, evoke considerable critical response.

December 1994

Notes

—

Bibliography

—

Index

Notes

Preface

1. Grigorii Svirskii, *Na lobnom meste: literatura nravstvennogo soprotivleniia (1946–1976)* (London: Overseas Publishing Interchange, 1979).

Introduction

1. Chingiz Aitmatov, interview with Norman Shneidman, 7 April 1976, *Russian Literature Triquarterly* 16 (1979): 268.

2. Chingiz Aitmatov, "Veriu v cheloveka," *Pravda*, 14 February 1987, 3, 6. In the article, Aitmatov condemns the "primitive politicization" of morality that characterized Soviet life for so long.

3. Chingiz Aitmatov, interview with author, Stetson University, 9 April 1991.

4. Igor' Dedkov lists Aitmatov among the contemporary Soviet writers responsible for preparing the ground for "new thinking" in Soviet society. See Igor' Dedkov, "Literatura i novoe myshlenie," *Kommunist* 12 (August 1987): 65.

5. These themes were prominent in the work of such contemporaries as Vasil' Bykau, Iurii Trifonov, Valentin Rasputin, Boris Mozhaev, Ion Drutse, Fazil' Iskander, Nodar Dumbadze, and others.

6. See Aitmatov's initial remarks on the subject at a roundtable discussion concerning the relations between writers and political authorities. Participating in the discussion were Christa Wolf, Kenzaburo Oe, Daniil Granin, Lev Anninskii, Georgii Gachev, Vladimir Makanin, and others: "Khudozhnik i vlast'," *Inostrannaia literatura* 5 (May 1990): 177–201.

7. See Vasilii Aksenov's attack on the Russian postmodernists of the 1990s and his defense of the 1960s generation in "The Dystrophy of the 'Thick' and the *Bespredel* of the 'Thin,'" *World Literature Today* 67 (Winter 1993): 18–23. Particularly irritating to him is the recent stereotype of the *shestidesiatnik* as an "old Komsomol fool romantically sobbing away."

8. Tat'iana Ivanova speaks of such works as the "yeast" that causes the cake dough to rise, noting that when the cake is done, "no one but the baker remembers the yeast." Tat'iana Ivanova, "Igra zakonchena," *Knizhnoe obozrenie*, 31 August 1990, 4.

9. Chingiz Aitmatov, "Zhivi sam i dai zhit' drugim. Po povodu proekta Zakona o iazykakh narodov SSSR," *Literaturnaia gazeta*, 22 November 1989, 3.

10. See Keneshbek Asanaliev, "Infantil'nye kriterii," *Literaturnaia gazeta*, 4 June 1986, 6.

11. Chingiz Aitmatov, "Pochva i sud'ba: o iazyke natsional'nykh literatur," *Literaturnaia gazeta*, 8 November 1989, 3. The same tactic—publishing in Russian in

the central literary journals—was adopted by the bilingual Moldavian writer Ion Drutse because of the extreme cultural conservatism of the literary establishment in Kishinev. See Joseph P. Mozur, "Ion Drutse: Contemporary Chronicler of Bessarabian History," *World Literature Today* 60 (Winter 1987): 13–18.

12. Comment made by Denis Mickiewicz during a roundtable discussion at a conference on Soviet censorship; in *The Red Pencil. Artists, Scholars, and Censors in the USSR*, ed. Marianna Tax Choldin and Maurice Friedberg (Boston: Unwin Hyman, 1989), 106.

13. Chingiz Aitmatov, "Dukhovnaia opora," in *Chingiz Aitmatov: V soavtorstve s zemleiu i vodoiu . . . : Ocherki, stat'i, besedy, interv'iu*, ed. A. Zalutskii (Frunze: Kyrgyzstan, 1978), 344.

14. The parabolic nature of Aitmatov's novellas was first discussed by Stepan Il'ev in reference to *Farewell, Gul'sary!* and *The White Ship*. See Stepan Il'ev, "Parabolicheskie povesti Chingiza Aitmatova," *Zagadnienia Rodzajów Literackich* 20 (1977): 61–70.

15. John P. Donahue, *The Gospel in Parables* (Philadelphia: Fortress, 1988), 5.

16. Ibid., 19.

17. See Alexander Gershkovich, "Soviet Culture of the Mid-1980s: A New Thaw?" in *Red Pencil*, ed. Choldin and Friedberg, 8.

18. For the most part, the last years preceding the demise of the Soviet state witnessed the publication of important works by Soviet authors who had been repressed in the past. Although talented "new" works appeared during this time—for example, Vladimir Makanin's "Utrata," Sergei Kaledin's "Smirennoe kladbishche," Mikhail Kuraev's "Kapitan Dickstein," and short stories by Tat'iana Tolstaia—they were overshadowed by the "recovered" works of Pasternak, Platonov, Grossman, Nabokov, and others. For a survey of Soviet literature in the mid-1980s, see Aleksandr Pankov, "Esli govorit' ob ideiakh: Zametki o novoi proze serediny 80-kh," *Sibirskie ogni* 11 (November 1989): 120–29. In the early 1990s many of the important "thick" literary journals are facing extreme financial difficulties and may be forced to cease publication, thus bringing to an end a cultural tradition unique in the world, an event that, in Vasilii Aksenov's opinion, threatens to drive contemporary Russian literature into banality and *chernukha* (literature depicting the dark and repulsive). See Aksenov, "Dystrophy of the 'Thick' and the *Bespredel* of the 'Thin,' " 21–23.

19. Chingiz Aitmatov, public lecture, Stetson University, 10 April 1991.

Chapter 1. Aitmatov and Kirghizstan

1. See, for example, Usen Kasybekov, *Narodnye epicheskie traditsii i genezis kyrgyzskoi pis'mennoi prozy* (Bishkek: Ilim, 1991). Also see P. M. Mirza-Akhmedova, *Natsional'naia epicheskaia traditsiia v tvorchestve Chingiza Aitmatova* (Tashkent: Fan, 1980), 3–8.

2. As quoted in V. M. Zhirmunskii, "Vvedenie v izuchenie eposa 'Manas,' " in *Kirgizskii geroicheskii epos "Manas,"* ed. M. I. Bogdanova and V. M. Zhirmunskii (Moscow: Akademiia nauk, 1961), 86.

3. Chingiz Aitmatov, interview with author, Stetson University, 10 April 1991.

The "birth" of a *manashci* is the subject of one of Aitmatov's most lyrical short stories, "The Cry of the Migrating Bird," written in 1972.

4. Keneshbek Asanaliev, "Chingiz Aitmatov: Poetika khudozhestvennogo obraza," Ph.D. diss., Kirghiz State U., Avtoreferat, Frunze, 1989, 18.

5. The articles were written in 1952 while Aitmatov was still a student. See Chingiz Aitmatov, "O terminologii kirgizskogo iazyka," and "Perevody, dalekie ot originala," in *Chingiz Aitmatov: V soavtorstve s zemleiu i vodoiu . . . Ocherki, stat'i, besedy, interv'iu,* ed. A. Zalutskii (Frunze: Kyrgyzstan, 1978), 65–67, 68–73.

6. See Kasybekov, *Narodnye epicheskie traditsii,* 90.

7. Lev Anninskii, for example, expresses dismay at how poorly sections of *The Place of the Skull* (journal publication, 1986) were written, but then asks himself whether he is not dealing with some kind of tactic used by the author to jar the readers to attention. Lev Anninskii, "Pamiatnik momentu?" *Literaturnoe obozrenie* 5 (May 1987): 43.

8. For a brief history of the ideological controversy surrounding *Manas* in Kirghizstan, see Ishengul' Bolzhurova, "Strasti vokrug 'Manasa,' " *Literaturnyi Kyrgyzstan* 1 (January 1992): 115–25.

9. See Alexandre A. Bennigsen, "The Crisis of the Turkic National Epics, 1951–1952: Local Nationalism or Internationalism?" *Canadian Slavonic Papers* 18 (1975): 472.

10. Chingiz Aitmatov, "Osvobodit'sia ot melochei povsednevnosti," *Literaturnyi Kirgizstan* 11 (1987): 6.

11. Chingiz Aitmatov, "Snega na Manas–Ata," in *Chingiz Aitmatov: Sobranie sochinenii v trekh tomakh* (Moscow: Molodaia gvardiia, 1984), 3:199. Volume 1 was published in 1982, volume 2 in 1983, volume 3 in 1984.

12. Guy Imart, "Yesterday's Kirghizstan: The Islamic Impact on Traditional Kirghiz Ethnicity," *Nationalities Papers* 14 (Spring–Fall 1986): 67.

13. Ibid., 69.

14. Ibid., 76–79.

15. Joseph Needham, "Time and Knowledge in China and the West," in *The Voices of Time: A Cooperative Survey of Man's Views of Time as Expressed by the Sciences and by the Humanities,* ed. Julius T. Fraser (Amherst: University of Massachusetts Press, 1981), 128–35. The culture of the nomadic Kirghiz was particularly imbued with a cyclical view of time because of the constant movement from *kyshtoo* to *koktoo* and *dzhailoo* (winter, spring, and summer pastures). They migrated from the valleys to the high mountain pastures and back again according to the seasons. See Kasybekov, *Narodnye epicheskie traditsii,* 43–44.

16. John L. Russell, "Time in Christian Thought," in *The Voices of Time,* 68.

17. See Kathleen F. Parthé, *Russian Village Prose: The Radiant Past* (Princeton: Princeton University Press, 1992), 52.

18. Samuel G. F. Brandon, "Time and the Destiny of Man," in *The Voices of Time,* ed. Fraser, 154.

19. An Indian scholar notes that "among Asian peoples . . . the conception of 'telos' is absent from thought. Western ethics generally aim at teaching a man to act to a purpose, Eastern ethics at forming character: in the words of Confucius, to rectify one must achieve rectitude!" To gain that rectitude, one must measure oneself against the past. The Asian outlook is "Epimethean; . . . the 'golden age' [lies] in the

past, not in the future as the Promethean West." Asoka Menta, *Perception of Asian Personality* (New Delhi: S. Chand, 1978): 18–19.

20. Imart, "Yesterday's Kirghizstan," 83–85.

21. See Tschingis Aitmatow and Daisaku Ikeda, *Begegnung am Fudschijama. Ein Dialog*, trans. Friedrich Hitzer (Zurich: Unionsverlag, 1992): 119. In the passage condemning religious fundamentalism, Aitmatov notes that Moslem fundamentalism "is particularly striking."

22. Aitmatov, interview with author, 9 April 1991.

23. Hu Zhen-hua and Guy Imart, *A Kirghiz Reader* (Bloomington: Indiana University, Research Institute for Inner Asian Studies, 1989), 214.

24. Chingiz Aitmatov, "Zametki o sebe," in *Chingiz Aitmatov: Sobranie sochinenii* 3:108. All biographical information on Aitmatov in this chapter is from this source, unless otherwise indicated.

25. For more on Torekul Aitmatov and the political situation in Central Asia, see Joseph P. Mozur, *Doffing "Mankurt's Cap": Chingiz Aitmatov's "The Day Lasts More than a Hundred Years" and the Turkic National Heritage* (Pittsburgh: University of Pittsburgh, Center for Russian and East European Studies, 1987): 6–12.

26. Northern Kirghizstan alone is reported to have lost 41.4 percent of its native population as a result of the rebellion and subsequent reprisals by Slavic settlers and the tsarist authorities. See Kushpek Usenbaev, *Vosstanie 1916 goda v Kirgizii* (Frunze: Ilim, 1967), 249.

27. Published biographical information on Torekul Aitmatov is scarce. A small article on his party positions appears in the Kirghiz encyclopedia: *Kyrgyz Sovet Entsiklopediiasy*, ed. Asanbek Tabaldiev (Frunze: Kyrgyz SSR Ilimler akademikilasy, 1976). See also Abdyldazhan Akmataliev, *Chingiz Aitmatov: Zhizn' i tvorchestvo: Kratkii ocherk* (Bishkek: Mektep, 1991), 8–9.

28. Aitmatov, interview with author, 9 April 1991.

29. Aitmatov's yearning for a lost father is, of course, not unique in contemporary Soviet literature. Among the more prominent Soviet writers losing parents during the Great Terror were Vasilii Aksenov, Bulat Okudzhava, and Iurii Trifonov. Trifonov, for example, was thirteen years old when his father, Valentin Aleksandrovich Trifonov, a prominent Bolshevik, was arrested and later liquidated. Trifonov spent years looking through government archives trying to "resurrect" his father by learning as much as he could about his life and contribution to the Soviet state. Those efforts resulted in a documentary work, *Otblesk kostra* (Reflection of the fire), 1965, in which Trifonov sought to vindicate his father's name. See Colin Partridge, *Yuri Trifonov's "The Moscow Cycle": A Critical Study* (Lewiston, N.Y.: Edwin Mellen, 1990), 6–9. Aitmatov has also expressed his desire to write a book about his father, but to date the project remains unrealized. Chingiz Aitmatov, "Otvetstvennost' pered budushchim," in *Chingiz Aitmatov: V soavtorstve*, 120.

30. Chingiz Aitmatov, interview with author, Duke University, 13 April 1991.

31. Ibid.

32. Chingiz Aitmatov, "Preodolet' sebia," *Literaturnaia gazeta*, 11 September 1991, 9.

33. Ibid. Among those executed was Kasym Tynystanov, prominent Kirghiz scholar and linguist. A virtual symbol of culture and enlightenment in the region, Tynystanov was an ardent supporter of the Latin alphabet in Kirghizstan. The exe-

cuted were accused of belonging to the fictitious Turan Social party, whose purported goal was "to bring down the young Soviet state by armed insurrection, withdraw Kirghizia from the USSR, and to create a bourgeois republic under the hegemony of Great Britain." See Kabai Karabekov, "Ustanovleny imena," *Vechernii Bishkek*, 1 August 1991, 1.

34. Aitmatov, "Preodolet' sebia," 9.

35. R. Khelimskaia, "Taina bol'shogo kamnia," *Slovo Kyrgyzstana*, 17 August 1991, 4. Published in the article are materials from Torekul Aitmatov's KGB file, no. 4418. These include biographical information on the arrested, as well as letters from Nagima Aitmatova and Chingiz requesting information on the place of Torekul's incarceration.

36. Aitmatov, interview with author, 13 April 1991. Another paternal uncle, Alymkul, was also later arrested. Like Ryskulbek, he was never heard from again.

37. Aitmatov, "Preodolet' sebia," 9.

38. Aitmatov, "Zametki o sebe," 113.

39. Aitmatov, interview with author, 13 April 1991.

40. Aitmatov, "Snega na Manas-Ata," 202.

41. Aitmatov, interview with author, 13 April 1991.

42. Aitmatov refers to the common grave found near Bishkek as "yet another Katyn' " ("Preodolet' sebia," 9).

Chapter 2. First Steps

1. Chingiz Aitmatov, "Zametki o sebe," in *Chingiz Aitmatov: Sobranie sochinenii v trekh tomakh*, ed. S. Shevelev (Moscow: Molodaia gvardiia, 1984), 3:115.

2. The articles reveal a very serious approach to technical and literary translation, and are devastating in their criticism of several existing Kirghiz translations of Aleksandr Griboedov and Nikolai Nekrasov. See Chingiz Aitmatov, "O terminologii kirgizskogo iazyka" and "Perevody, dalekie ot originala," in *Chingiz Aitmatov: V soavtorstve s zemleiu i vodoiu . . . Ocherki, stat'i, besedy, interv'iu*, ed. A. Zalutskii (Frunze: Kyrgyzstan, 1978), 65–67, 68–73.

3. For information on Kirghiz and Russian editions of Aitmatov's fiction from 1952 to 1987, see *Chingiz Aitmatov. Rekomendatel'nyi bibliograficheskii ukazatel'*, ed. Ol'ga S. Sukhomlinova (Frunze: Goskomizdat Kirgizskoi SSR, 1988).

4. Chingiz Aitmatov, "Otvetstvennost' pered budushchim," in *Chingiz Aitmatov: V soavtorstve*, ed. Zalutskii, 114.

5. Chingiz Aitmatov, "Gazetchik Dziuio," *Al'manakh Kirgizstan* 2 (1952): 76.

6. Chingiz Aitmatov, interview with author, Duke University, 13 April 1991.

7. Katerina Clark, "Political History and Literary Chronotope: Some Soviet Case Studies," in *Literature and History. Theoretical Problems and Russian Case Studies*, ed. Gary Saul Morson (Stanford: Stanford University Press, 1986), 231.

8. Ibid., 233.

9. Geoffrey Hosking, *Beyond Socialist Realism* (London: Granada, 1980), 197.

10. See Larisa Lebedeva, "Nerazdelennye kontrasty," in *Chingiz Aitmatov: Stat'i retsenzii o ego tvorchestve*, ed. Kerimkul Abdyldabekov (Frunze: Kyrgyzstan, 1975), 301.

11. Aitmatov was one of three young Kirghiz writers chosen by the head of the

Kirghiz Writers' Union, Aziz Saliev, for the honor of studying in Moscow (Abdyld-azhan Akmataliev, director of the Kirghiz Institute of Art and Literature, interview with the author, Bishkek, 19 June 1992).

12. *Kyrgyzstan madaniiaty*, 12 December 1978, quoted in Abdyldazhan Akmataliev, *Chingiz Aitmatov: zhizn' i tvorchestvo. Kratkii ocherk* (Bishkek: Mektep, 1991), 24.

13. The situation is autobiographical. During World War II, Aitmatov's mother had to struggle to feed her four children in Sheker. The relatives gave her a young cow which, when mature, would provide the family with milk. Just as the cow was about to produce the long-awaited milk, someone stole it (Aitmatov, interview with author, 13 April 1991).

14. See Heinz Plavius, "Gespräch mit Tschingis Aitmatow: Mensch und Welt in der Prosa der 70er Jahre," *Weimarer Beiträge* 2 (February 1977): 60–61.

15. Chingiz Aitmatov, interview with author, Stetson University, 9 April 1991.

16. Chingiz Aitmatov, introduction to *Litsom k litsu, Literaturnyi Kirgizstan*, March 1990, 7.

17. Louis Aragon, "The Finest Love Story in the World," *Culture and Life* 7 (July 1959): 39–43.

18. "Classic socialist realism" refers to the rigid literary method promoted by Communist party ideologues in the Soviet Union during the Stalin era. Frequently, those who sought to control literary activity would point writers to established and "recognized" (by the party) models. Among such models held up for emulation were Fedor Gladkov's *Tsement* (Cement), 1925; Nikolai Ostrovskii's *Kak zakalialas' stal'* (How the steel was tempered), 1934; Aleksandr Fadeev's *Molodaia gvardiia* (The young guard), 1946, 1951; Boris Polevoi's *Povest' o nastoiashchem cheloveke* (A story about a real man), 1946; and Vsevolod Kochetov's *Zhurbiny* (The Zhurbins), 1952. Such models display a sort of "master plot" that allegorically reflects what the ideologues believed to be the triumphant and inevitable march of history toward communism. Playing a key role in the master plot was the "positive hero" who, with the aid and inspiration of the Communist party, manages to overcome his private self, as well as any other obstacles in his way, in order to take on and successfully complete a "public task." Optimism, of course, was the primary mood pervading such literature. The use of nonrealistic elements, such as the fantastic, was taboo.

Although Stalin's death and the Thaw did much to weaken the slavish application of the method by Soviet writers, conservative writers, critics, and ideologues continued to espouse its principles until the 1980s. The presentation of Soviet literature in school text books was also influenced for decades by the principles of classic socialist realism. See Katerina Clark, *The Soviet Novel: History as Ritual* (Chicago: University of Chicago Press, 1985).

19. Chingiz Aitmatov, "Gorzhus' moim sovremennikom," in *Chingiz Aitmatov: V soavtorstve*, ed. Zalutskii, 99. Yevgenii Yevtushenko said that several years after Aitmatov penned the open letter, he asked Yevtushenko to forgive him for publishing it. According to Yevtushenko, the letter no doubt gained Aitmatov allies in the Moscow literary establishment who were able to help him with cultural conservatives back in Kirghizstan (Yevgenii Yevtushenko, interview with author, Springhill College, Mobile, Alabama, 4 January 1993).

20. It might be noted that Solzhenitsyn's *Matrenin dvor* (Matryona's house),

1963, published somewhat later, reveals a similar philosophy and would provide much inspiration for Village Prose in the 1970s.

21. See Saul Abramzon, *Kirgizy i ikh etnogeneticheskie i istoriko-kul'turnye sviazi* (Leningrad: Nauka, 1971), 275–80. Also refer to Toktobiubiu D. Baialieva, *Doislamskie verovaniia i ikh perezhitki u Kirgizov* (Frunze: Ilim, 1972), 45–46.

22. Chingiz Aitmatov, "Materinskoe pole," in *Chingiz Aitmatov: Sobranie sochinenii* 1:343.

23. Pavel Glinkin, *Chingiz Aitmatov* (Leningrad: Prosveshchenie, 1968), 69.

24. From 1961 to 1985, political power in the republic was wielded by Turdakun Usubaliev, first secretary of the Communist party of Kirghizstan. His rule was distinguished by strict loyalty to Moscow and an active policy of Russification. Literary works critical of central policies or conditions in the republic had little chance of appearing in print. Aitmatov thus found it easier to publish his controversial works first in Moscow and then "return" them to Kirghizstan in his own Kirghiz translations.

One event in particular provoked the anger of the Kirghiz political establishment and made it difficult for Aitmatov to publish in his native republic—the premiere in 1966 of a film by Andrei Mikhalkov-Konchalovskii, based on Aitmatov's script of his novella *The First Teacher*. Aziz Saliev, head of the Kirghiz Writers' Union and later Central Committee member responsible for cultural issues in the republic, asked Aitmatov not to release the movie because of its "graphic" content and its negative portrayal of Kirghiz reality. Aitmatov refused, and Saliev became one of Aitmatov's most vocal critics in Kirghizstan (Akmataliev, interview with the author, 19 June 1992). Saliev would later condemn *Farewell, Gul'sary!* and *The White Ship* for Aitmatov's distortion of the "age-old poetic traditions of the Kirghiz nation." See Keneshbek Asanaliev, "Traditsii—dukh ili bukva," *Literaturnaia gazeta*, 30 August 1972, 4. Also highly revealing of Aitmatov's difficulties with the Kirghiz cultural establishment in the late 1960s is the fact that from 1966 to 1975 no theater productions of Aitmatov's work were staged anywhere in the republic. See Dzhukun Imankulov, *Iskusstvo teatra. Proizvedeniia Chingiza Aitmatova na stsenakh teatrov respublik srednei Azii i Kazakhstana* (Frunze: Kyrgyzstan, 1985), 120–25.

25. Aitmatov, "Orbity vzaimodeistviia," in *V soavtorstve*, 283.

Chapter 3. *Farewell, Gul'sary!* Coming to Terms with the Stalinist Past

1. It has been suggested that Sholokhov's role in condemning the two writers and his calling for more severe punishment might have been partly motivated by the fact that the trial had "diverted attention from his reception of the Nobel Prize." See John Garrard and Carol Garrard, *Inside the Soviet Writers' Union* (New York: Free Press, 1990), 141.

2. See Alexandr Solzhenitsyn, *Bodalsia telenok s dubom: ocherki literaturnoi zhizni* (Paris: YMCA Press, 1975), 147–49. Both works were written in 1965. Aitmatov published several chapters of his novella in the April 1965 issue of *Literaturnyi Kirgizstan* under the title "Smert' inokhodtsa" (The death of an ambler). See Chingiz Aitmatov, commentary to *Farewell, Gul'sary!* in *Chingiz Aitmatov. Sobranie sochinenii v trekh tomakh*, ed. S. Shevelev (Moscow: Molodaia gvardiia, 1982), 1:605.

3. See Alexandr Tvardovskii, "Pis'mo K. Fedinu o Solzhenitsyne," 7–15 ianvaria 1968 goda, in *Sobranie dokumentov samizdata*, Radio Liberty AS-41, 1:3–4.

4. On the eve of the Twenty-third Party Congress (April 1966), the appearance of several pro-Stalinist newspaper articles in the Soviet press prompted a group of twenty-five prominent Soviet citizens to send a letter to Leonid Brezhnev, warning him of the dangerous consequences for the USSR of any efforts to rehabilitate Stalin. Among those signing were Andrei Sakharov, Viktor Nekrasov, Konstantin Paustovskii, and Valentin Kataev. For the text of the letter, see "Reabilitatsiia Stalina vyzvala by volnenie," *Posev*, 16 September 1966, 1.

5. See Aleksandr Zyrin, "Vremia, sud'ba, kharakter," *Zvezda* 2 (February 1967), 212; and S. Krutilin, "Obida Tanabaia," in *Chingiz Aitmatov (Stat'i i retsenzii o ego tvorchestve)*, ed. K. Abdyldabekov (Frunze: Kyrgyzstan, 1975), 228.

6. Typical of this position is the review of Georgii Radov, "Tanabai, drug Aitmatova," *Komsomolskaia pravda*, 6 May 1966, in *Chingiz Aitmatov (Stat'i i retsenzii o ego tvorchestve)*, ed. Abdyldabekov, 204.

7. N. Kruzhkov, "Tanabai dogonit svoikh," in *Chingiz Aitmatov: stat'i i retsenzii o ego tvorchestve*, ed. Abdyldabekov, 230. See also Nikolai Tikhonov, "Pafos tvorchestva—zhizn' naroda," *Pravda*, 10 November 1968; and Eduard Skobelev, "Put' Tanabaia," *Oktiabr'* 2 (February 1967): 210–13.

8. See A. Buchis, "Nad kartoi kritiki," *Druzhba narodov* 3 (March 1967): 238.

9. Georg Lukács, *Solzhenitsyn*, trans. William David Graf (Cambridge: MIT Press, 1970), 88.

10. See Keneshbek Asanaliev, *Otkrytie cheloveka sovremennosti. Zametki o tvorchestve Chingiza Aitmatova* (Frunze: Kyrgyzstan, 1968), 125.

11. Georgii D. Gachev, "O natsional'nykh kartinakh mira," *Narody Afriki i Azii* 1 (1967): 84.

12. See Mukhtar Auezov, "Kirgizskaia narodnaia geroicheskaia poema 'Manas'," in *Kirgizskii geroicheskii epos "Manas,"* ed. M. I. Bogdanova and V. M. Zhirmunskii (Moscow: Akademiia nauk, 1961), 65.

13. See M. Borbugulov, "Dzhanybar—imeiushchii dushu," in *Chingiz Aitmatov: Stat'i i retsenzii*, ed. Abdyldabekov, 255.

14. Gachev, "O natsional'nykh kartinakh mira," 85.

15. The word *inokhodets* also conjures up the Russian word for dissident—*inakomysliashchii*, which appropriately characterizes Tanabai's questioning of the authorities throughout much of the novella.

16. See Gachev, "O natsional'nykh kartinakh mira," 83. Gachev believes that the fear of enclosures goes back deep into the Kirghiz consciousness and is connected with their nomadic way of life. Aitmatov's last three works reveal his preference for open spaces—in *The Piebald Dog* it is the open sea, in *The Day Lasts More than a Hundred Years* and *The Place of the Skull* it is the steppes and mountains of Kazakhstan and Kirghizstan.

17. Chingiz Aitmatov, *Proshchai, Gul'sary!*, in *Chingiz Aitmatov. Sobranie sochinenii*, 1:382. Hereafter all references to the novella will be given in the text by page number.

18. See Toktobiubiu Baialieva, *Doislamskie verovaniia i ikh perezhitki u kirgizov* (Frunze, Ilim, 1972), 16–17.

19. Ibid., p. 18.

20. *Kodzhodzhash* (excerpt), trans. Mark Tarkovskii, in *Antologiia kirgizskoi poezii*, ed. K. Rakhmatullin and Tugel'bai Sydykbekov (Moscow: Gosizdatel'stvo khudozhestvennoi literatury, 1957), 85–92. Aitmatov has inspired another modern version of the ancient myth in the work of contemporary Kirghiz writer Mar Baidzhiev: *Odnazhdy ochen' davno* (Frunze: Mektep, 1984), 5–78.

21. Chingiz Aitmatov, speech presented at the Twenty-third Party Congress, *Pravda*, 9 July 1990, 2.

22. One of the variants of the lament, "Plach verbliuditsy, poteriavshei verbliuzhonka," (translated from the Kirghiz by Andrei Globa) can be found in *Antologiia kirgizskoi poezii*, ed. Rakhmatullin and Sydykbekov, 118.

23. Baialieva, *Doislamskie verovaniia*, 30.

24. "The Lament of the She-Camel" appeared earlier in Tugel'bai Sydykbekov's *Sredi gor* (In the mountains), 1955–1958. In his novel, however, the lament fulfills ornamental and illustrative functions, unlike in *Farewell, Gul'sary!* See P. M. Mirza-Akhmedova, *Natsional'naia epicheskaia traditsiia v tvorchestve Chingiza Aitmatova* (Tashkent: Fan, 1980), 20–21. Interestingly, in his criticism of Aitmatov at the 1966 Congress of the Kirghiz Writers' Union, Sydykbekov accused Aitmatov of precisely the oriental exoticism he himself had practiced.

25. Sheelagh Duffin Graham, "Chingiz Aitmatov's *Proshchay, Gul'sary!*," *Journal of Russian Studies* 49 (1985): 24.

26. In his discussion of Aesopian devices and texts, Lev Loseff speaks of the Aesopian text's system of "screens" and "markers." The former "are bent on concealing the Aesopian text," while the latter "draw attention to that same Aesopian text." Pointing to the inevitable "dual nature of an Aesopian utterance," Loseff notes that frequently both screen and marker can be realized in the same textual elements. Lev Loseff, *On The Beneficence of Censorship. Aesopian Language in Modern Russian Literature* (Munich: Verlag Otto Sagner, 1984), 51–52. That ambiguity is typical of Aitmatov's use of animal stories and folklore legends throughout his prose fiction. The parabolic subplot in Aitmatov's prose screens the Aesopian message while at the same time drawing the reader's attention to its presence in the text.

Chapter 4. *The White Ship*: Outcry in a Soulless World

1. See "Protiv chego vystupaet *Novyi mir*," *Ogonek* 30 (1969), 26–28. Signing the open letter were Petr Proskurin, Sergei Voronin, Vitalii Zakrutkin, Mikhail Alekseev, Vladimir Chivilikhin, and others.

2. The January 1970 issue of *Novyi mir* was the last one that Tvardovskii personally initialed for publication. On Tvardovskii's last days as editor, see Boris Zaks, "O Tvardovskom i starom *Novom mire* (stranitsy vospominanii)," *Russkaia mysl'*, 31 March 1983, 8–9, and *Russkaia mysl'*, 8 April 1983, 8–9.

3. Of course, historical subjects could be used effectively against the country's totalitarian authorities. Bulat Okudzhava's historical novels *Glotok Svobody* (A Taste of Liberty) (Moscow: Politizdat, 1971) and *Pokhozhdenie Shipova ili starinnyi vodevil'* (Merci, or the adventures of Shipov) (Moscow: Sovetskii Pisatel', 1975), make allusions to Soviet efforts to crush independent thinking. Similarly, throughout the 1970s and early 1980s, Vasil' Bykau's novels dealing with World War II would portray Stalinist attitudes on the battlefield as dehumanizing and treacherous.

4. Chingiz Aitmatov, "Tochka prisoedineniia," *Chingiz Aitmatov. Sobranie sochinenii v trekh tomakh*, ed. S. Shevelev (Moscow: Molodaia gvardiia, 1983), 3:403.

5. Mikhail Bulgakov, *Master i Margarita, Moskva* 11 (November 1966), 7–127, and 1 (January 1967), 56–144. Although there are a number of theories why *Master i Margarita* suddenly appeared in 1966, the year of the Siniavskii-Daniel trial, most probably party authorities suddenly felt compelled to placate the frustrated liberals and at the same time to deflect attention from Solzhenitsyn. See also Andrew Barratt, *Between Two Worlds: A Critical Introduction to The Master and Margarita* (Oxford: Clarendon, 1987), 36–37.

6. Aitmatov, "Tochka prisoedineniia," 405.

7. Chingiz Aitmatov, *Belyi parokhod (Posle skazki)*, in *Chingiz Aitmatov. Sobranie sochinenii*, 2:114. Hereafter all references to this edition of the novella will be given in the text by page number.

8. The words also serve as the title for Dobroliubov's 1860 essay on Ostrovskii's play. See Nikolai Dobroliubov, "Luch solntse v temnom tsarstve," in *Izbrannye stat'i* (Moscow: Sovetskaia Rossiia, 1978).

9. See Anuar Alimzhanov, "Tragediia na lesnom kordone," *Literaturnaia gazeta*, 8 July 1970, 5.

10. D. Starikov, "Ne skazkoi edinoi . . . ," *Literaturnaia gazeta*, 1 July 1970, 5.

11. See Aitmatov, "Neobkhodimye utochneniia," in *Chingiz Aitmatov. Sobranie sochinenii*, 3:382.

12. Ibid., 381.

13. Ibid., 382.

14. The first book edition of the novella appeared in 1970 in a selected collection of Aitmatov's works: *Povesti i rasskazy* (Moscow: Molodaia gvardiia, 1970).

15. See also Stepan Il'ev, "Parabolicheskie povesti Chingiza Aitmatova," *Zagadnienia Rodzajów Literackich* 20 (1977): 67. A different version of this fairy tale can be found in *Kirgizskie narodnye skazki*, trans. and comp. D. Brudnyi and K. Eshmambetov (Frunze: Kyrgyzstan, 1981), 230–31.

16. See Alimzhanov, "Tragediia na lesnom kordone," 5. Aziz Saliev also accuses Aitmatov of distorting Kirghiz folklore and attempting to "cast a shadow on the bright ideals of national legends." See Keneshbek Asanaliev, "Traditsii—dukh ili bukva," *Literaturnaia gazeta*, 30 August 1972, 4.

17. Aitmatov, "Neobkhodimye utochneniia," 383.

18. Vladimir Soloukhin, "Skazki pishut dlia khrabrykh," *Literaturnaia gazeta*, 1 July 1970, 5.

19. See Aitmatov, "My izmeniaem mir, mir izmeniaet nas," *Chingiz Aitmatov. Sobranie sochinenii*, 3:327.

20. See Toktobiubiu Baialieva, *Doislamskie verovaniia i ikh perezhitki u Kirgizov* (Frunze: Ilim, 1972), 149.

21. See James G. Frazer, *Totemism* (Edinburgh: Adam and Charles Black, 1887), 7.

22. See Chokhan Valikhanov, "Istoricheskie predaniia dikokamennykh Kirgiz," in *Izbrannye proizvedeniia*, ed. A. Kh. Margulan (Alma-Ata: Kazakhskoe gos. izdatel'stvo khudozh. lit., 1958), 297–305.

23. See Saul Abramzon, *Kirgizy i ikh etnogeneticheskie i istoriko-kul'turnye sviazi* (Leningrad: Nauka, 1971), 282.

24. See Valikhanov, "Istoricheskie predaniia dikokamennykh Kirgiz," 301.

25. Ibid., 297–98.

26. Ibid.

27. See K. Kasper, "Der menschheitsgeschichtliche Anspruch der Erzählungen Cingiz Ajtmatov," *Zeitschrift für Slawistik* 1 (1976), 70.

28. Today, the tribe is one of the largest subnational groups of the Kirghiz.

29. Ethnographers have established two different Kirghiz home territories. The earliest homeland was apparently in southern Siberia, on the Enisei River; at a later period, a second homeland emerged in the eastern part of Central Asia, in the mountains of Tian'-Shan and Pamiro-Altai. Some historians hypothesize a migration from Siberia to Issyk-kul'. See Abramzon, *Kirgizy*, 10–15. This hypothesis finds expression in Aitmatov's myth of the Deer-mother in *The White Ship*.

30. See also Alimzhanov, "Tragediia na lesnom kordone," 5.

31. For color and number symbolism in *The White Ship*, see Joseph P. Mozur, "Chingiz Aitmatov and the Poetics of Moral Prose," Ph.D. diss., University of North Carolina, 1983, 110–14.

32. Baialieva, *Doislamskie verovaniia*, 154.

33. See Tatyana and George Feifer, afterword to Chingiz Aitmatov, *The White Steamship*, trans. Tatyana Feifer and George Feifer (London: Hodder and Stoughton, 1972), 184.

34. I was alerted to this connotation by Abdyldazhan Akmataliev, director of the Kirghiz Institute of Literature and Art.

35. F. Papp, "Dva aspekta analiza khudozhestvennoi struktury povesti Chingiza Aitmatova 'Posle skazki (Belyi parokhod)'," *Slavia* 12 (December 1972): 147.

36. See Lev Arutiunov, "Vzaimodeistvie literatur i problema novatorstva," in *Edinstvo, rozhdennoe v bor'be i trude*, ed. V. M. Ozerov (Moscow: Izvestiia, 1972), 205–07.

37. Norman Shneidman, *Soviet Literature in the 1970s: Artistic Diversity and Ideological Conformity* (Toronto: University of Toronto Press, 1979), 39.

Chapter 5. Aitmatov in the 1970s: Confronting and Transcending Soviet Reality

1. See Heinz Plavius, "Gespräch mit Tschingis Aitmatow. Mensch und Welt in der Prosa der siebziger Jahre," *Weimarer Beiträge* 2 (1977), 46–47. This important interview appeared in abridged form in Russian in *Novyi mir* 12 (December 1977): 242–59. Passages that did not appear in the Russian deal with Aitmatov's criticism of the purists of socialist realism, who, in his opinion, were hurting the development of Soviet literature.

2. In actuality, Buddhists do not confess their sins to Mount Fuji. The ascent alone is popularly believed to cleanse the senses and increase longevity.

3. Chingiz Aitmatov and Kaltai Mukhamedzhanov, *The Ascent of Mount Fuji*, trans. Nicholas Bethell (New York: Farrar, Straus and Giroux, 1975), 53. The volume also contains both the original Russian and the English translation of the play. Hereafter all references to the play are from this volume and are given in the text by page. To my knowledge, the play was never published in the Soviet Union.

4. The lines are spoken by Osipbai Tataev, director of the historical institute

in the play. Out of respect for his power in the republic, some of the characters address him as Iosif Tataevich, the Russified version of his name. Needless to say, the Russian form of the name and patronymic seems to evoke Iosif (Joseph) Stalin. *Tata* (or *tiatia*) in Russian is a colloquial form for *father*, which thus conjures up the phrase *otets narodov* (father of the peoples), often used in reference to Stalin.

5. Hedrick Smith, "New Soviet Play Probes Issue of Collective Guilt for Stalinism," *New York Times*, 25 February 1973, sec. 1, 5.

6. Konstantin Simonov, "Strogoe iskusstvo," *Izvestiia*, 2 February 1973, 4.

7. Arkadii Anastas'ev, "Vysota nravstvennosti," *Literaturnaia gazeta*, 28 February 1973, 8.

8. Smith, "New Soviet Play."

9. Jack Kroll, "Ascent and Dissent," *Newsweek*, 30 June 1975, 44.

10. Rasputin's novel first appeared in the October 1974 issue of *Nash sovremennik*. It came out in book form in 1975 and was featured in the anniversary issue (May 1975) of the journal *Moskva*.

11. Virtually the same conflict is the subject of Aitmatov's *Face to Face* (1958), but as was pointed out in the discussion of Aitmatov's novella, Rasputin's plot resolution is more convincing.

12. Chingiz Aitmatov, *Rannie zhuravli*, in *Chingiz Aitmatov: Sobranie sochinenii v trekh tomakh*, ed. S. Shevelev (Moscow: Molodaia gvardiia, 1982), 1:514. Hereafter, all references to this work will be given in the body of the text by page number.

13. See Aitmatov, "Snega na Manas-Ata," in *Chingiz Aitmatov: Sobranie sochinenii*, 3:209–10.

14. The summaries of the plots of *Early Cranes* and *The Piebald Dog* are adapted from Joseph P. Mozur, "Chingiz Aitmatov: Transforming the Esthetics of Socialist Realism," *World Literature Today* 56 (1982), 435–39.

15. For a discussion of the symbolism of rite of passage in the Soviet novel, see Katerina Clark, *The Soviet Novel: History as Ritual* (Chicago: University of Chicago Press, 1985), 167–76.

16. Chingiz Aitmatov, "Zametki o sebe," in *V soavtorstve s zemleiu i vodoiu . . . Ocherki, stat'i, besedy, interv'iu*, ed. A. Zalutskii (Frunze: Kyrgyzstan, 1978), 106.

17. Chingiz Aitmatov, *Belyi parokhod*, in *Chingiz Aitmatov: Sobranie sochinenii*, 2:77.

18. See "Semetei" (excerpt), in *Antologiia kirgizskoi poezii*, ed. K. Rakhmatullin and Tugel'bai Sydykbekov (Moscow: Gosudarstvennoe izdatel'stvo khudozhestvennoi literatury, 1957), 48–54. See also V. M. Zhirmunskii, "Vvedenie v izuchenie eposa 'Manas'," in *Kirgizskii geroicheskii epos "Manas,"* ed. M. I. Bogdanova and V. M. Zhirmunskii (Moscow: Akademiia nauk, 1961), 172–73.

19. See Zhirmunskii, "Vvedenie," 182.

20. See lexical note in *Manas: kirgizskii geroicheskii epos*, ed. A. S. Sadykov, S. M. Musaev, and A. S. Mirbadaleva (Moscow: Nauka, 1988), 2:668.

21. See Z. G. Osmanova, *Khudozhestvennaia kontseptsiia lichnosti v literature vostoka* (Moscow: Nauka, 1972), 212.

22. In an interview with Norman Shneidman a year before the appearance of *The Piebald Dog*, Aitmatov commented on the complicated interaction between

socialist realist theory and literary practice in the Soviet Union: "The literary output of contemporary writers is ahead of the theoretical premises for contemporary literature. . . . The interaction of theory and practice in the Soviet Union is often complicated because certain representatives of the past in our literature endeavor to hold back its development." Chingiz Aitmatov, interview with N. N. Shneidman, 7 April 1976, *Russian Literature Triquarterly* 16 (1979): 268.

23. The Kirghiz mountain, Ala-too, which overlooks Bishkek, means "piebald mountain." Aitmatov "transfers" his native mountain to the shores of the Sea of Okhotsk.

24. A similar totemistic myth based on the union of man and fish is central to the plot of Iurii Rytkheu's *Kogda kity ukhodiat*, *Novyi mir* 7 (1975), 95–151. Rytkheu's "modern legend" is set in Chutkotka, on the shores of the Bering Sea.

25. Chingiz Aitmatov, *Pegii pes, begushchii kraem moria*, in *Chingiz Aitmatov: Sobranie sochinenii*, 2:135. Hereafter all references to this work will be given in the text by page number.

26. Chingiz Aitmatov, "Dukhu Khel'sinki al'ternativy net," in *Chingiz Aitmatov: Sobranie sochinenii*, 3:122.

27. Interestingly, in Chinese mythology, the world will come to an end when a crocodile swallows the sun.

28. The opposition between the land and the sea stems not from Nivkh mythology but from the author. See A. Rudenko, "Vladimir Sangi: Legenda, sozdannaia zanova: Dialog kritika i prozaika," *Druzhba narodov* 1 (1978), 256.

29. Organ, for example, "returns" to the sea, to the great Fish-woman.

30. The image has a remarkable similarity to the myth of the pelican in Western religion and culture. The mother pelican was believed to pierce her own breast with her sharp beak in order to feed her young with her own blood. This act of sacrifice became a frequent symbol for Christ's sacrifice for humankind. The myth predates Christianity by many centuries, however, and was recorded in the ancient Greek *Physiologus*. See Gilbert Cope, *Symbolism in the Bible and the Church* (New York: Philosophical Library, 1959), 56.

31. Rudenko, "Vladimir Sangi: Legenda, sozdannaia zanova," 257.

32. Ibid., 257.

33. See Keneshbek Asanaliev, *Chingiz Aitmatov: poetika khudozhestvennogo obraza*, Ph.D. diss, Kirghiz State University, Avtoreferat, Frunze, 1989, 21–22.

34. Rudenko, "Vladimir Sangi: Legenda, sozdannaia zanova," 257.

35. Vladimir Sangi notes that Aitmatov breaks with the animistic worldview of the Nivkh when he portrays the idea of humanity struggling between two opposing elements (land and sea). For the Nivkh people, nature is one unbroken continuum. By the same token, Mylgun's Jobian blasphemy of the wind-god in *The Piebald Dog* is inconsistent with the primal religion of the Nivkh. See ibid., 256–57.

36. Anatolii Bocharov, "Svoistvo, a ne zhupel," *Voprosy literatury* 5 (May 1977): 70–71.

37. Ibid., 69.

38. Lev Anninskii, "Zhazhdu belletrizma!" *Literaturnaia gazeta*, 1 March 1978, 5.

39. Aleksei Kondratovich, "Muzu v tumane," *Literaturnaia gazeta*, 12 April 1978), 5.

40. See Aitmatov, "Kirpichnoe mirozdanie ili energiia mifa," in *Chingiz Aitmatov: V soavtorstve*, 394.

41. Ibid., 397. Aitmatov would also refer to the "magical realism" of the popular Latin American writer Gabriel García Márquez. Soviet writers and critics of the time referred to the fiction of García Márquez, a socialist, to justify their demands for more experimentation in Soviet literature. Aitmatov spoke of García Márquez as offering new aesthetic possibilites for socialist realism. See Plavius, "Gespräch mit Tschingis Aitmatov," 35–36.

42. This is also the position of Murat Auezov, whose article in *Literaturnaia gazeta* concludes the paper's discussion of the use of the mythological in Soviet letters. See Murat Auezov, "Ostaetsia podlinnaia zhizn'," *Literaturnaia gazeta*, 7 June 1978, 4.

Chapter 6. *The Day Lasts More than a Hundred Years*: Defining Soviet Mankurtization

1. In the postscript to the *Novyi mir* edition (November 1980), Aitmatov notes that he wrote the novel from December 1979 to March 1980. While I suspect that Aitmatov has somewhat exaggerated the brevity of this time frame, it is significant in that it encompasses the invasion of Afghanistan by the USSR (December 1979), the exile of Andrei Sakharov (end of January 1980), and the subsequent worsening of superpower relations (February to March 1980), which culminated in the U.S. boycott of the Moscow Olympics in the summer of the same year.

2. Katerina Clark, "The Mutability of the Canon: Socialist Realism and Chingiz Aitmatov's *I dol'she veka dlitsia den'*," *Slavic Review* 4 (Winter 1984), 577.

3. Grigor Narekatsi, *Lamentations of Narek: Mystic Soliloquies with God*, trans. Mischa Kudian (London: Mashtots, 1977), 11.

4. Levon Mkrtchian, "Ptitsa Donenbai," *Literaturnoe Obozrenie*, October 1981, 36.

5. For the author's account of the problems he faced finding a title for his novel, see Chingiz Aitmatov, "Paradoksy perestroiki," *Literaturnaia gazeta*, 27 June 1990, 1, 4.

6. See Aitmatov's foreword to the publication of the belated chapter: Chingiz Aitmatov, *Beloe oblako Chingiskhana. Povest' k romanu*, *Znamia* 8 (August 1990), 7.

7. The novel in its entirety, including chapter 9, "The White Cloud of Genghis Khan,"appears in *I dol'she veka dlitsia den'* (*Beloe oblako Chingiskhana*); *Litsom k litsu* (Bishkek: Glavnaia redaktsiia kyrgyzskoi sovetskoi entsiklopedii, 1991). Hereafter, all references to the novel are from this edition and will be given in the text by page number.

8. The caricature manner in which Sabitzhan glorifies Soviet power finds expression in his name. In colloquial Kirghiz, *sabet* refers to Soviet power, while *zhan* means "soul." Thus with a slight shift in pronunciation the name has the meaning "Soviet soul."

9. The real setting of Aitmatov's novel is the area around the Baikonur cosmodrome in north-central Kazakhstan. After writing his novel, Aitmatov learned that a local cemetery had indeed been destroyed when the town servicing the Baikonur complex was built. Chingiz Aitmatov, "I slovo eto—vmesto dushi moei," in *Chingiz*

Aitmatov. Sobranie sochinenii v trekh tomakh, ed. S. Shevelev (Moscow: Molodaia gvardiia, 1984), 3:446–47.

10. See Evgenii Sidorov, "Utverzhdenie ideala," *Voprosy literatury* 9 (September 1981): 42–43; and Vladimir Lakshin, "O dome i o mire," *Literaturnoe obozrenie,* October 1981, 38.

11. See Clark's discussion of Soviet reviews of Aitmatov's novel in the context of Village Prose, "The Mutability of the Canon," 575–76.

12. Vladimir Chubinskii, "Sarozekskie metafory Chingiza Aitmatova," *Neva* 5 (May 1981): 176.

13. Alla Latynina, "Tsep' chelovecheskoi pamiati," *Oktiabr'* 5 (May 1981): 208.

14. See V. Turbin, "O khudozhestvennoi fantastike," *Oktiabr'* 9 (September 1981): 213.

15. Viktor Petelin, "Korni," *Ogonek* 12 (March 1981), 19.

16. N. Potapov, "Mir cheloveka i chelovek v mire: zametki o romane Chingiza Aitmatova," *Pravda,* 16 February 1981, 7.

17. Iurii Mel'vil', "Trud, gumanizm, kosmos," *Voprosy literatury* 9 (September 1981): 26.

18. See Klaus Mehnert, "Ein Tag—länger als ein Leben: Tschingis Aitmatows neuer Roman," *Osteuropa* 11 (1981): 989. Aitmatov confirmed that the novel could not have appeared without his agreeing to write the preface and that the real conclusion of the novel was the scene depicting the missile launches of Project Iron Hoop. The following two paragraphs, portraying the arrival of Edigei's two daughters at Boranly-Burannyi, were added because he was "requested" to smooth over the negative conclusion (Chingiz Aitmatov, interview with author, Duke University, 12 April 1992).

19. The danger of a powerful totalitarian China is always on the mind of a man whose native Kirghizstan shares a long border with China. Indeed, the infamous Zhuan'zhuany tribe has an indisputably Chinese sound to it. Despite the universality in which Aitmatov frames the moral lessons of *The Day Lasts More than a Hundred Years,* the main thrust of the novel deals not with Maoism, but with Stalinism and its remnants in the Soviet Union.

20. V. Dmitriev, "Vo imia idei—imia cheloveka," *Voprosy literatury* 9 (September 1981): 51.

21. Parts of the following discussion appeared earlier in Joseph P. Mozur, *Doffing Mankurt's Cap: Chingiz Aitmatov's "The Day Lasts More than a Hundred Years" and the Turkic National Heritage* (Pittsburgh: University of Pittsburgh, Center for Russian and East European Studies, 1987).

22. See Geoffrey Wheeler, *The Modern History of Soviet Central Asia* (London: Weidenfeld and Nicolson, 1964), 210–11.

23. *Manas: Kirgizskii epos; Velikii pokhod,* ed. U. Dzhakishev, E. Mozol'kov, I. Sel'vinskii, and K. Iudakhin (Moscow: Gosudarstvennoe izdatel'stvo khudozhestvennoi literatury, 1946).

24. Chingiz Aitmatov, interview with author, Stetson University, 10 April 1991.

25. Aitmatov would later use the term "historical syncretism" in *The Place of the Skull,* stressing that those endowed with the ability to "live mentally in several temporal dimensions simultaneously" are doomed to suffer bitter frustration when

reliving the tragedies of the past. Chingiz Aitmatov, *Plakha* (Moscow: Molodaia gvardiia, 1987), 162–63.

26. Aside from well-known written versions of the legend by Navoi (Uzbek) and Fizuli (Azeri), the story exists in numerous folkore versions in the genre of love *dastan* (lyrical narrative), precisely the form in which Aitmatov presents it in the plot of *The Day Lasts More than a Hundred Years*. The legend continues to fascinate the imagination of writers from the Soviet Union's Moslem republics, a fact attested to by the recent appearance of Elchin's *Mahmud i Mariam* (1987). (Elchin is a pseudonym for Efendiev Iliasogly.) Like Aitmatov, the Azeri author extends the significance of the lovers' story to encompass contemporary religious and political issues. See my review, Joseph P. Mozur, "Mahmud und Marjam: Eine orientalische Liebeslegende," in *World Literature Today* 63 (Summer 1989): 530–31. For a Central Asian version of *Laila u Majnun*, see Alisher Navoi, *Leili i Medzhun: Poema*, trans. Semen Lipkin (Moscow: Khudozhestvennaia literatura, 1945).

27. Interestingly, Aitmatov chooses the birch tree—a favorite Russian cultural symbol—as the execution site for his nonconformist bard. In a discussion of ethnolinguistics in Kirghizstan, Isabelle Kreindler wonders if that detail in Aitmatov's novel were a mere coincidence or, by implication, a subtle protest against years of cultural Russification in the republic. See "Forging a Soviet People: Ethnolinguistics in Central Asia," in *Soviet Central Asia. The Failed Transformation*, ed. William Fierman (Boulder: Westview, 1991), 277.

28. The Zhuan'zhuany (also called Muan'zhuany and Zhouzhan') were a nomadic tribe ethnically related to the Mongols. In the third and fourth centuries A.D., they waged war with the Turkic tribes of Central Asia. *Kyrgyz Sovet Entsiklopediiasy* (Frunze, 1977), 2:510. The method of torture employed by the Zhuan'zhuany in Aitmatov's novel may have been adapted by the author directly from a short story, "Ballada zabytykh let" (A ballad from forgotten years), by Abish Kekil'baev, a well-known Kazakh writer. In Kekil'baev's story the memory-depriving torture is used by a Turkmenian tribe on prisoners of Kazakh origin. There is even a striking resemblance in the vocabulary of Aitmatov's legend and that used by Kekil'baev in his description of the torture. See Abish Kekil'baev, "Ballada zabytykh let," in *Ballada stepei*, trans. from Kazakh by the author (Moscow: Molodaia gvardiia, 1975), 28–30.

29. Aitmatov coined the term *mankurt*. In his interpretation of the etymology of the word, the first syllable (*man*) is a form of the Kirghiz pronoun *men*, meaning "I." The second syllable (*kurt*) means "worm." *Mankurt*ization can also be found in *Manas*. When Manas was born, soothsayers predicted that he would grow up to be a great leader who would unite all the Kirghiz tribes. To prevent this from happening, seven jealous khans conspired to "turn the boy into a *mankurt*." The parents arranged the child's flight, however, and thus the plot was foiled (Chingiz Aitmatov, lecture at Duke University, 13 April 1991).

30. Today's Central Asia is dotted with such holy places. In Kirghizstan and Kazakhstan (areas of former nomadism), such sites are related not only to Sufi brotherhoods, but also to the pre-Islamic cult of ancestors. Ana-Beiit in Aitmatov's novel is typical of such sites, many of which have been destroyed by Soviet authorities. On holy places in Central Asia, see Alexandre Bennigsen and S. Enders Wimbush, *Mystics and Commissars: Sufism in the Soviet Union* (Berkeley: University of California Press, 1985), 129–56.

31. In Kirghiz folklore, *mother* (in Kirgiz, *ene*, in Kazakh, *ana*) is closely associated with one's native language (*ene til*) and culture. This is emphasized by a well-known Kirghiz proverb: "Ata—askar too, ene—shyldyr bulak, bala—ortodogu sham chyrak" (Father is the great mountain, mother the babbling spring, and their child the candle between them). See Sabyr Iptarov, "Tri sviashchennykh simvola—poniatiia v pedagogicheskom pansofii Kyrgyzsov," in *Narodnaia pedagogika i sovremennye problemy vospitaniia. Materialy vsesoiuznoi nauchno-prakticheskoi konferentsii* (Cheboksary, 1991), 84–86. Thus the matricide in the legend of the *mankurt* is paramount to killing one's cultural identity, something that is borne out by the other narrative planes of Aitmatov's novel as well.

32. See Latynina, "Tsep' chelovecheskoi pamiati," 206.

33. See Bess Brown, "Kazakhstan: Interethnic Tensions, Unsolved Economic Problems," *Report on the USSR* 3 (4 January 1991): 29. For a graphic account of the human suffering caused by Soviet nuclear testing in Kazakhstan, see Cordt Schnibben, "Stirb, Brüderchen, stirb," *Der Spiegel* 19 (1992): 164–83.

34. Aitmatov remarks in the introduction that to support such falsification, countries have to erect around themselves a "Chinese Wall," for only behind walls can the myth of their superiority continue to exist (11). Soviet readers at the time, of course, could just as readily interpret the Chinese Wall as corresponding to the Iron Curtain around the Soviet block.

35. Clark, "The Mutability of the Canon," 582.

36. A prominent Western specialist on Soviet policies toward the national republics, for example, calls Aitmatov's novel "one of the most forthright and uncompromising works passed by the Soviet censorship since destalinization was abandoned in the 1960s." See Bohdan Nahaylo, "Party Lines," in *Spectator*, 5 November 1983, 30.

37. Clark, "The Mutability of the Canon," 582.

38. Russification or mention of conflict between the dominant nation and smaller nationalities was listed by Efim Etkind in 1981 as a taboo topic for Soviet literature. See Efim Etkind, "Sovetskie tabu," *Sintaksis,* September 1981, 18.

39. Chingiz Aitmatov, "Tsena—zhizn'," *Literaturnaia gazeta*, 13 August 1986, 4.

40. Chingiz Aitmatov, "Zhivi sam i dai zhit' drugim. Po povodu proekta Zakona o iazykakh narodov SSSR," *Literaturnaia gazeta*, 22 November 1989, 3.

41. Hu Zhen-hua and Guy Imart, *A Kirghiz Reader* (Bloomington: Indiana University, Research Institute for Inner Asian Studies, 1989), 254. A prominent Kazakh poet, Olzhas Suleimenov, describes accurately the waves of repression following on the heels of "linguistic reforms" in Central Asia, noting that only as of 1989 had it become possible to examine works by important Central Asian intellectuals, provided one can read the languages in the Latin and Arabic alphabets. See Erden Zada-uly Kazhimbekov and Olzhas Suleimenov, "Tiurkologiia: vchera, segodnia, zavtra," *Sovetskaia tiurkologiia* 6 (November–December 1989): 83–109.

42. See Aleksandr Samoilenko, "Otchuzhdenie: Bespretsedentnyi reportazh iz Soiuza pisatelei Kirgizii," *Literaturnaia gazeta*, 16 June 1986, 7.

43. Chingiz Aitmatov, "Aktual'noe interv'iu," *Sovetskaia tiurkologiia* 3 (May–June 1988), 117–18.

44. See Zada-uly Kazhimbekov and Suleimenov, "Tiurkologiia," 100–01. Aitmatov no doubt would have been surprised to know that some ten years after the

appearance of *The Day Lasts More than a Hundred Years,* many of the cultural and linguistic grievances in the national republics would for the first time be seriously addressed by Soviet authorities.

45. In his 1980 Nobel Prize lecture, Czeslaw Milosz expressed similar ideas, remarking that "it is possible that there is no other memory than the memory of wounds." He warns Westerners of the danger of "the Earth inhabited by a tribe of children of the day, carefree, deprived of memory and, by the same token, of history, without defense when confronted with dwellers of subterranean caves, cannibalistic children of the night." Czeslaw Milosz, "The 1980 Nobel Lecture," *World Literature Today* 3 (Summer 1981): 408.

46. See Katerina Clark's "morphology" of the socialist realist novel in *The Soviet Novel: History as Ritual* (Chicago: University of Chicago Press, 1985), 159–76, 255–60.

47. Clark, "The Mutability of the Canon," 585.

48. Clark, *The Soviet Novel,* 168–69.

49. See Michael Rywkin, *Moscow's Muslim Challenge: Soviet Central Asia* (London: M. E. Sharpe, 1982), 97–98.

50. Levon Mkrtchian ("Ptitsa Donenbai," 38) compares Edigei to Ostrovskii's Pavel Korchagin. An important East German critic, likens Edigei to Sholokhov's Andrei Sokolov from *Fate of a Man.* See Anton Hiersche, " 'Der Tag zieht den Jahrhundertweg' von Tschingis Aitmatov," *Weimarer Beiträge* 2 (February 1982), 92.

51. Clark, "The Mutability of the Canon," 584. Another study of socialist realism emphasizes the indispensible element of kenosis in the lives of socialist realist heroes. Often there is a degree of masochism in the way such heroes endure cold and hunger, as well as other physical trials. See Igor' P. Smirnov, "Scriptum Sub Specie Sovetica," *Russian Language Journal* 138–39 (1987), 115–38.

52. Both Kazangap and Elizarov are present in Edigei's mind on his way to Ana-Beiit. His recollections of them influence him in resolving to complete the funeral and to fight for the doomed cemetery.

53. Markov discusses the novel in the context of what he perceived as the great need for Soviet literature "to take on the problems confronting production collectives." See Georgii Markov, "Sovetskaia literatura v bor'be za kommunism i ee zadachi v svete reshenii XXVI s"ezda KPSS," *Literaturnaia gazeta,* 1 July 1981, 2.

54. Clark, *The Soviet Novel,* 15–24, 84–89.

55. Chingiz Aitmatov, "Vse kasaetsia vsekh," *Voprosy literatury* 12 (December 1980): 6.

56. The funeral actually combines Moslem traditions with elements from contemporary Central Asian life. Kazangap's grave, for example, is prepared according to ancient rites, yet because of the hard soil of the arid steppe, the men must resort to use of an excavator, which violates the custom of hand-dug graves. Moreover, Edigei combines prayers from the Koran with his own ideas on God, which contradict the traditional Moslem concept of God. Edigei's concept is that of a God created by human beings—"If a man cannot secretly see himself as a god, struggling for the benefit of others, as You should struggle for people, then You, too, my God, will cease to exist" (366).

57. Aitmatov recalls that as a child he swam in the Aral Sea when his family traveled by train from Central Asia to Moscow (1935). In his youth the shore was

very close to the railroad line. It pains him very much to think that today the sea can no longer be seen from the tracks (Chingiz Aitmatov, interview with author, Stetson University, 9 April 1991). For a study of the enormity of the ecological disaster for Central Asia, see William S. Ellis, "A Soviet Sea Lies Dying," *National Geographic* 2 (February 1990), 73–92.

58. The subject was taboo in 1980. A novel, *Seṇ* (Duty), 1984, was published on the subject by the Kazakh writer Abdizhamil Nurpeisov. No doubt, Nurpeisov's novel, which explores the disaster in both ecological and human terms, was written much earlier but was held up by the censors. See my review, Joseph P. Mozur, *"Der sterbende See," World Literature Today* 63 (Summer 1989), 499–500.

59. See Toktobiubiu Baialieva, *Doislamskie verovaniia i ikh perezhitki u Kirgizov* (Frunze: Ilim, 1972), 34.

60. See Igor P. Smirnov, "Scriptum Sub Specie Sovietica, 2," in *Ideology in Russian Literature*, ed. Richard Freeborn and Jane Grayson (New York: St. Martin's, 1990), 157–73.

61. Geoffrey Hosking, *Beyond Socialist Realism: Soviet Fiction Since "Ivan Denisovich"* (London: Granada, 1980), 47.

62. Ibid., 197.

63. Clark, "The Mutability of the Canon," 577.

64. See Wolf Schmid, "Thesen zur innovatorischen Poetik der Russischen Gegenwartsprosa," *Wiener Slawistisches Almanach* 4 (1979): 66–87.

65. Aitmatov, foreword to *Beloe oblako Chingiskhana, Znamia* 8 (August 1990), 7.

66. The motif of the white cloud Aitmatov took from another Central Asian legend. It deals with an exceptionally holy mullah who is so favored by God that everywhere he goes a cloud accompanies him, shading the sun's rays from his face (Aitmatov, interview with author, 9 April 1991).

67. Aitmatov's portrayal of execution by camel is strongly reminiscent of the executions of Kodar and Kamka from Mukhtar Auezov's historical novel *Abai*. In the novel, Kodar (a widower) is falsely accused of having illicit relations with his daughter-in-law, Kamka. The two are hanged from a black camel. The tragic love story of Erdene and Dogulang in *The White Cloud of Genghis Khan* also closely mirrors the fate of Lang and Bibi, the main characters in a movie script Aitmatov wrote in 1986 with Tadjik movie director Bako Sadykov. See Chingiz Aitmatov amd Bako Sadykov, *Smerch. Kinopovest', Pamir* 4 (April 1986): 7–60. Like *The White Cloud of Genghis Khan, Smerch* portrays the fate of love under a totalitarian leader (named simply *Vozhd'* in the script), who seeks to subjugate everything to his authority and plans of conquest.

68. The scene is highly autobiographical. Aitmatov recalled seeing his father for the last time through the window of a train leaving Moscow for Central Asia. On the eve of his arrest, Torekul Aitmatov managed to arrange for his family's return to Central Asia. Aitmatov expressed the belief that his father was later transported from Moscow down the same railroad in a prison wagon, to be interrogated in Central Asia. The train would have passed in sight of Sheker, where the family was staying (Chingiz Aitmatov, interview with author, Duke University, 13 April 1991). In light of this information, the incessant movement of the trains in *The Day Lasts More than a Hundred Years*, expressed in the refrain ("The trains in those regions

moved from east to west and from west to east . . ."), takes on a very personal and tragic meaning for the author. Four months after that interview, in August 1991, the body of Torekul Aitmatov was discovered in the mass grave near Bishkek. Aitmatov learned that his conjecture had been correct.

69. Chingiz Aitmatov, public lecture, Stetson University, 10 April 1991.

70. Victoria Fyodorova and Haskel Frankel, *The Admiral's Daughter* (New York: Delacorte, 1979).

71. Chingiz Aitmatov, interview with author, Stetson University, 10 April 1991.

Chapter 7. Soviet Society at the Crossroads: "New Thinking" and *The Place of the Skull*

1. Chingiz Aitmatov, *Plakha* (Moscow: Molodaia gvardiia, 1987), 86. Hereafter, all references to this work will be noted in the text by page number.

2. Two works published just before the appearance of Aitmatov's novel eloquently document the perceived moral disintegration of Soviet society: Viktor Astaf'ev's *Pechal'nyi detektiv* (A sad detective story), appearing in the January 1986 issue of *Oktiabr'*, and Valentin Rasputin's *Pozhar* (The fire), published in the July 1985 issue of *Nash Sovremennik*.

3. Reference is made to the year 1983 in the present time of the narrative. The novel first appeared in *Novyi mir* in three installments: June, August, and September 1986. Although a Soviet critic reported that Aitmatov remarked in an interview that he wrote the novel in less than a month, such an assertion should be treated with skepticism. See A. I. Pavlovskii, "O romane Chingiza Aitmatova *Plakha*," *Russkaia literatura* 1 (1988), 93.

4. John Garrard and Carol Garrard, *Inside the Soviet Writers' Union* (New York: Free Press, 1990), 157.

5. Sergei Yurenen, "1984 USSR State Prizes for Literature: Socialist Realism at the Zero Point," *Radio Liberty Research*, 29 November 1984, 3.

6. Konstantin Chernenko, "Aktual'nye voprosy ideologicheskoi massovo-politicheskoi raboty partii," *Izvestiia*, 15 June 1983, 2.

7. See Christopher Andrew and Oleg Gordievskii, *KGB: The Inside Story of Its Foreign Operations from Lenin to Gorbachev* (New York: Harper Collins, 1990), 581–605.

8. See for example Aitmatov's essay, "Razum v iadernoi osade," *Pravda*, 4 February 1985, 6. In the article, the author calls for an end to the arms race and the establishment of a "global understanding of the unity of all life on the planet," and he equates the historical significance of the discovery of the atom to that of the crucifixion of Christ. The association of Christ and the destructive power of the atom would be developed further in *The Place of the Skull*.

9. Garrard and Garrard, *Inside the Soviet Writers' Union*, 199.

10. Other works regarded as harbingers of glasnost appearing about the same time are Valentin Rasputin's *Pozhar* (The fire), July 1985, and Victor Astaf'ev's *Pechal'nyi detektiv* (The sad detective story), January 1986. Both works document in naturalistic prose the moral degeneracy of Soviet provincial life. Deserving of mention in this context is also Tengiz Abuladze's searing antitotalitarian movie *Pokaianie*, which was first shown in Soviet Georgia in the summer of 1986 and in Moscow at

the end of the year. Roy Medvedev calls its Moscow premiere "the most important event in Soviet culture during the winter of 1986." See Roy Medvedev and Giulietto Chiesa, *Time of Change: An Insider's View of Russia's Transformation*, trans. Michael Moore (New York: Pantheon, 1989), 15.

11. On the genesis of the novel, see Chingiz Aitmatov, "Kak slovo nashe otzovetsia," *Druzhba narodov* 2 (February 1987): 238.

12. Aitmatov's novel was soon followed by two other important works emphasizing religious quests: Vladimir Tendriakov's *Pokushenie na mirazhi* (*Novyi mir*, April–May 1987) and Sergei Kaledin's *Smirennoe kladbishche* (*Novyi mir*, May 1987). Tendriakov's novel was first submitted to *Novyi mir* in 1979 and prepared for print in 1982. Its strong anti-utopian pathos made its publication impossible at that time.

13. The final installment (part 3) of the journal publication of the novel in *Novyi mir* was actually held up for a month because Aitmatov was still preparing it for publication.

14. Vladimir Lakshin, "Po pravde govoria," *Izvestiia*, 4 December 1986, 3. A. I. Pavlovskii ("O romane Chingiza Aitmatova *Plakha*," 93) notes that the word *glasnost'* began to become commonly used "almost simultaneously with the appearance of [Aitmatov's] novel."

15. Lakshin, "Po pravde govoria," 3.

16. Lev Anninskii, "Pamiatnik momentu?" *Literaturnoe obozrenie* 5 (May 1987): 41–43. Anninskii also remarks that the decisive manner in which Aitmatov broke with the traditional fears of portraying taboo themes makes the Soviet reader painfully aware of his own *malodushie* (faintheartedness). Ales' Adamovich refers to this technique as *sverkh"literatura* (superliterature), flourishing in the transition period between repression and full glasnost, designed to shock readers out of their complacency. In this category, the critic places *Plakha*, Rasputin's *Pozhar* (1985), and Astaf'ev's *Pechal'nyi detektiv* (1986). See Ales' Adamovich, "Protiv pravil . . . ?: O novom myshlenii i adekvatnom slove," *Literaturnaia gazeta*, 1 January 1987, 4. To Adamovich's list, one could certainly add Anatolii Pristavkin's *Nochevala tuchka zolotaia* (1988) as well.

17. Those who wish to attribute Aitmatov's "aesthetic fall" in *The Place of the Skull* to the new conditions created by emerging glasnost regrettably give credence to Miklós Haraszti's paradoxical assertion that art flourishes in a totalitarian society: "The need to create under the surface and deliver a hidden message forces the oppressed writer to search for structural and stylistic innovation and to look for new symbolic devices and metaphors." Quoted by Norman Shneidman, *Soviet Literature in the 1980s: Decade of Transition* (Toronto: University of Toronto Press, 1989), 20.

18. Among the diverse genres, one can identify the animal tale, the epistolary novel, the psychological novel, the ballad, the vita, and the production novel. See Irmtraud Gutschke, *Menschheitsfragen, Märchen, Mythen. Zum Schaffen Tschingis Aitmatows* (Leipzig: Mitteldeutscher Verlag, 1986), 120.

19. Guy Imart and Victoria Imart, "Le Procurator, L'Indigène et le Billot: Une 'Soupe-à-la Hache'. À propos du dernier roman de C. Ajtmatov," *Cahiers du Monde russe et soviétique* 28 (January–March 1987): 55–72.

20. The name Avdii–Obadiah designates three other people in the Old Testament as well: one of the twelve lesser prophets (the Book of Obadiah), a minister

of song at King David's court (1 Chron. 6:44), and a Levite whose son helped sanctify the temple under King Hezekiah (2 Chron. 29:12). By referring in the narrative to the Obadiah from the Book of Kings, Aitmatov suggests a certain degree of affinity between his hero and King Ahab's good stewart. It is also important to note that the Orthodox Church recognizes a Saint Avdii, who was martyred for his faith in A.D. 412, and whose memory is honored on 5 September. Finally, Avdii–Obadiah was the name of the founder of a heretical sect in fourth-century Mesopotamia. He taught that God had human form and that fire, water, and darkness preceded Creation. Like the Avdii in *The Place of the Skull*, he was excommunicated for his heresy. See *Polnyi pravoslavnyi bogoslovskii entsiklopedicheskii slovar'* (Saint Peterburg: Izdatel'stvo P. P. Soikina, 1913), 1:26–27. The surname of Aitmatov's hero, Kallistratov, is Greek, meaning "beautiful warrior." There was a historical personage, Kallistrat, who was martyred with his Christian soldiers in A.D. 304, during the reign of Diocletian.

21. By consciously repeating his portrayal of situations from *Farewell, Gul'sary!* twenty years later in *The Place of the Skull*, Aitmatov emphasizes the sense of social hopelessness in the Soviet village, the idea that time has indeed stood still and has been tragically wasted for Soviet citizens working on kolkhozes and *sovkhozes* throughout the USSR.

22. Kochkorbaev in Kirghiz is derived from *kochkor* (ram), which evokes the negative idea of a leader followed by a herd of submissive sheep. Kirghiz readers saw in the name a thinly veiled allusion to Turdakun Usubaliev, Kirghiz party boss from 1961 to 1986, whose hometown bears the name Kochkorka. During his time in power, Usubaliev became infamous in the republic for his gratuitous acquiescence to the Moscow party line (Abdyldazhan Akmataliev, director of the Kirghiz Institute of Literature and Art, interview with the author, Bishkek, 17 June 1992).

23. See also Carol J. Avins, "The Failure of *Perestroika* in Aitmatov's *The Executioner's Block*," *Studies in Comparative Communism* 21 (Autumn–Winter 1988): 260.

24. In *The White Ship*, the boy hero can only dream of shooting down Orozkul, a similar sadistic alcoholic.

25. The sense of impending apocalypse receives greater emphasis in the title Aitmatov chose for the Kirghiz version of his novel: *Akyr zaman (Kyiamat)* [The final age (Judgment day)]. Aside from emphasizing the end of the world, the Kirghiz title also evokes prerevolutionary opposition to Russian colonization in Kirghizstan. At the end of the nineteenth century, Kirghiz *akyns* (bards of the steppes) would sing of *akyr zaman*, decrying the loss of "heroic steppe ideals" and morals and blaming the "Russian infidels" for bringing about their decline. See Manuel Sarkisyanz, "Russian Conquest in Central Asia: Transformation and Acculturation," in *Russia and Asia: Essays on the Influence of Russia on the Asian Peoples*, ed. Wayne S. Vucinich (Stanford: Hoover Institute Press, 1972), 260. Guy and Victoria Imart note the nationalist dimension implicit in the title, but also suggest a possible word play: *akyr zaman* translates as final age, while *akyrky zaman* means present age. See Imart and Imart, "Le Procurator, L'Indigène et le Billot," 71. While Aitmatov's agenda in the novel is far more ambitious than simply to call attention to past misdeeds in Central Asia or to blame only the Russians for the moral decline of his people, allusions to the dark chapters in Central Asian history cannot be overlooked.

26. Pavlovskii, "O romane Chingiza Aitmatova *Plakha*," 92.

27. In Kirghizstan, the secretary of a regional party committee conducted a formal discussion of the novel, with the notable participation of a narcologist and the editors of the regional newspapers *Slava trudu* and *Kolkhoznaia nov'*. Sidestepping the religiosity in the novel, the party secretary offered his own interpretation of how to oppose evil, noting that "real opposition to evil could be achieved by living in accordance with the ideals of the party and people." See M. Ozmitel', "Chitateli o *Plakhe*," *Sovetskaia Kirgiziia*, 24 August 1988, 4.

28. See Mikhail Nazarov, "Mozhet li ateizm poumnet'?" *Veche* 30 (1988): 150; and Mikhail Nazarov, "A chto esli eto sposob torzhestva takikh idei?" *Posev* 2 (February 1987): 46.

29. Iosif Kryvelev, "Koketnichaia s bozhen'koi," *Komsomol'skaia pravda*, 30 July 1986, 4.

30. Yevgenii Surkov, "Tragediia v Moiunkumakh," *Pravda*, 22 December 1986, 3.

31. Suren Kaltakhchian, "Ne vera, a znaniia," *Komsomol'skaia pravda*, 10 December 1986, 2.

32. Vladimir Ilyich Lenin, letter to Alexei Maxsimovich Gor'kii, 13–14 November 1913, in *V. I. Lenin i A. M. Gor'kii. Pis'ma, vospominaniia, dokumenty*, ed. B. A. Bialik and S. S. Zimina (Moscow: Nauka, 1969), 1:122–25.

33. Chingiz Aitmatov, "Tsena—zhizn'," *Literaturnaia gazeta*, 13 August 1986, 4.

34. The Kryvelev article was soon ridiculed in the Soviet press. See Yevgenii Yevtushenko, "Istochnik nravstvennosti—kul'tura," *Komsomol'skaia pravda*, 10 December 1986, 2. Also see Georgii Gachev, "Sovest'! Stan' smelost'iu!" *Iunost'* 3 (March 1987): 83.

35. Gachev, "Sovest'! Stan' smelost'iu!" 85.

36. A. I. Pavlovskii, for example, characterizes Kryvelev's ideas as *dremuchee nevezhestvo* (abysmal ignorance) ("O romane Chingiza Aitmatova *Plakha*," 94).

37. V. Oskotskii, "Obsuzhdaem roman Chingiza Aitmatova *Plakha*," *Voprosy literatury* 3 (March 1987): 61.

38. See V. Verin, "Obsuzhdaem roman Chingiza Aitmatova *Plakha*," *Voprosy literatury* 3 (March 1987): 43.

39. Alla Latynina, "Obsuzhdaem *Plakhu* Chingiza Aitmatova," *Literaturnaia gazeta*, 15 October 1986, 4.

40. Lev Anninskii, "Skachka kentavra," *Druzhba narodov* 12 (December 1986): 249–52.

41. See Iraklii Abashidze, "Obrazets istinnoi literatury," *Literaturnaia Gruziia* 10 (October 1987): 148.

42. In Revelation 6:12, the Lamb opens the sixth of seven seals on the scroll of the "final day," and a violent earthquake begins, followed by cosmic catastrophes. When the seventh seal is broken (Rev. 8:1–5), seven angels appear; their trumpet blasts begin the various stages of the earth's destruction. The seventh trumpet (11:15) announces the end of the old world and the advent of the heavenly kingdom.

43. Chingiz Aitmatov, "Tsena—zhizn'," 4.

44. Aleksandr Kosorukov also notes the parallels between the "legend of the six and the seventh" and the biblical betrayal of Christ by Judas. See Aleksandr

Kosorukov, "*Plakha*—Novyi mif ili novaia real'nost'," *Nash sovremennik* 8 (August 1989): 145.

45. Chingiz Aitmatov, "Zachem cheloveku sovest'," *Literaturnaia gazeta*, 20 December 1989, 5. This statement and the legend of the "six and the seventh," appearing in *Plakha* earlier are the first indications Aitmatov has given that he sees the evil of Stalinism as having its roots in the very beginning days of Soviet power under Lenin.

46. Some of the narrative elements common to Bulgakov's and Aitmatov's depictions of Christ's encounter with Pilate are the heat of the day, Pilate's headache, a bird hovering overhead, and the idea that Christ's teachings are being distorted.

47. Lev Anninskii, "Skachka kentavra," 250.

48. See, for example, Chernenko's speech, "Aktual'nye voprosy ideologicheskoi massovo-politicheskoi raboty partii."

49. See Gennadii Bazarov, *Prikosnovenie lichnosti* (Frunze: Kyrgyzstan, 1983), 91.

50. See Irina Rishina, "Zachem cheloveku sovest' (beseda s Chingizom Aitmatovym i Kendzaburo Oe," *Literaturnaia gazeta*, 20 December 1989, 5.

51. Chingiz Aitmatov, "Otvetstvennost' pered Khristom i pered sovest'iu," *Inostrannaia literatura* 2 (February 1990), 247.

52. For more on Berdiaev's ideas in *The Place of the Skull*, see Joseph P. Mozur, "Chingiz Aitmatov's *Plakha*: A New Religion for Soviet Man?" *Studies in Comparative Communism* 21 (Autumn–Winter 1988): 263–73.

53. Nicolas Berdiaev, *Dostoevsky*, trans. Donald Attwater (New York: Meridan, 1964), 189–90.

54. The language of Christ in the dream was particularly irritating to a number of critics. Sergei Averintsev qualifies the clichéd language of Christ as "not the language of contemporaneity, but the *bez"iazykost'* (speechlessness) of contemporaneity." See "Paradoksy romana ili paradoksy vospriiatiia?" *Literaturnaia gazeta*, 15 October 1986, 4.

55. See F. Urmancheev, "Zolotaia volch'ia golova na znameni (k voprosu o proiskhozhdenii obraza volka v drevnetiurkskom epose)," *Sovetskaia tiurkologiia* 3 (March 1987), 68–73. Among the Kirghiz, the wolf was believed to have the power to ward off illness, injury, and evil. Women believed that a wolf hide would protect their newborn infants from death. It was also believed that by attaching wolf paws to children's cradles the infants would be protected from evil spirits. See Toktobiubiu Baialieva, *Doislamskie verovaniia i ikh perezhitki u Kirgizov* (Frunze: Ilim, 1972), 20–24.

56. For an excellent study of Mähmudov's novel, see William Fierman, "Cultural Nationalism in Soviet Uzbekistan: A Case Study of *The Immortal Cliffs*," *Soviet Union/Union Sovietique* 12 (1985): 1–41. In Kazakh literature there is also the powerful short story "The Vicious Gray," by Mukhtar Auezov.

57. Chingiz Aitmatov, "Tsena—zhizn'," 4. In *Kodzhodzhash* itself, the unity of the human and animal worlds is stressed by the marriage of Kodzhodzhash's son to the daughter of Sur-echki (the progenitress of all mountain goats). The epos portrays the lives and social organization of the goats as identical to that of humans. See Baialieva, *Doislamskie verovaniia*, 18–19.

58. It is Bazarbai's dependency on vodka that causes him stumble upon the

wolves' den in the first place. While he stops in the mountains to drink a bottle of vodka, he hears the pups whining (212–13). Thus, in a sense, alcohol is at the root of the tragedy in part 3 of the novel. Since the novel appeared at the height of Gorbachev's campaign against alcohol consumption in the Soviet Union, Aitmatov's Bazarbai—a striking illustration of the evil of drinking—can be viewed as the author's contribution to the efforts of the temperance program. Two other prominent works of the time, Valentin Rasputin's *Pozhar* (The fire), 1985, and Viktor Astaf'ev's *Pechal'nyi detektiv* (A sad detective story), 1986, likewise reveal the danger of unrestrained alcohol abuse for Soviet society.

59. The pre-Islamic deity of the Kirghiz was Tengri, the blue boundless sky.

60. A. Krasnovas discusses the novel from the point of view of precisely this passage. See A. Krasnovas, "Prizyv i preduprezhdenie," *Druzhba narodov* 12 (1986): 246–48.

61. For a discussion of the ideological shift from "developed socialism" to "socialist pluralism," see Gerald M. Easter and Janet E. Mitchell, "Cultural Reform in the Soviet Union," in *Toward a More Civil Society? The USSR Under Mikhail Sergeevich Gorbachev*, ed. William Green Miller (New York: Harper and Row, 1989), 87–91.

62. Aitmatov chooses a fitting name for his villain. The German word *ober* evokes the idea of "high" rank, and the Kirghiz word *kanda*, which is the second component in the surname, means "bedbug" and calls to mind bloodsucking.

63. Chingiz Aitmatov, "Veriu v cheloveka," *Pravda*, 14 February 1987, 3.

Conclusion

1. Alla Latynina, "Shturm zimnego nakonets otrazhen," *Literaturnaia gazeta*, 28 August 1991, 3.

2. Ibid., 7.

3. A number of notorious literary conservatives and party bureaucrats from the *sekretariat* of the Writers' Union (Nikolai Gorbachev, Iurii Verchenko, Iurii Gribov, Feliks Kuznetsov, Anatolii Prokhanov, and others) spoke in support of the coup at an August 20 meeting of the governing body. See "Oboidemsia bez raskola? Reportazh s zasedaniia sekretariata pravleniia SP SSSR, 28 avgusta 1991," *Literaturnaia gazeta*, 28 August 1991, 9.

4. The words of Aleksandr Fadeev, who as head of the Writers' Union under Stalin countersigned the arrest warrants of numerous talented writers epitomizes the party's approach to morality. Discussing his novella *Razgrom* (The rout), 1927, Fadeev remarks that he had tried to develop the idea that "there is no such thing as abstract, eternal, universally human morality. Lenin demanded from every class-conscious worker, communist, and Komsomol member such an understanding of morality so that all of their deeds and actions would be directed in the interests of the revolution and would proceed from the interests of the working class. Immoral is everything that runs counter to the interests of the Revolution and the working class." Quoted from Natal'ia Ivanova, "Nauka nenavisti," *Znamia* 11 (November 1990): 224. In such an environment, the creation of amoral monsters like Pavlik Morozov should have surprised no one.

5. Natal'ia Ivanova, "Samoobman i prozrenie," *Druzhba narodov* 10 (October 1990): 244.

6. The expression "Russian apocalypse" is used by Aleksandr Tsipko to describe the holocaust of the Stalin era. See Aleksandr Tsipko, *Is Stalinism Really Dead?* trans. E. A. Tichina and S. V. Nikheeva (New York: Harper Collins, 1990), vi.

7. Natal'ia Ivanova, "Samoobman i prozrenie," 250.

8. Ibid., 254. Vladimir Soloukhin takes a similar position in respect to the beginnings of Village Prose in the Thaw years. While it was good that writers like Valentin Ovechkin exposed the inefficiencies of collective farms, Soloukhin suggests that in the final analysis they actually prolonged the agony of village life by not denouncing collectivized agriculture as "fundamentally flawed." See Kathleen Parthé, *Russian Village Prose: The Radiant Past* (Princeton: Princeton University Press, 1992), 127. For a sensitive discussion of the problems of "rewriting and rereading the literary history" of Village Prose, see 113–28.

9. Aleksandr Tsipko, "Khoroshi li nashi printsipy?" *Novyi mir* 4 (April 1990): 201–02.

10. Ibid.

11. Josephine Woll, *Invented Truth. Soviet Reality and the Literary Imagination of Iurii Trifonov* (Durham: Duke University Press, 1991), 141.

12. Ivanova, "Samoobman i prozrenie," 246.

13. Typical of such journalistic work are Aitmatov's "Uberech' sekvoii ot SOI," *Literaturnaia gazeta*, 1 January 1986, 9; "Edinenie millionov," *Literaturnaia gazeta*, 29 December 1982, 1; "Razryvaia dymovuiu zavesu predubezhdenii: Chingiz Aitmatov beseduet s amerikanskimi radioslushateliami," *Sovetskaia kul'tura* (25 June 1982), 6–7; and "Glavnoe—sovremennost'!" *Literaturnaia gazeta*, 18 August 1982, 3.

14. For an illuminating, subjective discussion of the complex relationship between a Soviet writer and the censors, see Yevgenii Yevtushenko, "Plach po tsenzure," *Ogonek* 5–7 (February 1991); 24–26, 14–16, 22–25. Yevtushenko believes firmly that much of Aitmatov's journalistic work should not be taken seriously because it was part of a strategy aimed at ensuring the publication of his more controversial fiction (Yevgenii Yevtushenko, interview with author, Springhill College, Mobile, Alabama, 4 January 1993). Aitmatov's party positions and journalistic work were viewed far more critically, however, by Soviet writers who found themselves exiled in the West during the last decade of Soviet power. See, for example, Vladimir Voinovich, "O literature razreshennoi i napisannoi bez razresheniia," *Kontinent* 37 (1983): 439–40.

15. Arthur Miller, *The Archbishop's Ceiling* (New York: Dramatists' Play Service, 1985), 62.

16. Tschingis Aitmatow, "Traditionsquellen des östlichen Denkens," in Tschingis Aitmatow and Daisaku Ikeda, *Begegnung am Fudschijama: Ein Dialog*, trans. Friedrich Hitzer (Zurich: Unionsverlag, 1992), 213.

17. James Woodward, "Chingiz Aitmatov's Second Novel," *Slavonic and East European Review* 69 (April 1991), 219.

18. Aitmatow, "Traditionen und Besonderheiten der russischen Literatur," in Aitmatow and Ikeda, *Begegnung am Fudschijama*, 80.

19. "Pis'mo v redaktsiiu gazety *Pravda*," *Literaturnaia gazeta*, 5 September 1973, 5. To my knowledge, this is the only public letter denouncing dissidents that

Aitmatov signed. Among those who also signed were Vasil' Bykau, Oles' Gonchar, Konstantin Simonov, and Sergei Zalygin. Although Solzhenitsyn is mentioned in the letter, it was published as part of a campaign directed against Andrei Sakharov, a circumstance that caused Hedrick Smith to mistakenly assert that Aitmatov had never signed any public letters denouncing Solzhenitsyn. See Hedrick Smith, "Soviet Writer, Though Critical, Is Favored," *New York Times*, 4 June 1974, 10. Sergei Zalygin would also later "redeem" his guilt before the Nobel laureate by fighting hard for permission to publish Solzhenitsyn's *Archipelago Gulag* in *Novyi mir* at a time when glasnost was still tentative in the Soviet Union.

20. Tschingis Aitmatow, "Was wünschen wir der Jugend?" in Aitmatow and Ikeda, *Begegnung am Fudschijama*, 33–34. Elsewhere in the volume, Aitmatow calls himself an "advocate of the Great Evolution," a term he borrows from Yevgenii Zamiatin. See "Eugene Carrs Ansichten über die russische Revolution," 313.

21. The remark was made in the Russian original of *Begegnung am Fudschijama*, but not included in the German edition. Chingiz Aitmatov, "Novoe myshlenie i budushchee," *Plach okhotnika nad propast'iu* (unpublished manuscript provided to the author by Aitmatov), 329.

22. Tschingis Aitmatow, "Zerstörung der Umwelt und das philosophische Prinzip der Einheit von Subjekt und Objekt," in Aitmatow and Ikeda, *Begegnung am Fudschijama*, 238.

23. This comment has been attributed to Igor' Zolotusskii. See A. I. Pavlovskii, "O romane Chingiza Aitmatova *Plakha*," *Russkaia literatura* 1 (1988), 92.

24. Samuel G. F. Brandon, "Time and the Destiny of Man," in *The Voices of Time: A Cooperative Survey of Man's Views of Time as Expressed by the Sciences and by the Humanities*, ed. Julius T. Fraser (Amherst: University of Massachusetts Press, 1981), 154.

25. The author's parabolic genre and use of folklore have fallen on fertile ground in Central Asia. For a brief discussion of Aitmatov's influence on Kirghiz, Kazakh, Uzbek, Tartar, Karakalpak, and Turkmen letters see Abdyldazhan Akmataliev, *Slovo ob Aitmatove* (Bishkek: Ilim, 1991), 78–111.

26. Soko Gakkai unites over ten million families in Japan and a million outside the country. It is affiliated with the Japanese Buddhist priestly order Nichiren Shoshu (True school of Nichiren). Nichiren Buddhism emphasizes one's present life. The faithful believe that the three cardinal goals of benefit, beauty, and goodness can enable people to change the accumulated effects of past causes as well as usher in beneficial future effects. Daisaku Ikeda, current president of Soko Gakkai International, is a well-known public figure in Japan and a prolific writer with a profound knowledge of Russian literature, theology, and philosophy.

27. The remark was made in the Russian original of *Begegnung am Fudschijama* but not included in the German edition. Aitmatov, "Novoe myshlenie i budushchee," 329.

28. Chingiz Aitmatov, "Preodolet' sebia," *Literaturnaia gazeta*, 11 September 1991, 9.

29. Chingiz Aitmatov, public lecture, Stetson University, 10 April 1991. Whereas the metaphor Aitmatov uses expresses the writer's difficulty in adapting to new conditions, it also captures the idea of new opportunities for a writer who has had to deal with limits all his creative life. Victor Erofeev, on the other hand, speaks

of "liberal" literature in the Soviet Union as dying from an "abundance of oxygen." Since "the main purpose of liberal literature was to tell as much truth as possible in resistance to the censorship, which was trying not to let this truth through," the absence of *glavlit* (Soviet censorship authorities), in his opinion, inevitably dooms liberal writers and their works to irrelevancy.

While Erofeev gives the liberals their due, he calls upon writers in the former Soviet Union to turn away from "social assignments" and "public enlightenment" to embrace the "playful element" in literature: "The socially linear literature of resistance in its liberal and dissident hypostases has fulfilled its social mission, the mission, alas, that literature was obliged to take upon itself in the period of the closed state. In post-utopian society, it is time, finally, to return to literature" (Viktor Erofeev, "A Funeral Feast for Soviet Literature," *Soviet Studies in Literature*, Fall 1990, 16–17.

30. Tschingis Aitmatow, "Soziale Verantwortung der Literaten," in Aitmatow and Ikeda, *Begegnung am Fudschijama*, 67–68.

Bibliography

Literary Works by Chingiz Aitmatov

The Ascent of Mount Fuji In English, *The Ascent of Mount Fuji*, with parallel Russian text, *Vozkhozhdenie na Fudziiamu* (with Kaltai Mukhamedzhanov), translated by Nicholas Bethell. New York: Farrar, Straus and Giroux, 1975.

"Ashim" In Russian: "Ashim." *Al'manakh Kirgizstan* 2 (1952).

The Camel's Eye In Russian: *Verbliuzhii glaz*. In *Sobranie sochinenii v trekh tomakh*, edited by S. Shevelev, vol. 1. Moscow: Molodaia gvardiia, 1982. In English: *The Camel's Eye*, translated by Eve Manning. *Soviet Literature* 1 (June 1962).

"The Cry of the Migrating Bird" In Russian: "Plach pereletnoi ptitsy." In *Sobranie sochinenii v trekh tomakh*, edited by S. Shevelev, vol. 3. Moscow: Molodaia gvardiia, 1984.

The Day Lasts More than a Hundred Years In Russian: *I dol'she veka dlitsia den'*. In *Sobranie sochinenii v trekh tomakh*, edited by S. Shevelev, vol. 2. Moscow: Molodaia gvardiia, 1983; a later version with the new chapter "Beloe oblako Chingiskhana" (The white cloud of Genghis Khan) is found in *I dol'she veka dlitsia den' (Beloe oblako Chingiskhana); Litsom k litsu*. Bishkek: Glavnaia redaktsiia kyrgyzskoi sovetskoi entsiklopedii, 1991. In English: *The Day Lasts More than a Hundred Years*, translated by John French. Bloomington: Indiana University Press, 1988.

"Difficult Crossing" In Russian: "Trudnaia pereprava" (also "Na reke Baidamtal"). In *Sobranie sochinenii v trekh tomakh*, edited by S. Shevelev, vol. 3. Moscow: Molodaia gvardiia, 1984.

"On Dry Fields" In Russian: "Na bogare." *Sovetskaia Kirgiziia*, 11 April 1954.

Dzhamilia In Russian: *Dzhamilia*. In *Sobranie sochinenii v trekh tomakh*, edited by S. Shevelev, vol. 1. Moscow: Molodaia gvardiia, 1982. In English: *Dzhamilia*. In *Tales of the Mountains and Steppes*, translated by Fainna Glagoleva and Olga Shartse. Moscow: Progress Publishers, 1973.

Early Cranes In Russian: *Rannie zhuravli*. In *Sobranie sochinenii v trekh tomakh*, edited by S. Shevelev, vol. 1. Moscow: Molodaia gvardiia, 1982; a later version with new passages, which could not be published under censorship, is found in *I dol'she veka dlitsia den' (Beloe oblako Chingiskhana); Litsom k litsu*. Bishkek: Glavnaia redaktsiia kyrgyzskoi sovetskoi entsiklopedii, 1991.

Face to Face In Russian: *Litsom k litsu*. In *Sobranie sochinenii v trekh tomakh*, edited by S. Shevelev, vol. 1. Moscow: Molodaia gvardiia, 1982; a later version with new passages, which could not be published under Soviet censorship, is found in *I dol'she veka dlitsia den' (Beloe oblako Chingiskhana); Litsom k litsu*. Bishkek: Glavnaia redaktsiia kyrgyzskoi sovetskoi entsiklopedii, 1991.

Farewell, Gul'sary! In Russian: *Proshchai, Gul'sary!* In *Sobranie sochinenii v trekh tomakh*, edited by S. Shevelev, vol. 1. Moscow: Molodaia gvardiia, 1982. In English: *Farewell, Gyulsary!* translated by John French. London: Hodder and Stoughton, 1970; and *Farewell, Gyulsary!* translated by Eve Manning. *Soviet Literature* 1 (January 1967).

The First Teacher In Russian: *Pervyi uchitel'*. In *Sobranie sochinenii v trekh tomakh*, edited by S. Shevelev, vol. 1. Moscow: Molodaia gvardiia, 1982. In English: *The First Teacher*, translated by Eve Manning. *Soviet Literature* 1 (January 1963); and *Duishen*. In *Tales of the Mountains and Steppes*, translated by Fainna Glagoleva and Olga Shartse. Moscow: Progress Publishers, 1973.

"Gold" In Russian: "Zoloto." *Sovetskaia Kirgiziia* (30 November; 1–4, 8 December 1960).

Meeting at Mount Fuji. A dialog In German: *Begegnung am Fudschijama. Ein Dialog* (with Daisaku Ikeda), translated by Friedrich Hitzer. Zurich: Unionsverlag, 1992.

"A Meeting with a Son" In Russian: "Svidanie s synom." In *Sobranie sochinenii v trekh tomakh*, edited by S. Shevelev, vol. 3. Moscow: Molodaia gvardiia, 1984. In English: "A Meeting with a Son." *Soviet Literature* 3 (March 1979).

Mother's Field In Russian: *Materinskoe pole*. In *Sobranie sochinenii v trekh tomakh*, edited by S. Shevelev, vol. 1. Moscow: Molodaia gvardiia, 1982. In English: *Mother's Field*, translated by J. Lynott. *Soviet Literature* 11 (November 1963).

"Newsboy Dziuio" In Russian: "Gazetchik Dziuio." *Al'manakh Kirgizstan* 2 (1952).

The Piebald Dog Running Along the Seashore In Russian: *Pegii pes, begushchii kraem moria*. In *Sobranie sochinenii v trekh tomakh*, edited by S. Shevelev, vol. 3. Moscow: Molodaia gvardiia, 1983.

The Place of the Skull In Russian: *Plakha*. Moscow: Molodaia gvardiia, 1987. In English: *The Place of the Skull*, translated by Natasha Ward. New York: Grove Press, 1989.

My Poplar in the Red Scarf In Russian: "Topolek moi v krasnoi kosynke." In *Sobranie sochinenii v trekh tomakh*, edited by S. Shevelev, vol. 1. Moscow: Molodaia gvardiia, 1982.

"The Red Apple" In Russian: "Krasnoe iabloko." In *Sobranie sochinenii v trekh tomakh*, edited by S. Shevelev, vol. 3. Moscow: Molodaia gvardiia, 1984.

"Soldier Boy" In Russian: "Soldatenok." In *Sobranie sochinenii v trekh tomakh*, edited by S. Shevelev, vol. 3. Moscow: Molodaia gvardiia, 1984.

"Water Lords" In Russian: "Sypaichi." In *Sobranie sochinenii v trekh tomakh*, edited by S. Shevelev, vol. 3. Moscow: Molodaia gvardiia, 1984.

"We March Onward" In Russian: "My idem dal'she." *Komsomolets Kirgizii* 17 (20 August 1952).

The Whirlwind In Russian: *Smerch. Kinopovest'* (with Bako Sadykov). *Pamir* 4 (April 1986).

The White Cloud of Genghis Khan In Russian: *Beloe oblako Chingiskhana*. Znamia 8 (August 1990); later included in *The Day Lasts More than a Hundred Years* as chapter 9: *I dol'she veka dlitsia den' (Beloe oblako Chingiskhana); Litsom k litsu*. Bishkek: Glavnaia redaktsiia kyrgyzskoi sovetskoi entsiklopedii, 1991.

"White Rain" In Russian: "Belyi dozhd'." In *Sobranie sochinenii v trekh tomakh*, edited by S. Shevelev, vol. 3. Moscow: Molodaia gvardiia, 1984.

The White Ship In Russian: *Belyi parokhod (Posle skazki)*. In *Sobranie sochinenii v trekh tomakh*, edited by S. Shevelev, vol. 2. Moscow: Molodaia gvardiia, 1983. In English: *The White Ship*, translated by Mirra Ginsburg. New York: Crown, 1972; and *The White Steamship*, translated by Tatyana Feifer and George Feifer. London: Hodder and Stoughton, 1972.

Secondary Sources

Akmataliev, Abdyldazhan. *Chingiz Aitmatov: Zhizn' i tvorchestvo (kratkii ocherk).* Bishkek: Mektep, 1991. Most recent biographical information on the author's life.

———. *Chingiz Aitmatov i vzaimosviazi literatur.* Bishkek: Adabiiat, 1991.

Clark, Katerina. "The Mutability of the Canon: Socialist Realism and Chingiz Aitmatov's *I dol'she veka dlitsia den'*." *Slavic Review* 43 (Winter 1984), 573–87.

Falica, Anica. "Die provinziellen Apokalypsen des Čingiz Aitmatov." In *Perestrojka und Literatur*, ed. Eberhard Reissner. Berlin: Arno Spitz, 1990.

Gachev, Georgii. *Chingiz Aitmatov v svete mirovoi kul'tury.* Frunze: Adabiiat, 1989.

Gutschke, Irmtraud. *Menschheitsfragen, Märchen, Mythen: zum Schaffen Tschingis Aitmatows.* Halle: Mitteldeutscher Verlag, 1986.

Imart, Guy, and Victoria Imart. "Le Procurator, L'Indigène et le Billot: Une 'Soupe-à-la Hache' (À propos du dernier roman de C. Ajtmatov)." *Cahiers du Monde russe et soviétique* 28 (January-March 1987): 55–72.

Kleinmichel, Sigrid. "Annäherung an das Wesen der heutigen Welt: Aitmatows Roman *Die Richtstatt*." *Weimarer Beiträge* 4 (1988): 615–25.

Latchinian, Adelheid. "Der Mensch als Richter und Schöpfer: Aitmatows Roman *Die Richtstatt*." *Weimarer Beiträge* 4 (1988), 626–40.

Paton, Steward. "Chingiz Aitmatov's First Novel: A New Perspective," *The Slavonic and East European Review* 62 (October 1984): 496–510.

Pittman, Riitta. "Chingiz Aytmatov's *Plakha*: Novel in a Time of Change." *Slavonic and East European Review* 66 (January 1988), 356–79.

Sukhomlinova, O. S., ed. *Chingiz Aitmatov: Rekomendatel'nyi bibliograficheskii ukazatel'.* Frunze: Ministerstvo kul'tury Kirgizskoi SSR, 1988. Contains a bibliography of Aitmatov's works in Russian and other Soviet languages; a bibliography of Soviet articles, reviews, and monographs about his fiction; and information on theatrical and cinematographic productions based on his works.

Woodward, James. "Chingiz Aitmatov's Second Novel." *Slavonic and East European Review* 69 (April 1991), 201–20.

Index

Pitt Series in

Russian and East European Studies

Jonathan Harris, Editor

Perceptions and Behavior in Soviet Foreign Policy
Richard K. Herrmann

Plekhanov in Russian History and Soviet Historiography
Samual H. Baron

The Russian Empire and Grand Duchy of Muscovy: A Seventeenth-Century
French Account
Jacques Margeret
Chester S. L. Dunning, trans.

The Soviet Socialist Republic of Iran, 1920–1921: Birth of the Trauma
Cosroe Chaqueri

The Soviet Union and the Threat from the East, 1933–41: Moscow, Tokyo
and the Prelude to the Pacific War
Jonathan Haslam

That Alluring Land: Slovak Stories by Timrava
Norma L. Rudinsky, trans.

Troubled Waters: The Origins of the 1881 Anti-Jewish Pogroms in Russia
I. Michael Aronson

The Truth of Authority: Ideology and Communication in the Soviet Union
Thomas F. Remington

Varieties of Marxist Humanism: Philosophical Revision in Postwar Europe
James H. Satterwhite